Lesser Antilles

Barbados to the Virgin Islands

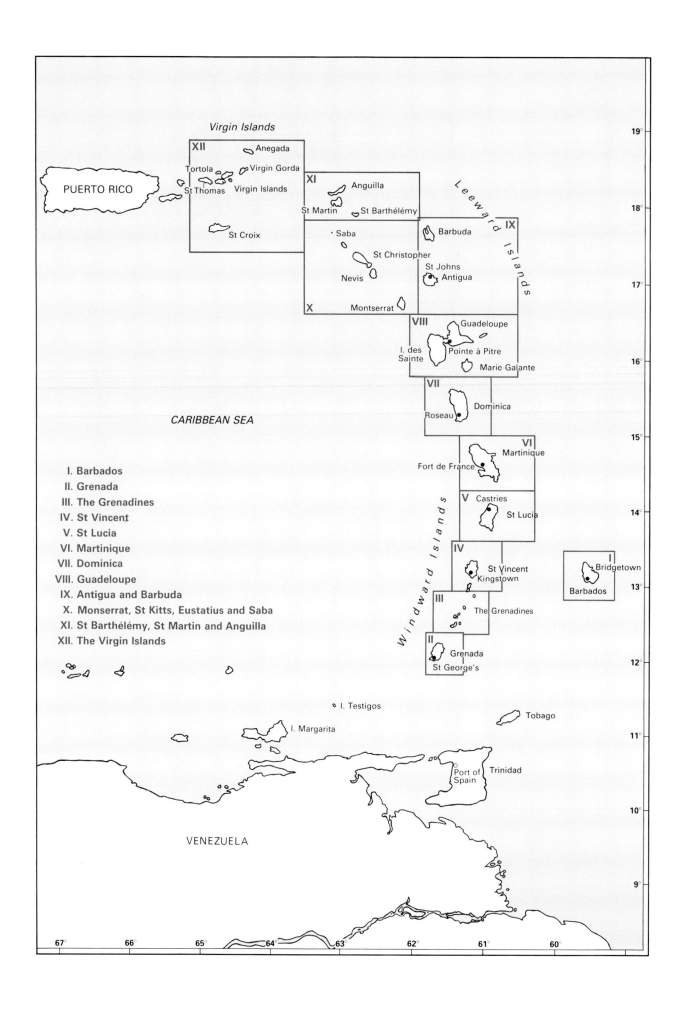

Virgin Islands

XII

Anegada

Tortola
Virgin Gorda
St Thomas   Virgin Islands

XI

Anguilla

St Martin
St Barthélémy

St Croix

Saba

Barbuda

IX

St Christopher
St Johns
Antigua

Nevis

X

Montserrat

VIII

Guadeloupe

I. des
Sainte
Pointe à Pitre

Marie Galante

Leeward Islands

CARIBBEAN SEA

VII

Dominica

Roseau

VI

Martinique

Fort de France

V   Castries

St Lucia

Windward Islands

I. Barbados
II. Grenada
III. The Grenadines
IV. St Vincent
V. St Lucia
VI. Martinique
VII. Dominica
VIII. Guadeloupe
IX. Antigua and Barbuda
X. Monserrat, St Kitts, Eustatius and Saba
XI. St Barthélémy, St Martin and Anguilla
XII. The Virgin Islands

IV

St Vincent
Kingstown

III

The Grenadines

I

Bridgetown

Barbados

II

Grenada
St George's

I. Testigos

Tobago

I. Margarita

Port of
Spain
Trinidad

VENEZUELA

PUERTO RICO

19°
18°
17°
16°
15°
14°
13°
12°
11°
10°
9°

67°   66°   65°   64°   63°   62°   61°   60°

Lesser Antilles

Barbados to the Virgin Islands

SHOM/RCC PILOTAGE FOUNDATION
Edited by Oz Robinson

Imray Laurie Norie & Wilson Ltd
St Ives Cambridgeshire England

Published by
Imray, Laurie, Norie & Wilson Ltd
Wych House, St Ives, Huntingdon,
Cambridgeshire, PE17 4BT, England

Translation by Janine Bide from the book *Ports et Mouillages-Antilles* by the Service Hydrographique et Océanographique de la Marine (SHOM-PARIS) with the authorisation of SHOM. Additional text by Hugo du Plessis and Oz Robinson.

ISBN 0 85288 153 3

British Library Cataloguing in Publication Data
A catalogue record for this title is available from the British Library.

CAUTION
Every effort has been made to ensure the accuracy of this book. It contains selected information and thus is not definitive and does not include all known information on the subject in hand; this is particularly relevant to the plans which should not be used for navigation. The Pilotage Foundation believes that its selection is a useful aid to prudent navigation but the safety of a vessel depends ultimately on the judgement of the navigator who should assess all information, published or unpublished.

PLANS
The plans in this guide are not to be used for navigation. They are designed to support the text and should always be used with navigational charts.

The last input of technical information was September 1991.

Printed in England by Tabro Litho Ltd, Ramsey Forty-Foot, Huntingdon, Cambridgeshire.

Contents

Foreword

RCC Pilotage Foundation was asked to undertake an English translation of *Ports et Mouillages Antilles*, prepared and published by SHOM, the hydrographic department of the French Navy, in collaboration with M. Jacques Anglès. This volume, however, is not a direct translation; as work progressed it first became clear that developments in the Antilles necessitated a new input of information and then, separately, the idea emerged that whereas SHOM had described the area from the Virgins to Grenada, it would be better for Europeans crossing the Atlantic if the order were reversed. The outcome is a pilot very different from the original.

The Pilotage Foundation was able to undertake the work through the resources of the Royal Cruising Club itself whose net included the translator, Janine Bide, and the corrector, Hugo du Plessis. Besides producing a skilled translation, Janine Bide also read proofs with an eye for detail. Hugo du Plessis provided a mass of information from his yacht, *Samharcin*, based in Grenada. He was also instrumental in engaging the support of David and Jean Milligan-Smith aboard *Calvados Spirit*, who commented on Antigua, of Jerry and Wanda from Marina Cay and Roy Starkey aboard *Sea Loon* who commented on the Virgin Islands, and Marcus Steele aboard *Mara* who commented on St Martin. The Foundation is very grateful for these contributions.

Anne Hammick provided many of the colour photographs and gave valuable advice whilst proof reading.

The index has been compiled by Elizabeth Cook.

O. H. Robinson
Director
The RCC Pilotage Foundation
July 1991

Anchored in Devil's Bay, the southernmost of the sandy beaches at The Baths, Virgin Gorda.
Elizabeth Hammick

Inside the market at Castries, St Lucia.
Anne Hammick

THE RCC PILOTAGE FOUNDATION

The Foundation was established through the generosity of an American member of the Royal Cruising Club, Dr Fred Ellis. Its charitable object is to advance the education of the public in the science and practice of navigation. This it does by publishing and revising pilot books and charts and by promoting the development and maintenance of pilotage, navigation and other aids to safety at sea. Its titles include *North Brittany* and *North Biscay Pilots*, *Atlantic Spain and Portugal*, *Atlantic Islands*, *North Africa – Strait of Gibraltar to Tunisia* and *The Atlantic Crossing Guide*. Comment on and corrections to its works sent to Publishers will reach the Foundation and will be welcome.

CONVENTIONS

M = nautical mile or miles. kt = knot or knots (nautical miles per hour) m = metre or metres. Wind speed is measured by the Beaufort Scale of Force denoted F, for instance F6. Pressure is measured in millibars (mb); although Pascale has been designated as the name of the basic unit for measuring atmospheric pressure (1hPa = 1 millibar), its use has not yet spread to the English speaking community. Bearings are true from seawards.

Brown pelican in flight (taken at Peter Island in the BVI).
Anne Hammick

View westwards to the Caribbean Sea from Grenada's lush and lovely interior.
Anne Hammick

General

Geography

The Lesser Antilles are an excellent cruising ground with a multitude of well sheltered and charming anchorages. They stretch approximately 500M between Puerto Rico and Venezuela and form an arc into the North Atlantic. They consist of a dozen comparatively large islands and about 100 small islands close to one another. Except for the 70M passage between the Virgin Islands and Anguilla, it is possible to travel through the whole archipelago without going out of sight of land. Most of the islands are of volcanic origin – some of the volcanoes are still active – and the rest are limestone or coral.

Politically, the Lesser Antilles are a mosaic of states. Many have become independent within the last 20 years and are members of the British Commonwealth whilst the remainder, under various statutes, are dependencies of France, the United Kingdom of Great Britain and Northern Ireland, the Netherlands and of the United States.

The Caribs, who inhabited the islands when they were discovered, were almost completely exterminated by the colonists who imported slaves on a massive scale from West Africa. The population is now mainly black. The exceptions are St Bartholomew and the Saints, where the population is 90% white, and Dominica, where some Caribs survive.

The languages spoken are English and French but accents vary between islands and native speakers of those two languages may have difficulty with some of the local dialects.

Local economy

The economy of the Lesser Antilles is still largely based on agriculture, with almost no industry. Although some big plantations, now mainly company-owned, remain from Colonial times a great deal is grown by small farmers. Bananas are a principal export crop followed by spices; sugar is grown largely for rum. Inter-island trade is being encouraged but the export business is orientated towards Europe, especially in the case of the French islands which are overseas *departements* of metropolitan France.

Tourism which has grown considerably in the last 10 years provides a useful source of wealth. It is very well established in the American islands where it is the principal source of income, a little less in the French islands. Development in the Commonwealth islands is variable; where it has taken place, it tends to be less obtrusive following an effort to avoid the 'Mediterranean wall effect' of high-rise buildings.

Marine tourism is growing rapidly through the number of centres chartering yachts. Chartering is now a main feature of yachting; in some areas over 50% of the boats are on charter with, as is inevitable, crews of varying experience.

Formalities

The traveller in this archipelago frequently crosses an international boundary and must each time comply with the entry and exit formalities. This is true even for yachts sailing between French islands where three customs zones are maintained: St Martin, Guadeloupe and Martinique. All Commonwealth islands require clearance papers from the previous port authority. This particular paper is not required in the French islands; thus, if for some reason it has been necessary to leave a Commonwealth island without obtaining formal clearance, the situation can be remedied by calling at a French island. In most places formalities can be carried out very quickly. A charge is made in some Commonwealth islands and overtime may be charged outside 'normal' office hours (generally 0900–1600 hours on weekdays; Saturdays and Sundays are overtime).

Health

There are no mandatory inoculations unless you have come from a yellow fever area. Dengue fever is known in Grenada and the Grenadines though the chance of infection may be small. Bilharzia has been reported uniquely from St Lucia so do not go paddling there in freshwater up country streams. The Antilles, however, are in the tropics and you may wish to take advice from your doctor, particularly with regard to exposure.

There are certain water hazards. Damage from coral and sea urchins can be most painful for long periods and infect easily; wear shoes underwater. Jelly fish are painful; apply alcohol to the tentacle – even gin. Sea snakes can be lethal.

There are few poisonous animals but scorpions are common. The greatest danger is from the Manchineal Tree (Hippomane Mancinella) very commonly found along beaches and elsewhere. Its small green apples are deadly poisonous and even drips from its small oval leaves in rainstorms can raise an uncomfortable rash.

Rabies: some Commonwealth islands have laws similar to the UK prohibiting the landing of dogs and cats. In St Lucia and Antigua the offending animal is shot. Grenada has an inoculation service and pets should have a current certificate. In the Grenadines it is the unofficial custom to exercise dogs on quiet beaches. Whatever your destination, inquire first.

Security

Overall security is much the same as in the UK. Minor theft is known and may often be attributed to other yachts short of gear. Major crimes occur at much the same rate and for the same reasons as in Europe but they attract attention and their significance becomes distorted. It is quite unnecessary to have firearms and they are a great administrative nuisance. They must be declared, logged, locked up and on some islands they are impounded.

Drugs have become a menace and yachts have been involved. US Coast Guard vessels may search a US ship on the high seas and some claim they have the right to search any ship within the Caribbean whether in international waters or not.

Communications

The telephone service on most islands is being modernised. Pay card call boxes are being installed but the systems, which are not compatible, vary with the provenance of the holding company. All French call boxes are card, those on Commonwealth islands both card and coin. Reverse charge calls are known as collect calls. International connections are good.

Cable and Wireless, which run telecommunications in most Commonwealth islands, have introduced boat phones. The system is based on US standards and is not compatible with European systems. Equipment may be bought or hired and gives worldwide communication.

Both European and US standards are used on VHF. A table of frequencies is given on pages 9 and 239. Ch 16 is common to both and is unnecessarily occupied with forbidden calls. There are many local rules – in Antigua, St Vincent and the Grenadines calling is done on VHF Ch 68 which becomes like an exchange used by taxis, restaurants and so forth. Ch 6 in some areas is reserved for government, not intership.

Martinique's reef-fringed east coast, seen from just north of the village of La Trinité.
Anne Hammick

In St Vincent a special permit is needed to import any kind of radio transmitter. This is easy to obtain for bona fide users.

The post. Several Poste Restante facilities are noted. Addresses should not include abbreviations or honorifics – WI may be sent to London W1, mail addressed to Sir Willoughby Willoughby KCMG will be filed under *K* and the more humble *Esq* will find his mail under E. Include the name of the yacht as *Yacht Willoughby*, not *Aux Ktch, s.s.* or whatever else might be thought appropriate.

Repairs, maintenance and laying up

The islands which have yacht yards with major facilities are Grenada, St Lucia, Martinique, Guadeloupe, Antigua, St Martin and the US Virgins; details are given in the text.

On most islands spares and indeed anything for a foreign registered yacht can be imported duty and tax free. All packages must be marked 'Ships stores in transit'. It is necessary to claim the package from the main post office where it will be examined (take a knife to open the package) and if over a certain value may also involve a customs examination. In this case it generally pays to employ an agent for the bureaucracy is formidable.

Equipment

Sailing in the Antilles calls for proper offshore equipment. We will only mention two items which might otherwise escape attention:
a. SSB communications. These are very useful in the hurricane season.
b. A rope cutter mounted on the propeller shaft. The seas, especially around the French islands abound with fish traps.

Tourism

Tourist information

A number of well-informed guide books on the Antilles exist in English and French. There is an English bibliography at page 245 which also suggests other reading. Charts are available from British, French and US sources; the basic surveys are old and the seabed changes, especially in coral areas where both growth and storm damage can change contours quite rapidly. The *Imray-Iolaire* series, published by Imray, Laurie, Norie & Wilson, Wych House, The Broadway, St Ives, Huntingdon PE17 4BT ☎ 0480 62114, Fax 0480 496109, has been designed especially for yachting and is maintained by inputs from yachtsmen. Chart diagrams are included in the Appendix. This information can be supplemented by leaflets and charts available locally.

Points of confusion:
Martinique Petite Martinique is in the Grenadines and belongs to Grenada.
Nevis Petit Nevis is south of Bequia.

Local schooners use the Careenage at St George's Grenada for loading and unloading. *Anne Hammick*

St Vincent Petit St Vincent is also in the Grenadines, next door to Petite Martinique, but belongs to St Vincent.
Sisters There are Sisters off Carriacou and Trinidad's Tobago – the latter are outside the area of this guide.
Soufrière St Vincent, St Lucia, Dominica, St Kitts and Guadeloupe have one each.
Tobago Trinidad has a Tobago (outside the area of this guide), and there are two Petit Tobagos, one off Trinidad's Tobago, one in the Grenadines. Great Tobago and Little Tobago are in the Virgin group. The Tobago Cays are in the Grenadines.
Tyrrel Bay is in Carriacou, Tyrrel's Bay is in Trinidad's Tobago.

There are a host of others no less significant in terms of their geography but not such pitfalls in the sense that their names are recognisable as being descriptive – Grande Anse and so forth.

Sailing season. Length of cruises

In the Antilles it is possible to sail throughout the year, assuming proper attention is given to storms in the hurricane season. For many the best time is in the dry season and from December to March when heavy rain is exceptional, the trade winds are well established and sometimes strong – Force 6–7, with seas to match. A fortnight's charter allows enough time to visit a fair number of islands at a gentle pace providing the prevailing wind and currents are taken into account – there are hazards. For instance, setting off from Guadeloupe one can easily reach St Martin and from St Martin, the Virgin Islands appear as an attractive and easily accessible cruising area. Getting back to base up-wind against the current is a different matter. For guidance on planning, see page 5.

Excursions

Most of the places of interest to tourists in the Antilles are on the coast and cruising is a good way to visit them; indeed pottering from anchorage to anchorage, rather than passage making, is one of the pleasures. However, on the larger islands there are a number of natural curiosities in the interior which are worth a visit and are noted in the appropriate place. In many places on the larger islands it is possible to rent a car. But in all islands the state of the roads and the standard of driving (the technique seems to be to avoid the pothole, not the pedestrian) is low. If you are accustomed to driving on the right, then in Commonwealth islands where traffic is supposed to keep to the left, it may be prudent to hire a taxi.

Currency. Exchange

In most areas the US dollar is acceptable. It is the currency in the Virgin Islands (including the British Virgins) and in the Dutch islands. In Commonwealth islands the currency is the East Caribbean dollar known as the EC which is tied to the US dollar (but the exchange is not one for one). Barbados has its own dollar. The French franc is used only in the French islands and other currencies are not acceptable there. Take traveller's cheques denominated in US dollars (Barclays in the UK can provide them) and change them into EC dollars or French francs locally.

The use of international credit cards is common. In the Commonwealth and French islands, cash advances can be made against certain credit cards – Barclays, which has branches throughout the Commonwealth islands, accepts both *Visa* and *Access* and in the French islands, Banque National de Paris accepts *Visa* and Banque Credit Agricole, *Access*.

The excellent market at Castries, St Lucia.
Anne Hammick

Holidays

The following table indicates some of the holidays.

	Grenada	St Vincent Grenadines	St Lucia	French islands	Barbados	Antigua Barbuda
New Year's Day	•	•	•[1]	•	•	•
Good Friday	•	•	•	•		•
Easter Monday	•	•	•			•
Ascension Day				•		
Whit Monday	•	•	•		•	•
Corpus Christi	•			•		
1 May Labour Day		•		•	•	
1st May Monday		•			•	•
Queen's Birthday				•		•
2 July			•			
Caricom Day						
1 Aug					•	
1st Monday	•[1]	•	•	•	•	•
August Bank Holiday						
15 August				•		
1st Monday Oct	•					
Thanksgiving						
25 Oct			•			
1 Nov All Saints				•		
Christmas Day	•	•	•	•	•	•
Boxing Day	•	•	•		•	•
National Days		22/1	13/12	14/7		
Independence Days	7/2	27/10	22/2		30/11	1/11 Nov
UN Day					1st Mon Oct	
Kadoment Day					1st Mon Jul	
Carnival		2nd wkend Aug	Last wk Jun/Jul	Mardi Gras	Last wk Jul/Aug	
Other				8 & 11/5		

1. And the following day.

Some islands also observe US holidays, especially Columbus Day, officially or otherwise:
15 Jan (Martin Luther King), 19 Feb (Washington's Birthday), 28 May (Memorial Day), 4 Jul (Independence Day), 3 Sep (Labour Day), 8 Oct (Columbus Day), 11 Nov (Veterans Day), 22 Nov (Thanksgiving Day).

Routes, landings, inter-island navigation, ports

Transatlantic routes

The best time for a westward crossing is between mid-November and late March when the trades blow well and the risk of hurricane is minimal. The most usual route is by the Canaries and the first stage of the voyage, to the Canaries, may be more testing both for boats and crews than the crossing itself, especially if it involves a late autumn departure down the English Channel and across the Bay of Biscay. Those with time to spare go early and cruise en route before making the crossing. The Trade Winds can be picked up from the Canaries – 25°N 25°W is the classic turning point – and carried all the way to the Antilles, a passage which may take less than 3 weeks in a modern yacht. A longer route, but with a shorter crossing, is to go via Cape Verde which has the advantage of an undeveloped cruising ground.

Barbados has, for good reason, been the traditional landfall on the western passage but in recent years formalities there have become tiresome. By-passing it does not add significantly to the length of the voyage and Grenada is an option if you wish to start at the windward end of the chain. French yachts tend to make straight for Guadeloupe or Martinique.

The return to Europe is best timed to clear Bermuda before the early hurricanes, which may strike in June. Timing has to be balanced against arriving early in waters still recovering from the winter. Most yachts call at the Azores but a direct passage is feasible except in unusually unfavourable conditions.

For guidance on all aspects of the crossing, see the *Atlantic Crossing Guide*, (RCC Pilotage Foundation, Adlard Coles); routes are also covered in *World Cruising Routes* (Jimmy Cornell, Adlard Coles) and for a pilot to the Canaries, Cape Verde and the Azores as well as Madeira see *Atlantic Islands* (RCC Pilotage Foundation, Imray, Laurie, Norie and Wilson).

Sailing between the islands

Passage making in the Antilles is almost always a matter of moving from one island to the next which on a clear day can usually be seen. However visibility is quite often less than 5M and rain squalls can cut it to 100m. Islands disappear and can be missed if currents are not taken into account. Coastal navigational skills are necessary for safety. Night sailing is particularly hazardous because of the lack, and unreliability, of lights and several charter companies forbid it.

Navigational aids

In general terms aids under the control of the UK, France and the US are maintained at the standards of those in home waters. Reliability elsewhere is very low on both main and ancillary lights and buoys, the latter often non-conforming or non-existent. Official publications cannot be relied on for up-to-date information on such areas.

Buoyage in use in the Antilles is theoretically the IALA Buoyage System 'B'. The principle is the same as that of System 'A' (in use in Europe) but the colours are reversed in the channels (on entry leave red markers to starboard and green markers to port). The shape of markers and buoys is unchanged and cardinal buoys are unaffected.

Radiobeacons are designed for use by aircraft and are widely spaced; besides range problems, paths at sea level are often distorted by land.

Radar is valuable by day or night but, as usual, requires skill and experience to interpret the screen. For instance, a harbour full of yachts may look like unbroken coastline.

Sailing through the reefs

'You only hit what you see.' Eric Hiscock

The growth of the coral reefs (a maximum of 5cm per year) and the movement of coral debris affects the depth of the sea. This has to be taken into account particularly as in this respect very few charts indeed are both accurate and up to date. Furthermore, as the edges of coral reefs are more often vertical than not, it is generally impossible to tell from the echo sounder how close they are.

Take careful note of the changes in the colour of the sea. Weeds tend to show black as do some reefs. Other reefs show brown – brown is a sure indicator. Blue water tends to pale as it shoals. As with many skills, experience is the best guide. Favourable conditions for reef spotting are: light behind, the sun more than 20° above the horizon – in practice between 1000 and 1600. Height when observing is advantageous and the use of polarised glasses can be helpful especially if the light is to one side. Reefs can be seen in time to take avoiding action but reduce speed and go slowly. Do not venture among reefs in cloudy weather or with the sun in your eyes (think about this when planning an anchorage to be entered in the morning and left in the afternoon. See page 7).

Marigot Harbour, St Lucia, in which Admiral Rodney is said to have concealed the British fleet from the French.
Anne Hammick

Ports, marinas and anchorages

There are perhaps a dozen real yacht harbours in all the Lesser Antilles. The term 'marina', above all as used in the English speaking islands, more often means a simple landing stage offering a few services for yachts (water, fuel, washing facilities, ice, etc.) rather than a well equipped yacht harbour. Generally speaking such marinas are established in sheltered bays and have few quay-side berths. Anchoring is the most common method of coming-to. You must have good ground tackle and, if your boat is of any size and since you are likely to handle the anchor several times a day, a reliable powered winch with manual back-up.

Holding is variable, ranging from mud in some harbours to sand. Some mud bottoms have been ploughed up so much by anchors that the holding is no longer reliable. A patent anchor is liable to skate over sand laid on dead coral. Do not anchor on bare coral; you can destroy centuries of growth in an hour. It is bad holding and since you must use chain it will give you a noisy night. If you must anchor on coral, use a fisherman's anchor. Some of the volcanic islands are steep-to (St Lucia and St Vincent in particular) and it may be necessary to take lines ashore.

Swell. In most islands the direction of swell is immaterial since it refracts round headlands – a northerly swell produces a swell on the south coast. In conditions of heavy swell an island itself gives no shelter.

Climate and weather

General remarks

The area covered by this book lies entirely within the zone of the North Atlantic trade winds. Winds from the east predominate most of the year accompanied by partially overcast skies and passing showers.

Visibility is often above 20M but strong trade winds can bring haze when visibility is cut to 5M or less. Fog is almost unknown.

Temperatures are high and the air generally damp throughout the year. There are however two seasons, distinguished from each other by rainfall. The dry season begins around the end of December and lasts to April. It is the coolest time of year with day temperatures from 26°C to 29°C. The wet season, or 'winter season', is from May to November with the highest rainfall in the latter month. Temperatures are on average 5° higher than in the dry season.

In the dry season, rainfall is usually in the form of short, heavy showers or stormy squalls. In the wet season there can be showers for several consecutive days but continuous rain is rare.

Winds

Throughout the year the trade winds come from the eastern sector. Only for some 10% of the time are they less than Force 3–4 and they are often stronger. They blow with almost equal frequency from NE to ENE or from ESE to SE, less often from the east.

Breezes and local phenomena

As a general rule the sea breeze augments the trade winds on the windward coasts. The wind strengthens very markedly at the northern and southern ends of mountainous islands where there is a compression effect and where you must always be prepared for sudden changes of wind and strong gusts. On the leeward side of these islands the wind can be very irregular and there is quite often a calm area extending several miles out to sea. Near the coast westerly eddies may be encountered at irregular intervals. In stormy weather water spouts have been seen in the channel of Les Saintes to the south of Guadeloupe.

Squalls are frequent in the Antilles and show up well on radar. They are usually very local and accompanied by heavy rain ('black squalls') so that they can be seen approaching from a distance. The wind may quickly build up to Force 8 and the squall is usually followed by a calm, the wind then returning to normal. As they move in the direction of the wind it is possible to alter course to avoid them. There are also 'white squalls', most often encountered in the lee of islands; they are less frequent but more dangerous because it is difficult to see them coming. The surface of the water whitened by gusts of wind is the only indication of their approach.

You must always be ready to 'greet the squall' by reducing sail.

Tropical revolving storms

The whole Caribbean is subject to tropical storms; when the wind exceeds Force 8, the storm is given a name, the first name for the year beginning with A and so on, and when it exceeds Force 12 in this area it is called a hurricane – elsewhere they are called differently, e.g. cyclone, typhoon. Not all tropical storms develop into hurricanes but they can be equally dangerous in the sense that an anchorage safe in the prevailing wind may be quite unsafe in a Force 8, let alone a Force 12, from the opposite direction.

The incidence of hurricanes can be summarised as follows:

a. The hurricane season is from June to November and they very rarely occur unseasonably
b. The worst months are August to October
c. There are on average 7 hurricanes per year but as many as 21 have been recorded (1933) and as few as 2.

By far the greatest number of cruises in this area are timed to avoid the hurricane season and for this reason hurricanes are not discussed here in any detail. If you plan to sail in the hurricane season, see appendix A for further information; but storms can occur any time of year and a crew cannot depend on the conditions which accompany a prevailing wind.

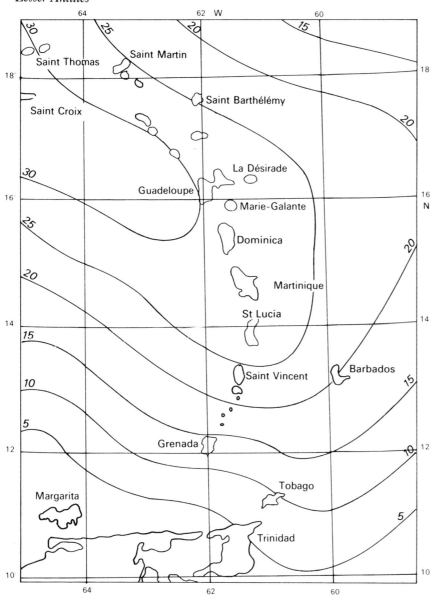

Frequency of hurricanes expressed as a % of observations

	J	F	M	A	M	J	J	A	S	O	N	D	Av.
Station San Juan......................	1017	1017	1016	1016	1015	1016	1017	1016	1015	1013	1013	1016	1016
Fort-de-France........................	1015	1015	1015	1015	1014	1014	1015	1014	1013	1012	1012	1013	1014
Grenada	1013	1013	1013	1012	1013	1013	1013	1012	1012	1011	1011	1012	1013

Barometric pressures (mb)

Currents – Sea

Movement of water – Currents and tides

Water movement in the Lesser Antilles is the result of the combination of a general current, the equatorial current flowing WNW at a speed of 0·5–1 knot in the open sea – faster in the channels – and the tidal streams. The latter alternate between west and east in the channels, reinforcing or reducing the equatorial current, with considerable variations near coasts. The Equatorial current generally predominates and particularly when the trade winds have been blowing strongly. A westerly movement can be expected of up to 2 knots in open waters but it sometimes exceeds 4 knots in channels. The tide changes twice daily (though one may be negligible) and the tidal range is small, about 0·5m. The ebb tide flows east. Its speed rarely exceeds 1 knot but in some areas it can reverse the equatorial current for a short time, for instance to the south of Martinique (the St Lucia channel) and in the Grenadines.

The strongest currents are likely to be encountered in the following areas:

● North of Grenada and in the Grenadines (4 knots towards the west in the narrow channels)
● In the St Lucia channel (3 knots towards the west close to the islands)
● In the Virgin Islands between St John and Tortola (3–4 knots)
● Near the south coast of Antigua (3 knots towards the west in June) Near the windward coast of Martinique (3 knots towards the north and north-west)
● To leeward of the islands where they vary considerably, are hard to predict and frequently cause eddies near northern and southern headlands.
● In channels amongst coral where they are often extremely strong and can carry a yacht onto a reef.

Tidal information for the area is compounded with predictions based on places as far apart as Georgetown, Guyana, and Galveston, Texas, not necessarily sharing the same tidal pattern, and one difficulty is finding the time of the tide at the standard port. The whole area is covered by the Admiralty *Annual Tide Tables Volume 2*. Those not needing the range of that book get by on the basis of local inquiry. Barbados Radio (900 kHz) gives the times of high and low waters with the weather forecast at 0710 hours; tides in the Windwards are two to three hours ahead.

The sea

To windward of the Lesser Antilles the Atlantic swell is almost permanent.

It comes most often from NE to E, less frequently from E to SE. Most often its height is from 1m to 2·5m but it can reach a height of 3–4m.

In general the swell is not a problem for yachtsmen. It increases noticeably in the channels exposed to the open sea particularly if they are narrow.

To leeward of the islands the sea is normally calm. The swell can however come round northern and southern headlands although it is greatly diminished. It is almost imperceptible while sailing but enough to cause yachts at anchor to roll.

Radio communications

VHF

European and US standards differ in their allocation of channels. Simplex channels in common are:
06, 08, 09, 10, 11, 12, 13, 14, 15, 16, 17, 67, 68, 69, 70, 71, 71, 73, 74. UK channel 77 is US channel 75.

Duplex channels in common are:
84, 85, 86, 87

Transmissions on WX1, WX2, WX3, WX4, WX5 and WX6 are on a common frequency.

Other channels may evoke no response or promote confusion; thus Ch 04 is a European duplex channel 160·800(RX)/156·200(TX) MHz but a US simplex channel 156·200(RX & TX) MHz.

The following islands have shore radio stations:

Barbados (8PO)

TX	RX	Hours	Type	Traffic lists
RT MF & HF				
2182	2182	24hrs	H3E	
2582	2182	24hrs	J3E R3E	0050, 1250, 1650, 2050
2723	2182	On request	J3E R3E	
4376	4081·6	On request	J3E R3E	
8765.4	8241·5	1200–2000	J3E R3E	0050, 1250, 1650, 2050
8793·3	8269·4	On request	J3E R3E	
13138	12367·2	1200–2000	J3E R3E	
17353·8	16580·9	On request	J3E R3E	

VHF 16, **26**. Traffic lists 0050, 1250, 1650, 2050

Grenada St George's

VHF 06, 11, 12, 13, **16**, 22

Martinique, Fort de France (FFP)

RT MF				
2182	2182	H3E, J3E, R3E		1100–2300
2545				Ev. odd H+33

VHF Ch 16 See Morne Bigot
VHF at Morne Bigot (14°31'N 61°04'W)
Ch 26, 27 Yachts must call Morne Bigot, not Fort de France

Automatic VHF stations

Morne Bigot 14°31'N 61°04'W Ch 87
Morne Aca 14°27'N 60°54'W Ch 86
Morne Bellevue 14°44'N 61°04'W Ch 28
Morne Calebasse 14°48'N 61°09'W Ch 84
Morne Beau Séjour 14°32'N 16°52'W Ch 81, 83

Guadeloupe, Pointe-à-Pitre (FFQ)

VHF Ch 16, **25**. Traffic lists 1100–2300

Automatic VHF stations

Piton St Rose 16°20′N 61°46′W Ch 03, 82, 87
Morne à Lois 16°11′N 61°45′W Ch 61, 86
Citerne 16°02′N 61°39′W Ch 21, 62, 63

Saba (PJS)

Ch 16, 26 24hrs. Traffic lists ev. H+05

Virgin Islands, Tortola (VPV)

Ch 16, **27**. Ch 16 24hrs Ch 27 1100–2300

St Thomas (WAH)

RT MF & HF

2182	2182	0300–1600	H3E	
2506	2009	(all freqs)	R3E	0000, 1200, then ev. 2 hrs
4357·4	4063		(all subsequent	
6515·7	6209·3		freqs)	
6518·8	6212·2			
8728·2	8204·3			
13100·8	12330			
13103·9	12333·1			
17236	16463·1			
17239·1	16466·2			
22664·2	22068·2			

VHF Ch 16, 24, 25, 28, **84**, 85, 86, 87, 88 0300–1600.
Traffic lists 0000, 1200 then ev. 2hrs

Puerto Rico (NMR)

RT MF

2182	2182	24 hrs	H3E, J3E

VHF Ch 16. 24 hrs

The station is run by the US Coast Guard and does not accept public correspondence.

Note

H3E Single Sideband, amplitude modulated, full carrier.
J3E Single Sideband, amplitude modulated, suppressed carrier.
R3E Single Sideband, amplitude modulated, reduced carrier.

Radiobeacons

AERO RADIOBEACONS

Windward Islands

Grenada 12°00′·50N 61°46′·90W GND 362kHz 0·15kW 24hr

Barbados 13°04′·11N 59°29′·49W BGI 345kHz 200M 24hr

Arnos Vale, St Vincent 13°08′·52N 61°12′·55W SV 403kHz 0·25kW 24hr

Hewanorra, St Lucia 13°44′.13N 60°58′.87W BNE 305kHz 0·1kW 24hr

Vigie, St Lucia 14°01′·15N 60°59′·73W SLU 415kHz 100M 24hr

Fort de France, Martinique 14°35′·97N 61°05′·72W FXF 314kHz 100M 24hr

Leeward Islands

Dominica 15°32′·81N 61°18′·16W DOM 273kHz 0·1kW 24hr

Grand Bourg, Marie Galante 15°52′·33N 61°16′·02W MG 376kHz 50M 24hr

Pointe-à-Pitre, Guadeloupe 16°15′·77N 61°31′·77W PPR 300kHz 250M 24hr

Antigua 17°09′·46N 61°47′·47W ZDX 369kHz 1·2kW 24hr

Saint Barthélémy 17°53′·45N 62°51′·17W BY 338kHz 50M 24hr

I. Barbados

Charts
Imray-Iolaire *B2*
Admiralty *2485, 502*
SHOM *3200*
US *25485*

General remarks

Geography

Arriving by air, Barbados can look disconcertingly similar to the UK. Go to the west coast and the scene is reminiscent of Scotland with atlantic rollers breaking on the rocky shore. But on the east coast the scene is entirely Caribbean with a beach unknown in Europe, Sandy Bay, miles of white sand and blue sea. Situated approximately 80M to windward of the Antilles arc, Barbados is different from most islands of the Antilles in that it is low lying with the only high points, Mounts Hillaby (336m) and Misery (309m), close together in the middle. There are no rivers and hardly any forest. The heart of the island is dominated by sugar plantations and its long colonial history has left a distinctly British flavour to the food and in the shops in Bridgetown. Few Bajans walk about with water-melon grins but crack the right joke and they will literally fall about with laughter.

Barbados became an independent state on 30 November 1966. It has a bi-cameral legislature of 21 senators appointed by the governor general, mostly nominated by the prime minister and the leader of the opposition, and 27 elected assemblymen.

Immediately after the Second World War agriculture, mainly sugar and cotton, produced about half the island's overseas income. The proportion fell to less than 7% by 1983 and though sugar production remained high (100,000 tons in 1985) electrical exports earned six times as much. Other light industries include clothing, plastics and electronics and the island's income is helped by petroleum and gas production, and by tourism.

History

Colonised by the Portuguese in 1536, Barbados was occupied by the British in 1627 and, unusually for a Caribbean island, remained British until 1966. There are other unusual features. Although the island has been chronically over-populated, the abolition of slavery did not result in the same chaos as it is did elsewhere in the British Caribbean. There was a greater degree of political and economic integration between the white settlers and the African population than in other islands, with the possible exception of St Kitts and Antigua, and this comparison still holds good.

Coasts, dangers

Transatlantic arrivals can best approach via the southern end of the island. There are remarkably tall radio masts close to Mount Misery, 183m above ground and 504m above sea level, with aircraft warning lights. The southeast coast consists of cliffs about 15–20m high with flat country behind and has a reef, 1¼M offshore at Kitridge Point and ½M offshore at South Point. The atlantic current divides at Kitridge Point, which is the most easterly headland, and sweeps along the northeast as well as the southeast coast; Ragged Point light stands about a mile northwest of Kitridge Point and does not mark the end of the island. Grantley Adams International airport with conspicuous lights lies about 2½M northeast of South Point and a large bank, the shallows, about 4M southeast; this area can be very rough when a westerly swell meets an east-going current and should be avoided. Needham Point, the southern extreme of Carlisle Bay, has a hotel and a sectored light. The coast from Bridgetown round North Point to Ragged Point is fringed by a reef; there are anchorages along the lee coast but it is not good cruising.

Approach and anchorage

Carlisle Bay is open. For permission to enter Deep Water Harbour call Bridgetown Harbour Signal Station on VHF Ch 12 or if out of hours anchor in the approved holding area, a radius of 500m from a point 750m south of the Careenage molehead; a yacht should then enter Deep Water Harbour as soon as possible after 0600. Fly the Q Flag and keep Ch 12 open.

After clearing, yachts are requested to anchor in an area north of the bandstand in the vicinity of the Esso jetty. It may be possible to anchor in the south-eastern part of the bay where local yachts are on moorings near the Holiday Inn pontoon.

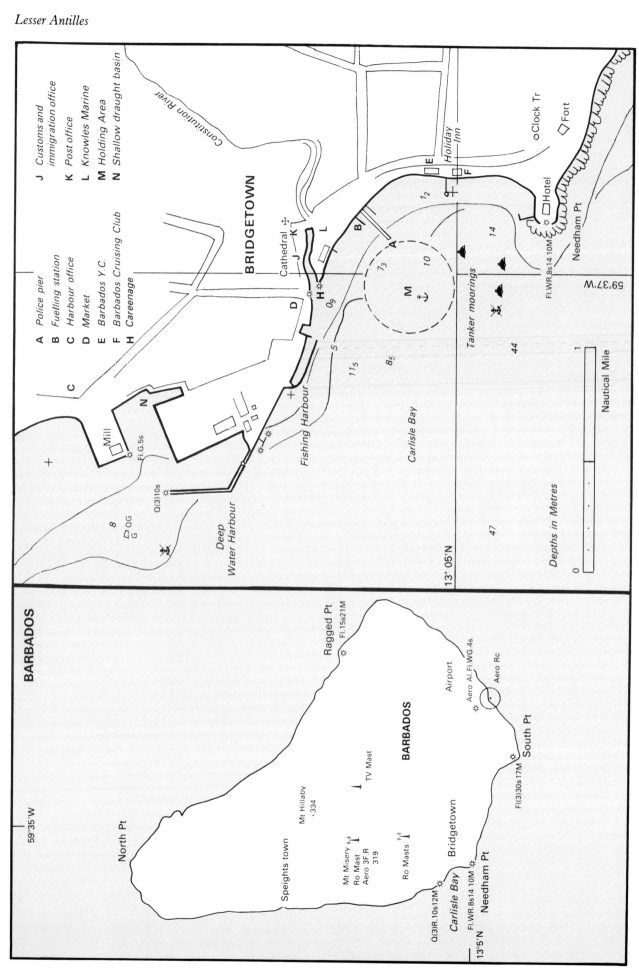

BRIDGETOWN

A Police pier
B Fuelling station
C Harbour office
D Market
E Barbados Y.C.
F Barbados Cruising Club
H Careenage

J Customs and
   immigration office
K Post office
L Knowles Marine
M Holding Area
N Shallow draught basin

Constitution River

Cathedral
J K
L
B
Holiday Inn
E
F
Clock Tr
Fort
Hotel
Needham Pt
Fl.WR.8s14 10M
59°37'W

H
D
0₉
5
11₅
8₅
Fishing Harbour
Carlisle Bay
1₂
7₃
10
A
M
14
Tanker moorings
44
13° 05'N
47
1

Mill
Fl.G.5s
N
Q(3)10s
8
G QG
Deep Water Harbour

Depths in Metres
0   Nautical Mile
1

BARBADOS

59°35'W
North Pt
Speights town
Mt Hillaby .334
TV Mast
Mt Misery
Ro Mast
Aero 3F.R 319
Ro Masts
BARBADOS
Ragged Pt
Fl.15s21M
Airport
Aero Al.Fl.WG.4s.
Aero Rc
South Pt
Fl(3)30s17M
Bridgetown
Carlisle Bay
Needham Pt
Fl.WR.8s14 10M
Q(3)R.10s12M
13°5'N

Formalities

Because the formalities are so tedious many yachts skip Barbados and go straight to a more friendly port downwind.

Yachts must clear customs and immigration in Deep Water Harbour; this is said to be possible any day of the week between 0600 and 2200. Besides the usual papers, a health report and in common with all British Commonwealth islands, a clearance certificate from the port of departure are required. There are charges.

In Barbados outward clearance can only be obtained in Deep Water Harbour. First the harbour dues have to be paid and the port authority's clearance obtained; this is taken to customs. The crew list and passports have then to be taken to emigration; after this, clearance is valid for 24 hours only and the yacht must leave Deep Water Bay to sea towards her next port of call. A yacht leaving on Saturday or Sunday must start the procedure with the port authority by 2100 on Friday. A crew member leaving a yacht must be taken to emigration by the master; if transferring to another, both masters must be present.

Flag

Three vertical stripes of blue, gold, blue, with a black trident in the centre.

Facilities

Water, fuel and supplies at the Holiday Inn pontoon. Minimal maintenance.

Communications

Car hire, taxis, buses.
Airport with European, mainland American and island connections.
VHF and SSB shore stations

Hurricane holes

None.

Bougainvillea is found in various colours throughout the Lesser Antilles. Admiral de Bougainville was prominent in the American War of Independence and besides this flower has a Pacific Island and a bay in the Straits of Magellan named after him.
Anne Hammick

II. Grenada and neighbouring islands

Charts
Imray-Iolaire *B32*
British Admiralty *2821*
SHOM *3273*
US *25481*

General remarks

Geography

Grenada, the southern island of the windward group, like most others of the chain, is volcanic. The middle of the island is mountainous, wooded and picturesque, with crater lakes, mineral springs, nutmeg groves and ruined sugar plantations. Mount St Catherine (836m) in the north is the highest point. A series of off shore islands and islets extend northeast towards Carriacou and the state itself extends even further to Petite Martinique. Grenada has an area of 344 sq km and an estimated population of 95,000, primarily of African origin but with noticeable Indian, Maltese and Madeiran inputs, of whom about 35,000 live in St George's. The island has many anchorages, particularly on its south coast.

Grenada became an independent state on 7 February 1974 and is a member of the British Commonwealth. Under its constitution, promulgated in 1973, there is a bicameral legislature with 13 senators appointed by the governor and 15 elected representatives.

The island depends on agriculture and tourism. It principle exports are cocoa, nutmegs, bananas and that secondary product of the nutmeg, mace. It is the world's second largest producer of nutmeg and has the nickname 'Spice Island'.

History

Grenada was named Concepción by Columbus when he sailed by in 1498 and the name Grenada only appeared in the 16th century on Spanish charts. The Caribs, who earlier displaced the Arawaks, successfully resisted various attempts at colonisation until the middle of the 17th century when a French expedition from Martinique arrived and waged a merciless war. After a year, in 1651, rather than surrender the surviving Caribs threw themselves off a cliff on the north coast which is still called Morne des Sauteurs, Hill of the Jumpers. The island remained a French possession until 1762 when it was captured by the British, to be thrown out during the distraction of the American War of Independence. It was returned to the British by the Treaty of Versailles in 1783 and remained a British possession until independence. Five years after independence a revolution established an alternative government. However the new government failed to satisfy the perceptions of some islanders or indeed the perceptions of its island neighbours and amid turmoil, in 1983 the latter requested armed intervention by the USA and the 1973 constitution was restored. Evidence of the original French occupation is strong: many place names and much of the patois derive from French and 60% of the population remains Roman Catholic.

Tourism

Grenada has several interesting ports of call, among them St George's, one of the more attractive of the Antilles capitals. The interior of the island with its particularly luxuriant vegetation is no less attractive. A day's outing from St George's can be made to see the huge banana plantations as well as nutmeg and cocoa estates. The Dougaldstone estate near Gouyave is the best known banana plantation. Gouyave and Grenville have many stations preparing nutmeg for shipment and a visit to one of them is extremely interesting.

Diamond Island, on the approach from the north, is a major bird colony with boobies, terns, petrels and frigate birds. Better known as Kick'em Jenny its nick name may be derived from 'Cay qu'on géne', the cay which gets in the way, an indication of the currents in the vicinity.

Carnival has been revived and transferred to the August tourist season. It is very colourful and very noisy with steel bands and elaborate costumes.

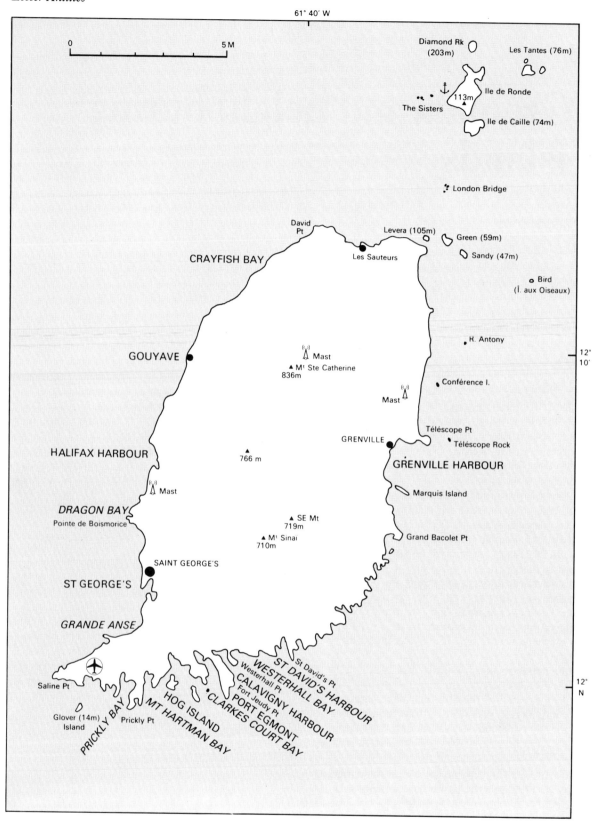

61° 40' W

0   5 M

Diamond Rk
(203m)

Les Tantes (76m)

Ile de Ronde

The Sisters   113m

Ile de Caille (74m)

London Bridge

David
Pt

Levera (105m)

Green (59m)

CRAYFISH BAY

Les Sauteurs

Sandy (47m)

Bird
(Î. aux Oiseaux)

R. Antony

GOUYAVE

Mast

Mt Ste Catherine
836m

Conférence I.

Mast

Téléscope Pt

GRENVILLE

Téléscope Rock

HALIFAX HARBOUR

766 m

GRENVILLE HARBOUR

Mast

Marquis Island

DRAGON BAY

Pointe de Boismorice

SE Mt
719m

Grand Bacolet Pt

Mt Sinai
710m

SAINT GEORGE'S

ST GEORGE'S

GRANDE ANSE

St David's Pt

WESTERHALL BAY

ST DAVID'S HARBOUR

Westerhall Pt

CALAVIGNY HARBOUR

Fort Jeudy Pt

Saline Pt

PORT EGMONT

CLARKES COURT BAY

HOG ISLAND

PRICKLY BAY

Glover (14m)
Island

Prickly Pt

MT HARTMAN BAY

12°
10'

12°
N

Arrival

From the Atlantic yachts tend to go south about to Prickly Bay or St George's and the island mass is easily identifiable; the point to watch is the current which is strongest to the northeast on the north side of the island and the southwest on the south side. From the Grenadines the northeast set is even more important and it may be better to pass along the lee side of Ile Ronde and then go down the west coast to avoid the strong currents in the channels. It is often necessary to motor when in the lee of Grenada; if there is wind it is likely to be gusty.

In clear weather, a tall radio mast on the northeastern spur of Mount St Catherine may be seen.

Formalities

Ports of entry are St George's, Prickly Bay and Grenville.

Flag

Divided into four triangles of yellow, top and bottom, and green, hoist and fly; in the centre a red disc bearing a gold star; along the top and bottom edged red stripes each bearing three gold stars; on the green triangle near the hoist a pod of nutmeg. Since the sailmaker is unlikely to be able to knock one up in a hurry, make sure you have it on board before starting.

Maintenance

St George's and Prickly Bay

Communications

Airport at Port Salines with European, US and Caribbean connections. Inter-island shipping.

Telephone system recently re-furbished, call boxes accepting coin, cards and call-collect. Faxes are common.

Mail has to be collected from the post office. Mail addressed care of the Grenada Yacht Club in St George's and the Spice Island Marina at Prickly Bay will be collected and held. Parcels have to be examined at the main post office. Outward mail has to be posted at a post office; there are no convenient post offices outside St George's.

Hurricane holes

Several possibilities; see Appendix.

East and south coasts of Grenada: Levera Point to Saline Point

Coasts, dangers

The Ile Ronde group, 4M north of Grenada, is described on page 34. South of them, less than a mile off Levera Point, the north eastern tip of the island, are three islets: Levera (105m), Green (59m) and Sandy (47m), the first of which, shaped like a pointed cone, is easy to identify from afar. Currents are strong close to the islets and if going south from the Grenadines it is better to pass west of them. Midway between them and the Ile Ronde group, is London Bridge (23m), a rock with a hole in it surrounded by smaller rocks and reefs. A mile south of Sandy Island there is a submarine breaking reef one mile off shore. Further on, towards Telescope Point, the reefs are within ½M of the shore, with Black (10m), Pearls (19m) and Telescope (20m) Rocks well out of the water. The radio mast (43m), near the old airport at Pearls, about 1·2M NNW of Telescope Point, is conspicuous.

- Grenville Bay, page 18, starts at Telescope Point, a small conical promontory, and continues to Marquis island, a conspicuous steep sided plateau.

- The coast between Marquis Island and Saline Point is deeply indented with a series of bays providing well protected anchorages. Off shore there is generally a 2 knot current moving towards Saline Point. Also towards Saline Point is a wide coastal shelf with 3–8m depths with the dangerous Porpoises (1m), which are difficult to see in an unfavourable light and Glover Island (14m), very low with a small lighthouse (Q(6)+LFl), on it; the Porpoises lie 0·5M SSE of Prickly Point and are marked by a small S cardinal buoy. Unless entering one of the bays, it is advisable to stay more than 0·5M outside this coastal shelf which breaks in heavy swell. Reefs extend up to 1M offshore between Fort Jeudy Point and Prickly Bay. There are few significant landmarks until Westerhall Point (50m) whose southeastern face is edged by a very white beach and coconut palms between the cliffs. Further west, Prickly Point (26m) is the southern tip of a prominent headland edged with cliffs with

Saline Pt

Yellow tank (conspicuous)

Control tower

SW point of Grenada

several hotels and villas on it and the control tower and hangars with white roofs of the airport are clearly visible about 1M east of Saline Point.

Grenville

12°07'·4N 61°37'·0W

About midway on the windward coast of the island, Grenville is a welcoming little town in which the three areas of activity are the market, the small nutmeg factory and the landing stage. It is situated in the northwest corner of a large bay on the shores of a lagoon totally sheltered from the swell by a large coral barrier. As a port of entry it is much used by local boats but rarely visited by yachts because of a difficult approach made worse by lack of marks. If entering without local knowledge, do so in the morning with the sun in the east and with no more than a moderate swell.

Approach

The outer channel is about 60m wide between shoals of 2·5–4m on which the swell does not always break. The leading line is marked by a triangle and a white square which in practice are impossible to see.

From a line between Telescope Point and the eastern tip of Marquis Island the entrance is on bearing of 297° to the police station, a conspicuous pink building with red roof near the landing stage. Enter on this bearing between the reefs until the entrance to the inner channel is reached. In 1988 it was reported that the first buoy on the north side of the channel was missing.

Entrance

The inner channel, known as the Luffing Channel, 3m deep, runs south to north between reefs which are awash and is marked by two pairs of small red and green buoys and a pole on the eastern side.

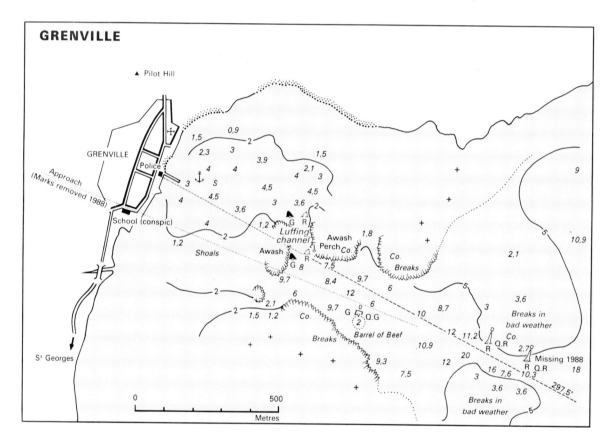

Grenville. Police building on 297°

Anchorage
Anchor in 3–4m, 150m ENE of the landing stage.

Formalities
Customs and immigration at the police station.

Facilities
A well-supplied market, several restaurants.

St David's Harbour

12°01'·4N 61°40'·5W

St David's Harbour, limited to the east by the headland of the same name, is the most beautiful and the best protected of the bays on this coast. At the head of the bay there is a long deserted beach fringed with coconut palms in a landscape of green hills. During the troubles, when threatened by a hurricane, elements of the English and French fleets made a truce and both sheltered here.

Approach
Having identified St David's Point, off which there is a small rock, enter the bay heading NNW following the east coast about 100m off. This course clears the line of reefs which separate St David's Bay from Little Bacolet Bay situated just to the west of it.

Anchorage
Anchor in 6–7m on sand about 100m from the beach.

Bacaye Harbour

12°01'·0N 61°42'·0W

Bacaye Harbour, also known as Westerhall Bay, is well protected but one of the less attractive anchorages with a difficult entrance. The ground around it is private and landing is difficult. Do not enter or leave in bad light or in a strong southeasterly wind.

Approach
Identify Westerhall Point (see page 19) and clear the shoals which extend 750m ESE of it. Enter the bay heading 292° towards the cape on the south coast where a landing stage can be seen. This course passes north of two clearly visible rocks 130–150m, and then south of a large steep-sided reef which extends off the north coast. When Westerhall Point is on the port beam, move away from the south coast in order to follow, at a distance of 50–60m, the reef which extends from it. When west of the landing stage mentioned above close the coast again to a distance of 60–70m to clear the very irregular shoals which extend for a considerable distance from the north shore.

Anchorage
The best anchorage is near the southern shore of the inlet in 4–5m on light mud with poor holding. The west and northern shores of the inlet are unsafe.

Grenada. Calavigny Harbour entrance. *Hugo du Plessis*

Westerhall Point looking NW

Calavigny Harbour

12°01'·0N 61°42'·3W

Calavigny Harbour, not to be confused with Calavigny Island, lies in a well protected inlet between luxuriant green hills, protected by a spit of sand covered with coconut palms. It has a housing estate on the east side but it is well planned and the anchorage is one of the more beautiful on the island.
This would be a good hurricane hole but it is small; six boats would make a crowd. Get into the mangroves in the N arm, 4m, or the silted W arm, less than 1m and with danger from debris in the flooding rivers.

Approach

It is essential to see the reefs and the entry should only be attempted in proper light. No charts agree and all have errors.

Westerhall Point (see page 19) is a good landmark northeast of the entrance. From the west, Fort Jeudy Point, a long headland with cliffs and an almost flat top sloping gently towards the south, a good mark but the next point, ½M northeast, is false and not at the entrance. The true point has a beach backed by a row of palm trees and a reef off it. Fort Jeudy Point has two rocks awash, reefs and often a race off it. The charts mark a 2m patch in the middle of the entrance but this has not been noticed recently. Head on 312° with a tin-roofed house on top of a small hill

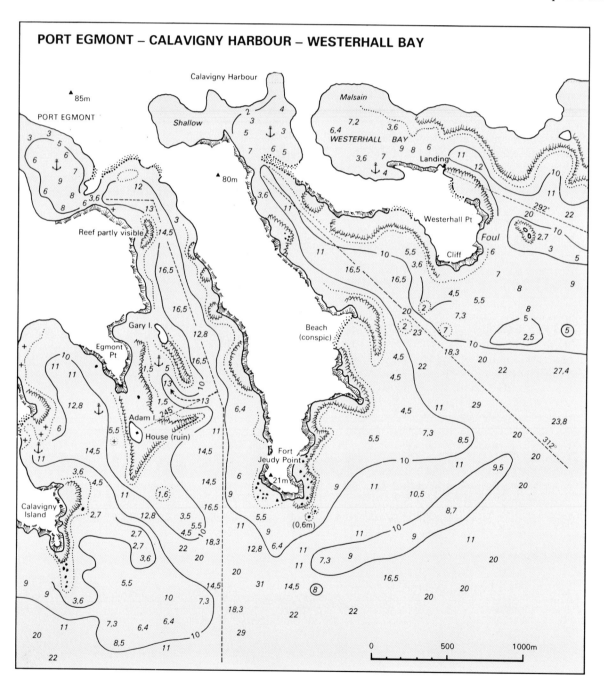

PORT EGMONT – CALAVIGNY HARBOUR – WESTERHALL BAY

immediately behind the harbour in line with the middle of the beach. The reefs on either side are well defined and quite easy to see.

Entrance

At the inner entrance the west part of the spit on the east side is now under water; keep close to the west side which is rocky and steep-to. The closest point to the reef is reached when inside and apparently safe.

Anchorage

When safely inside, anchor in the centre, 4–6m, mud. The western arm of the harbour is silted up but there is a narrow 2m channel close to the south side.

Port Egmont

12°00'·5N 61°42'·7W

At the head of this bay is a harbour which is completely enclosed and provides the best protection from hurricanes in the area. The anchorage, surrounded by high green hills on which a few villas are situated, is on the whole little frequented. Though it gives good shelter from hurricanes, it is well known as a hurricane hole and the anchorage becomes unsafe through over-crowding and through vessels not being properly anchored.

Approach

From the west round Fort Jeudy Point (see above) which has reefs and a rock (0·6m) up to 200m off it. From the east it is worth keeping a mile off shore to avoid the reefs off Calavigny Island and the shallow banks which can break. Either way, enter heading north and 200m west of Fort Jeudy to avoid the shoal off the west side of this point. Then, when Adam Island is abaft the beam and the northeast shore has opened up, keep in mid channel along the axis of the bay. This clears the reefs which lie ENE of Adam Island and SSE of Gary Island which are generally marked by breakers but beware the barely covered reef extending 100m from the west coast just before turning west towards the entrance of the harbour. The entrance is narrow but has 5m in the centre.

Anchorage

Anchor in 5–7m on mud in the middle of the harbour. The shores are clear of dangers. The holding is moderate.

The following anchorages should only be attempted by really experienced reef navigators and then only good sea conditions; they all entail an unusual degree of risk.

One in clear water at the entrance to the bay near Gary Island is more airy than Port Egmont. To reach it, start from a point along the axis of the bay and head 245° towards a ruined house on Adam island. When inside the quite well-defined western edge of the reef SSE of Gary Island, turn to about 340° and follow the line of the reef 60–80m off. Anchor in 5–7m on sand, 100m southwest of the southern point of the island. Depths decrease rapidly to below 2m north of this position and the passage north of the island is for dinghies.

Others between Adam Island and Calavigny Island are accessible from the channel between the reefs which extend from both islands. There are also anchorages WSW of Point Egmont (8–10m) and in the extreme south of the beach on the northeast of Calavigny island (8–10m – it has coral heads and beware of the reef in the northern two thirds of the beach).

Clarkes Court Bay

12°00'·7N 61°43'·9W

Wide and quite well protected (the wind tends to funnel up the bay), Clarkes Court Bay provides several anchorages in varied settings: mangrove shores or beaches fringed with coconut palms. In the northwestern inlet there is a small fishing hamlet, Lower Woburn, near which big piles of conch shells can be seen on the shore.

Shipping and large yachts use Clarkes Court Bay as a hurricane hole. Smaller vessels can get up to the mangroves by Woburn.

 Adam I.

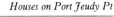 *Houses on Port Jeudy Pt*

Grenada. Entrance to Port Egmont. *Hugo du Plessis*

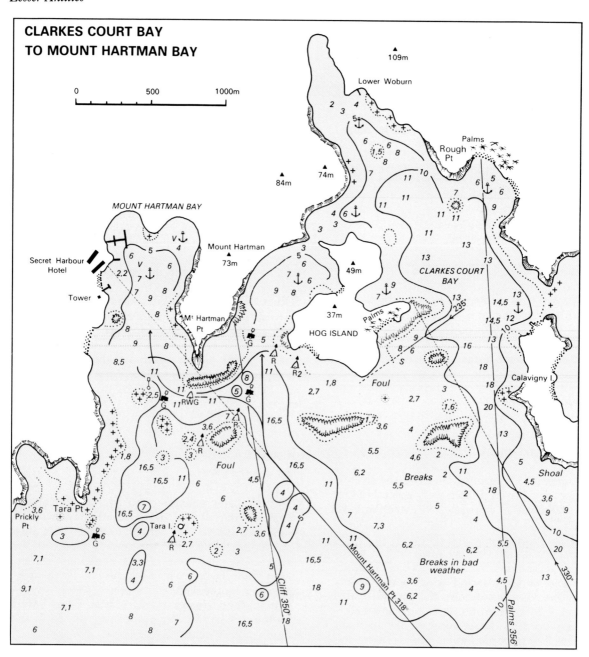

CLARKES COURT BAY
TO MOUNT HARTMAN BAY

0   500   1000m

109m

Lower Woburn

MOUNT HARTMAN BAY

Palms
Rough
Pt

Secret Harbour
Hotel

Tower

Mount Hartman
73m

84m

74m

49m

37m

HOG ISLAND

Mᵗ Hartman
Pt

CLARKES COURT
BAY

Palms

Calavigny I.

Foul

RWG

Foul

Breaks

Shoal

Tara Pt

Prickly
Pt

Tara I.

Breaks in bad
weather

Cliff 350°

Mount Hartman Pt 318°

Palms 356

Lower Woburn   Point W of Calivigny
              Petit Calivigny Bay

Entrance Clarkes Court Bay.

Village of Woburn   *Shoal patch*   *Woburn Pier*

Grenada. Clarkes Court Bay. *Hugo du Plessis*

Approach

Keep clear of Calavigny island – see above. There are also foul ground and shoals south of Hog Island. The best line from a point about half a mile south of Calavigny Island is 356° on to a group of Palm Trees behind the beach in Rough Island Bay which can be identified from a distance by the fields behind. This line passes very close to the reef off the west point of Calavigny Island but there is water to the west. (Rough Island Bay also known to the cartographers as Petit Calavigny Bay though the village of that name is high on the cliffs and has no path down.)

Anchorages

1. In the northwestern inlet. Anchor in 4–5m on mud SSW of the small landing stage of Lower Woburn. In the middle of the northwest arm leading to Lower Woburn there is a 1·5m patch which is difficult to see because the water is usually turbid; 100m either side there is 5m of water. Lower Woburn is on the bus route to St George's.
2. The inlet north of Hog Island. There are 3–4m in the centre on a bed of soft mud. Beware of the small reef which is difficult to see, 100m off the northeastern point of the island. Small yachts can get good shelter in 3–4m close inshore in the bay on the north side.
3. Inlet in the northeast of Hog Islet. There are 9m in the centre of this inlet, the shores of which are edged with mangrove. Beware of the reef, easily visible through the clarity of the water, which extends about 150m eastwards from the east point of the islet.
4. Petit Calavigny. In the north and the east of this spacious and deserted inlet, there are two beaches of grey sand fringed with coconut palms. Beware of a round reef, easy to see as it is barely covered with water, about 120m south of the northwest point of the inlet.

5. Beach on the northwest of Calavigny Island. This is the most beautiful anchorage in the bay in front of a very white beach surrounded with coconut palms and where there is a small landing stage. It is deep for anchoring and shelves sharply at the E end between the land and the mainland. The mainland side is foul. Anchor in 12–14m on sand about 100m from the shore. It is safe to go close in to the beach (5m, 30m from the shore). The channel of Calavigny Island is only usable by local boats.

Hog Island

12°00′N 61°44′W

Hog Island is a fair storm shelter where it is possible to get well up the mangroves and it does not have the same notorious rolling effect on boats as Prickly Bay. It used to be well-used only during the hurricane season but since buoys were laid by The Moorings Ltd it is now crowded all the year round. It is a good place for bird watching; in summer thousands of violet eared doves fly in to roost and there is usually a resident osprey. It was also a principal settlement of the Arawaks and pottery and other artifacts can still be picked up. Good diving and goggling.

Approach

From the southeast, aim 318° on the right hand cliff of Hartman Point. The reefs are usually marked by breakers. This route meets the buoyed channel coming from Secret Harbour (see page 24) and note the first buoy encountered is a red, starboard handed, buoy for the other channel and it lies well to the west of the channel you are in, with a shoal in between; do not turn into the east-west channel until it opens up.

From Secret Harbour the channel is buoyed but when approaching Hog Island, the buoys are close to the reef which extends into the channel beyond the line joining them; keep 100m from the port side. There is an uncharted 3m patch in the middle of the channel W of Hog Island 50m NW of the last starboard-hand buoy. Deep draught yachts should favour either side.

There is 2·5m at high water in the dog-leg north channel which is a useful cut to Lower Woburn but do not attempt it without local knowledge.

Anchorage

Anchor in 4–7·5m northwest of Hog Island on a muddy seabed. For best shelter get as far over to the east as possible.

Facilities

A few vegetables from the farm. Try Little Woburn or Secret Harbour.

Mount Hartman Bay

12°00′N 61°44′·5W

This bay is also known as Secret Harbour, a name useful to the charter company turning the bay into a major base, and has rocky coasts overlooked by green hills. On the west coast the white Mediterranean-style buildings of Secret Harbour Hotel, which are very easy to see near a square tower, are a good landmark for the entrance. It is a better place to leave a yacht, either on moorings or in the marina, and has less swell than Prickly Bay.

The local charter boats are on heavy moorings; in times of hurricanes, a chief danger may be from boats moved hurriedly round from Prickly Bay.

Approach

A buoyed channel has been established by The Moorings Ltd starting at Tara Island, a very small low mound of coral standing on a wide shallow patch. Note there is a 3m (not 3·5m) bank southwest of Tara Island, in the middle of the channel. It may break in a bad swell – there is water to the west but further in a reef extends 100m off the west shore.

Anchorage

Anchor in 4–8m on mud in the N or NE part of the bay; beware the shoal 75m W of the point on the N shore dividing the bay. The centre of the bay is full of moorings.

Facilities

Bar and restaurant in Secret Harbour Hotel. Water and fuel at The Moorings Ltd. Marina berths available.

Conspicuous grey cliff   *Hog Island*
                                             Note breakers on outlying reef

Grenada. S entrance to Hog Island and also entrance to Secret Harbour. *Hugo du Plessis*

Secret Harbour   NNE   *Mount Hartman Point*   *Hog Island anchorage*

Grenada. Entrance to Secret Harbour and Hog Island. *Hugo du Plessis*

Entrance to Mount Hartman Bay. Cliff S of Mount Hartman Pt on 318°

Prickly Bay

12°00'·0N 61°45'·4W

This wide bay, well protected from the trade wind by Prickly Point, is the most easily accessible and most popular anchorage in Grenada. However it is frequently made uncomfortable by swell and the dock is subject to surge. It is one of the world's cross-roads for yachts and although large, can at times get crowded with fifty or more yachts of all sizes. It is surrounded by wooded heights where several hotels and villas can be seen and edged in the northeast by a beach and coconut palms. On the east coast there is a small dock run by Spice Island Marine Services.

There is a good deal of aircraft noise by day, especially in the north bay.

Approach

Sail in.

Anchorage

There is an unmarked shoal in the middle, 1·5m over brain coral, very hard, its centre marked by a round white buoy. To clear it, keep the east peak of the distant twin peaks open of the hill on the north side of the harbour, heading 025°. There are also other coral patches roughly between this shoal and the conspicuous cliffs 300m north which although not hazardous are unwise spots to drop an anchor; it gets dangerously shallow within 100m of these cliffs. There is a prohibited anchorage within 150m of Calabash Beach on the northeast side, marked by a line of buoys, a wreck in the northeast corner and another south of the Spice Island Marine dock marked by a white buoy.

Anchor in the entrance to the northeastern inlet in 6–7m on sand. There may be places at the quay in the dock with 2–4m but note this is evacuated if a storm threatens. A quieter anchorage which may be welcome on disco nights is in the northern bay. The shoal in the middle is seldom visible but easy to avoid by keeping close to either side, 5m except for a shallow patch south of the point on the east side. Otherwise anchor where you can.

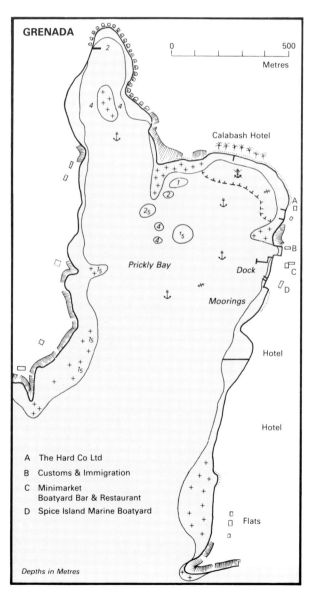

GRENADA

Calabash Hotel

Prickly Bay

Dock

Moorings

Hotel

Hotel

A   The Hard Co Ltd
B   Customs & Immigration
C   Minimarket
    Boatyard Bar & Restaurant
D   Spice Island Marine Boatyard

Flats

Depths in Metres

The Moorings Ltd Marina and Charter Base

Grenada. Secret Harbour. *Hugo du Plessis*

Leading line to avoid shoal in middle.
Twin peaks open of nearer hill W of Calabash Beach

Spice Island Marina
dock, boatyard and bar, etc.

Grenada. Prickly Bay. *Hugo du Plessis*

Glover Island looking E

Prickly Point looking E

Prickly Bay looking NE

Facilities

Customs north of Spice Island Marine Dock. Fuel and water at the dock but visitors may have to wait to get in. Call on VHF Ch 16 0800–1200 and 1300–1600 (no answer out of hours). 35-ton travel-lift but little room. Limited workshop facilities. The Hard Company specialises in procuring chandlery and handling clearance of imported items, boat minding (☎ and fax 809 444 4638).

Mini market. Bar and restaurant and many others nearby.

Transport

An unreliable bus service in and out of St George's, frequent crowded minibuses on the main road at the Sugar Mill (1M). Otherwise taxis, usually waiting for custom.

North and west coasts of Grenada

Coasts, dangers

Saline Point is the extreme southwest of the island with the unmarked Long Point Shoal extending for 0·5M off it. The airport runway stretches to the end of the point which has a light (Q(9)15s). The runways lights and the airport beacon, green and white, are conspicuous but are switched off when the airport closes. Another light, which has not yet appeared in notices and indeed which does not always work, is located on the hill north of the airport, 12°01′N 61°46′·1W approximately, Fl(2+1)20s18M.

• Between Saline Point and Long Point the coast is unsafe except for one anchorage. There is an unmarked shoal, almost awash, 0·5M off Long Point which has two high radio masts (Radio Grenada) each with two fixed red lights visible from a distance; there is space to pass between the shoal and the point keeping 100m off the point to avoid rocks and reefs on which the sea heaves and breaks.

Grenada and its northern islands looking SW

There is often a strong current off the point which seems to coincide with a strong west-going current on the south coast. Grande Anse has shoals and should not be entered on passage.

- North of St George's there is a conspicuous group of large white oil tanks in Grand Mal Bay. A mile north, Molinière Point has a rock at the end of it which appears almost separated from it. Between Molinière Point and David Point, 11M to the NNE, the coast is unobstructed, steep-to and covered with a dense vegetation. There are a number of villages and hamlets here and there, but only a few anchorages, (see page 30). The best landmarks in this area are the red and white radio mast at the head of Beauséjour Bay, three churches, one without a belfry, one with a square belfry, one with a spire south of Gouyave and Gouyave itself, with a large yellow building near the beach.
- Between David Point and Levera Point there is no good anchorage, several inshore reefs and a strong west-going current. The best landmark is Sauteurs Church.
- North of Levera Point is London Bridge, an arched rock, and 4M north of Grenada is the Ile de Ronde group, Ile de Caille, Ile de Ronde with the Sisters rocks a mile to the west, Diamond Rock (Kick'em Jenny) on the north side and Les Tantes to the east. The north- and west-going currents flow the most strongly through the channels between the islands.

Morne Rouge

12°01′·3N 61°46′·1W)

This small bay lies immediately south of Long Point. It is shallow and shelves to 1m. Although it looks better than Grande Anse, if the swell is bad there it usually turns out to be dangerous in Morne Rouge.

Anchorage

Anchor according to depth on the line into the middle of the bay. The holding must be the worst in the Caribbean, bottom weed over a hard surface. Try a fisherman's hooked into one of the holes; a trip may be useful to recover it.

Facilities

Bars and restaurants. The disco can be noisy.

Grande Anse

Grande Anse is bordered by a long white beach with low-roofed hotels visible beneath the palms, some at the northern end badly damaged during the US incursion. It provides a pleasant anchorage in very clear water but the northern swell – particularly in winter – can make it uncomfortable, particularly since the yacht will most probably be lying head to the prevailing wind. Though rolly, it may be a welcome change from the lagoon in St George's.

In August 1990 Grande Anse was declared a prohibited anchorage; as there is no other pleasant and swimmable anchorage within easy reach of St Georges, the prohibition may not last.

Approach

The southwestern half of the beach is skirted by a coral shelf for 150–300m with several dangerous heads. There are two shoals with little water over them and difficult to see, one about 200m from the middle of the beach, the other approximately 350m off the northeastern extremity of the beach. From

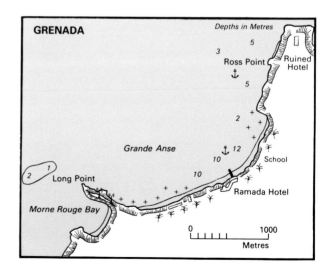

the north, keep the conspicuous sheds in the port open of Ross Point. From either direction, do not turn east until opposite the anchorage, 300m off the stone pier of the Ramada Hotel near a modest school building with a red tin roof, a little to the east of the centre of the beach (4m depths, sand). Anchoring is now forbidden within 500m of the shore – the bay is shallow and anchoring is possible well offshore.

An alternative anchorage is on Ross Point shoals, S of the harbour entrance, in 3–6m. Although less sheltered it is within convenient dinghy distance of the town.

Facilities

Some of the best hotels in Grenada. Shopping centre in Grande Anse.
Barclays Bank.

St George's

12°03′N 61°45′W

St George's is a small town with a warm and lively atmosphere. The town is in flights of steps and steep little alleyways, with houses smacking of Georgian architecture, and getting around is both arduous and, given the state of the paving, mildly hazardous; make your visit in the morning. It covers the two slopes of a rocky promontory which protects an excellent natural harbour from the north west. Thus one half of the town looks out towards the open sea whilst the other forms a semi-circle around the old port which is situated in the northern branch, the Careenage, of a double bay. The yacht anchorage is in the totally enclosed southern branch of this bay, the Lagoon. Part of the Lagoon is taken up by the marina, Grenada Yacht Services (GYS), which has some services for yachts. As the capital and principal town, small though it is, everything is concentrated here and if it is not available in St George's, it is not available on the island.

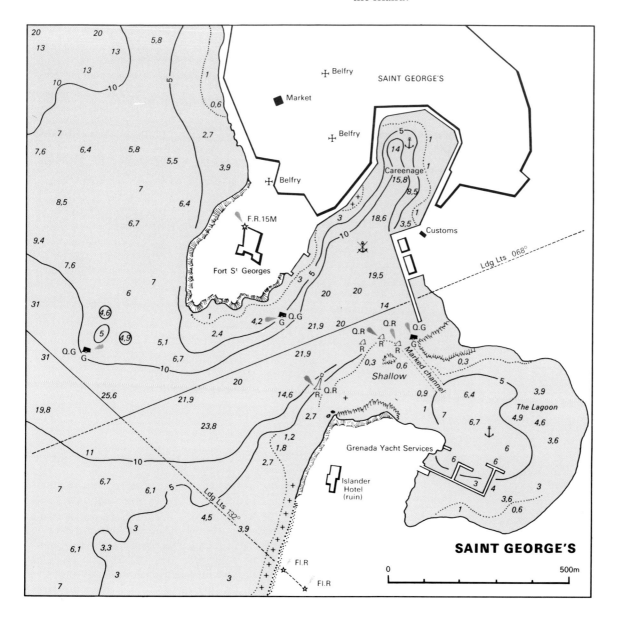

SAINT GEORGE'S

TV tower   Fort St George's

Saint George's looking E

Fort St George's Pt   Warehouses of new commercial port   Conspicuous hotel

Saint George's. Port entrance leading line (068°)

E side (green)   W side (red)

Grenada. St George's. Entrance to the Lagoon. *Hugo du Plessis*
Note First post projects further than first green post

It is a poor hurricane hole, not only for reasons described under 'Anchorage' but also because the reef would not keep out a heavy swell.

Approach

From the south, the entrance is 400m beyond the prominent ruined Islander Hotel, 62m. The harbour is open from this side and cruise liners can be seen at the dock. Although there is adequate water in the approach outside the buoyed channel, keep 200m off the point and when inside keep northeast of the starboard marks which are on the edge of the lagoon reef.

From the north, the entrance is not obvious and may be marked by a cruise liner emerging from a hole in the cliffs. It lies behind Fort St George's Point which merges with the background but is marked by battlements, flag staffs and the green-roofed police buildings. Get the ruined Islander Hotel open of Fort St George's, keep it so until the harbour has been opened up and keep more than 200m off the point.

Grenada. St George's lagoon. *Hugo du Plessis*

At night, the orange floodlights of the prison above St George's are conspicuous from a distance. Fort St George's is floodlit; a fixed red light is visible between SE and NW. The Lagoon buoys have reflective patches. The navigational lights are fairly reliable and even if out of action, a night approach is not impossible.

Entrance

The entrance to the Lagoon is through a narrow, marked, silting channel with 3m and it is necessary to get the channel in line before making the turn into it. The channel is marked by a lit red post Fl.R and three red buoys to starboard and a lit green post Fl.G and two buoys to port; because of the line of the channel the first starboard mark is west of the first port mark. It is very shoal outside the channel and it is advisable to wait for another yacht to clear the channel before entering.

Anchorage

Unfortunately the Lagoon is one of the most noisome, noisy and least secure anchorages of the Caribbean. The mud has been ploughed up over the years and is now unreliable holding. The long wooden jetty of GYS may now be quite unserviceable. Anchor where you can, with as short a scope as safety allows.

In the Anchorage, holding is poor on light mud, berthing at the decrepit pontoons at the marina should be done with caution.

It is possible to anchor for a short time in the middle of the Careenage, north of the prohibited area, poor holding and in the northeast part of the harbour but it is tricky because of shoals and the steep shelf. The berths at the quays of the old port are reserved for local craft unless the harbour master permits otherwise.

Formalities

Customs and immigration for arrivals and departures at GYS. Goods clearance at the Careenage – use an agent.

Facilities

Water, electricity and fuel at GYS. The fuel is duty-free which means dealing with the customs; duty-paid fuel in cans from Ottways Garage on the Lagoon Road. Gas from Huggins, the Careenage; if handed in early, the bottles can be returned by the evening.

GYS franchises a chandlery, not very well stocked, mechanical, electrical and woodworking shops and casual painters. There is a 230-tonne syncrolift. Showers, washing facilities; laundresses call.

Food Fair in the Careenage and the larger Foodland in the Lagoon are accessible by dinghy. Restaurants.

Barclays Bank at the top of the hill in Halifax St, 0800–1300 weekdays plus 1430–1700 Fridays.

Taxi boats run a cheap and irregular service to and from the town centre.

The harbour and lagoon at St George's, Grenada, (looking south).
Note shallow coral reefs on either side of the entrance to the
lagoon.
Anne Hammick

Mail holding facility and telephone at GYS
The post office, burnt down in April 1990, is now at
the southwest end of the Careenage. Open 0800–1500
weekdays but the parcel department closes between
1200 and 1300.
Grentel (Cable and Wireless) office on the Careenage,
telephone and telex.
Geest Line every week from Barry, Wales, United
Kingdom useful for anything heavy but use an agent
to clear.
Car hire. Buses.

The Careenage at St George's, Grenada (looking east).
Anne Hammick

Anchorages on the west coast of Grenada

Between St George's and David Point there are only a few anchorages and they can only be used when there is no northeasterly swell.

Dragon Bay
12°05'·1N 61°45'·4W

A quite pleasant bay with a sandy beach and a river immediately north of Molinière Point. Keep in the centre and away from the shores which have submerged rocks. There are 3m coral patches in the entrance but inshore the seabed is sandy with 3m depth 50m from the beach.

Halifax Harbour
12°06'·7N 61°44'·6W

A beautiful bay with room for two or three yachts in front of the continuously burning island rubbish dump which makes it easy to identify. The outer part is deep and shelves quickly to 4m. A moderate draught yacht can get well into the inner cover where there is good shelter in depths down to 2m. Alternatively anchor in less shelter approximately 60m from a little grey beach on the north coast, 7m. Beware of a coral shelf off the southern point of the bay.

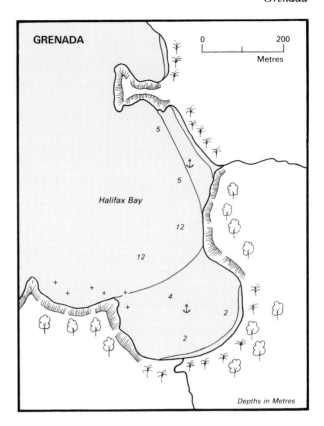

GRENADA

Halifax Bay

Depths in Metres

Grenada. Dragon Bay. *Hugo du Plessis*

Gouyave
09'·7N 61°43'·6W

Gouyave, an old whaling station, is one of the most picturesque villages of the island. It stretches over a sandy headland where a large number of small boats are hauled out in the shade of coconut palms. Gouyave can be identified easily from the sea and the approach is safe. Anchor in 6–7m depths approximately 150m from the beach north of the headland.

Gouyave village looking NE

Crayfish Bay

12°12'·8N 61°41'·2W

Anchor in front of a beach fringed by coconut palms
with the hamlet of Nonpareil behind. It is a luxuriant
setting. There are 3–5m depths and a sandy bottom,
100–150m from the beach. In both Gouyave and
Crayfish some supplies and very simple eating places
are to be found in the village.

Both Crayfish and Gouyave are uncomfortable in
any swell.

Isle de Ronde

12°18'N 61°35'W

Ile de Ronde is not circular; possibly it takes it name
from the surrounding waters constantly dancing their
round. If so the name carries its own warning about
currents. It lies 5M NNE of Grenada and is inhabited by a few fishermen. The one anchorage protected from the prevailing winds is in the bay on the
west coast. It bordered by several deserted beaches
(almost completely covered at high tide) at the foot
of steep slopes. The best anchorage is in front of the
north beach where the seabed is even and sandy, in
3–5m depths, 150–200m from the shore. The central
beach is edged by a coral shelf with little water over
it which extends for about 200m from the land in the
southern part of the bay. The swell can make this anchorage uncomfortable, even untenable. Kick 'em
Jenny is a major bird colony (see page 15) but access
is very difficult.

Isle de Ronde seen from the southwest.
Anne Hammick

III. The Grenadines

Charts
Imray-Iolaire *B3, B32, B311, B30*
Admiralty *2821, 2872, 791*
SHOM *3208*
US *25481, 25482*

General remarks

Geography

The Grenadines stretch for about 52M between Grenada and St Vincent. They consist of some 100 islands, islets and rocks, some islets mountainous, rising to 335m, and some rocks awash. Sovereignty is divided between Grenada and St Vincent.

The chain provides a number of well sheltered anchorages in varied settings which has attracted hundreds of yachtsmen. It must be emphasised that there are unmarked and uncharted shallows and coral reefs; and whilst marks might appear on charts they do not necessarily appear on the water. Further, currents are strong, particularly so near reefs. The rule of thumb is that serious obstructions between major islands have been located though not necessarily marked but inshore obstructions may not have been. When in doubt inshore, reef sailing techniques should be adopted – see page 6. The remains of the M.V. *Antilles*, wrecked in 1973 on a reef north of Mustique, will serve as a reminder.

In terms of pilotage, the Grenadines are best considered in three groups and are dealt with on this basis from south to north: the Carriacou group from Bonaparte Rocks to Petit St Vincent; the Union group from Frigate Island to Petit Canouan and the Bequia group from Savan Rock to Bequia. This division is, however, politically inconvenient and attention must be drawn to the fact that the boundary between the states of Grenada and St Vincent lies in the southern group, between Petite Martinique and Petit St Vincent.

The islands are poor. Cotton was grown but the economy is now either subsistence or based on the tourist. There are about 6500 citizens of Grenada and 11,000 citizens of St Vincent.

History

The Grenadines did not feature in the wars like their neighbours. They were by themselves too small to quarrel about.

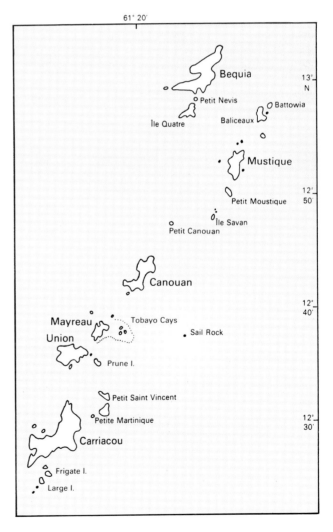

Arrival

See under Carriacou, Union Island and Bequia. From the Atlantic, make for Grenada or St Vincent; hitting the chain amidships is dangerous from this angle and is not recommended. Most islands have reefs on their East side, there are no navigational lights whatever the charts may say and on some islands there are not even town lights. If it has to be done, go S of Carriacou or N of Canouan which are clearer than the Martinique Channel between Carriacou and Union Island. Petite Martinique's conical peak of 227m is more conspicuous from the East than Carriacou's 290m peak at its northern end. Unlit Sail Rock (57m) is an isolated danger east of Mayreau and nearer in are the reefs of Worlds End. The peaks of Union Island, 300 and 270m, will tend to look like one hill. Radar will be helpful.

Formalities

Clear at Hillsborough, Carriacou (Grenada); Clifton, Union Island and Admiralty Bay, Bequia (St Vincent)

Do not forget to change the courtesy flag when crossing the boundary; omission may affect your reception. The flags are:

Grenada Divided into four triangles of yellow, top and bottom, and green, hoist and fly; in the centre a red disc bearing a gold star; along the top and bottom edged red stripes each bearing three gold stars; on the green triangle near the hoist a pod of nutmeg.

St Vincent Three vertical stripes of blue, yellow and green, with the yellow of double width and charged with three green diamonds.

Non-nationals are forbidden to spear fish in St Vincent. The following areas have been designated as preserves: Petit St Vincent, Palm Island, Mayreau, the Tobago Cays, Mustique (west coast), Ile Quatre, Bequia (northwest and north east coasts).

Hurricane holes

Tyrell Bay, Carriacou.

Maintenance

Carriacou Boatyard, Tyrell Bay, Carriacou.

Communications

Airstrips on Carriacou, Union, Canouan, Mustique. Frequent ferries between St Vincent and Bequia. Thrice weekly mail boat from St Vincent to Union Island calling at all islands en-route. Island schooners between Grenada, Carriacou and Petite Martinique and between Carriacou and Union Island.

The Carriacou group

Charts

Imray-Iolaire *B32, B31, B311*
Admiralty *2872*
US *25482*
SHOM

General

The first European settlers on Carriacou were French who turned to cotton for their livelihood. The island was acquired by Britain in 1763, together with Grenada, but it changed hands again to be recovered in 1783. The cotton plantations fell into decay after the abolition of slavery and were killed off by American cotton, then still grown by slaves, undercutting their market. At the beginning of the 19th century Scottish shipbuilders developed boatyards here which rivalled the yards on Cayman Island. Their successors still build with an adze on the shores of Tyrrel Bay and Windward. It is volcanic and steep, but a dry island as the hills are not high enough to provoke rain. Carriacou lives from agriculture, stock breeding and fishing. It is a hospitable island with an individual atmosphere and a genuine folklore which has not been exploited for the benefit of tourism; amongst the traditions is that of smuggling, which is by no means dead.

Coasts, dangers

This group consists of the islets lying immediately to the south of Carriacou, Carriacou, Petite Martinique and Petit St Vincent. In winter the passage from Grenada to Carriacou is one of the harder, normally close hauled with the current pushing strongly westwards. A sailing yacht should consider tacking east near Point David where the set is less. From the southwest the group starts inauspiciously with Bonaparte Rocks, which have a 4·5m patch to their southwest, Large Island (64m), Frigate Island (57m) and Saline Island (62m) where landing is prohibited. Currents are always strong in the channels between these islands and in the surroundings. See page 9.

Carriacou, the largest of the Grenadine Islands, is traversed by a range of hills. Chapeau Carré (292m) in the southwest is the highest and the range declines northeastwards. In the central part there is a large radio mast with several parabolic aerials standing on the highest peak of the Mont d'Or range (252m). On the west coast between Southwest Point and Cistern Point is Tyrrel Bay, one of the best anchorages in the Grenadines (see page 38). Sisters Rocks, white and clearly visible (14 and 22m), lie 0·75M west of Cistern Point (one wonders about a possible confusion between cisterns and sisters). Between Cistern and Rapid Point the bay is encumbered first by Mabouya Islet (41m) and Sandy Isle (very low) with shoals inshore, then, beyond Hillsborough, Jack a Dan standing on the eastern edge of a ledge with depths less than 1m. Rapid Point, at the northern tip

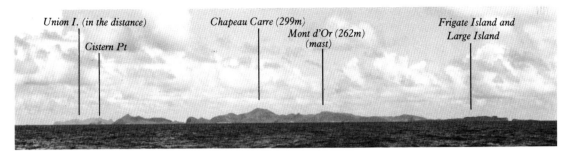

Union I. (in the distance)
Cistern Pt
Chapeau Carre (299m)
Mont d'Or (262m)
(mast)
Frigate Island and
Large Island

Carriacou looking NE

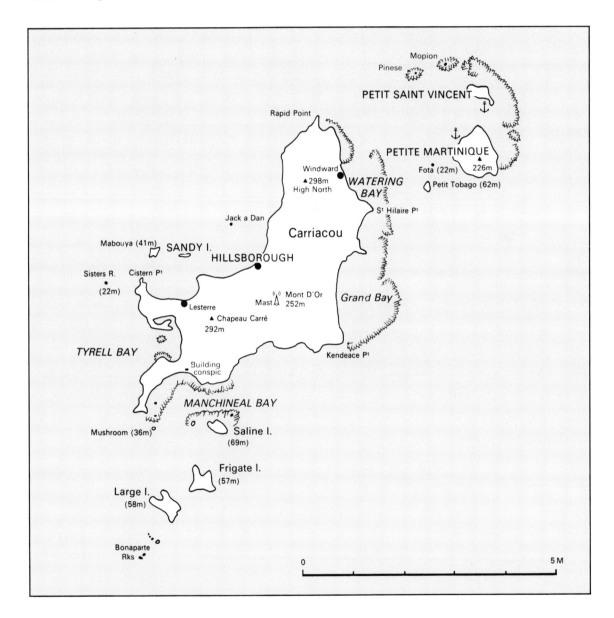

of the island, is low, tapering and has a yellow house with a red roof on it.

The east coast has an offshore reef all along it on which the sea always breaks. Watering Bay in the northeast and Grand Bay in the southwest lie behind the reef but are not of interest. The reefs and shoals, which are often difficult to see, extend as far as Saline Island. There is a conspicuous group of light grey buildings to the northeast of Manchineal Bay.

Northeast, between Carriacou and Petite Martinique (225m), lie Fota Rock (22m) and Petit Tobago (62m). Shallows (2·7m) extend for 250m SSW of Petit Tobago. Currents in these channels can reach 3 knots and flow NNW for longer than they flow SSE. SSE.

The conical peak of Petite Martinique, together with its height, makes the island easy to identify. It has some good anchorages partly because it shares with Petit St Vincent the protection of an offshore reef to windward, starting near Pinese northwest of Petit St Vincent and passing in a crescent east and south to a point east of Petite Martinique. Petit St Vincent, wooded and 83m high, is commonly called PSV. There is a channel between Pinese and Mopion. When crossing between Petite Martinique and Petit St Vincent bear in mind that an international boundary is also being crossed.

Formalities

Although customs are at Hillsborough, those arriving at Tyrrel Bay may take a bus there to clear. For some unknown reason, yachts clearing inwards will be given permission to stay 24 hours only and they must leave for St George's within this time to clear again.

Carriacou: Southwestern Point and Saline Island

12°26′N 61°28′·5W

These deserted anchorages in the south of the island should only be contemplated in fine weather when there is no southeasterly swell. There are strong eddies round the islands; the current sets across the rocks off Southwest Point and onto all reefs and islands

Manchineal Bay

There is a coral reef about 0·2M off the eastern side of the headland and the islets, Little Mushroom and Mushroom, (36m, shaped like a button mushroom) extend southwards from it. To reach the lagoon en-

closed by this reef pass about 100m west of Mushroom islets and One Tree Rock 0·3M further north. If coming from the north, do not turn east until the south side of White Island is open south of Mushroom Island. One Tree Rock now has three trees, windswept and stunted.

Anchor northwest or north of, and as close as possible to, the latter in 2·5–2·8m on sand. Keep to the E third of the lagoon; the west is foul with shallow coral patches. Use two anchors; there is a 2 knot current on the flood.

Saline Island

Approach between Saline and White Island, from the southwest. The reef stretches the mile between White and Cassava Islands. The channel is 150m wide with depths of 10–12m. The current in it reaches 3 knots. Anchor between Saline Island and the reef, at the entrance to a small inlet in the north coast of Saline which shoals to 1m.

Further south there are two anchorages marked on the charts near Frigate Island and Large Island. Neither is recommended as most of the time they are uncomfortable and affected by strong currents.

Carriacou, Tyrrel Bay

12°27′·5N 61°29′·3W

This large area of water, well sheltered from the prevailing winds and surrounded by green hills, is the best anchorage on Carriacou. Near the beach which fringes the east coast there are several houses, a fuel depot near a landing stage and often one or two local-style boats being built. It is permissible to take

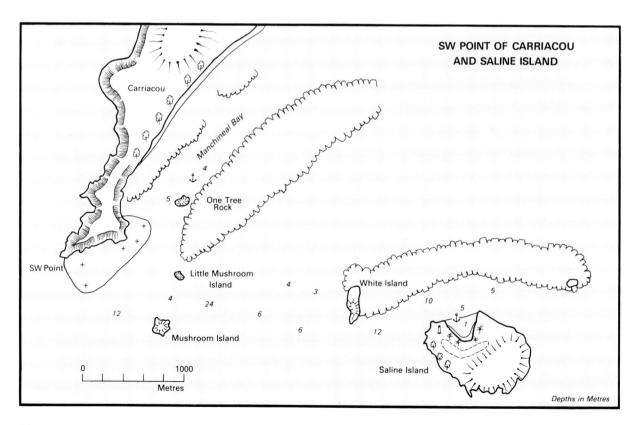

Landing and tanks (conspicuous)

Carriacou. Tyrrel Bay looking N. General view

a bus from Tyrrel Bay to clear customs in Hillsborough – but see the warning on page 40.

In the north of the bay a lagoon in the mangrove provides one of the better hurricane holes in the area – if you can get through the channel, 1·5m or less. The Careenage soon fills up with the heavily built trading schooners and sloops on receipt of a hurricane warning.

Approach

Tyrrel Bay is easy to identify from the sea because of several bright tanks in the fuel depot south of the jetty. There is an isolated shoal in the northern part of the bay, marked on its north side by two red buoys, with less than 1·5m and another hazardous reef, steep-to, off the south arm of the bay. The channel between the two is wide with an even sandy bottom at 4–5m. Either enter through this channel by keeping the three silver tanks in line with the saddle of the shallow twin peak hill behind (shown on the right of the photo on page 39); keep 200m off the south shore until you are within 200m of the east shore. The red buoy on the south side of the harbour marks the end of the boatyard slip, not the reef. Alternatively, come in by the deeper channel north of the reef.

Anchorage

Anchor in 3–4·5m about 150m from the east shore or in 8–10m west of the landing stage. The charter boats crowd in of an evening but tend to keep well inshore; an offshore anchorage may be quieter. Keep clear of the pier which is used by island sloops and the tanker.

In the north of the bay, there is an inlet banked by mangroves leading to the Careenage. The Careenage

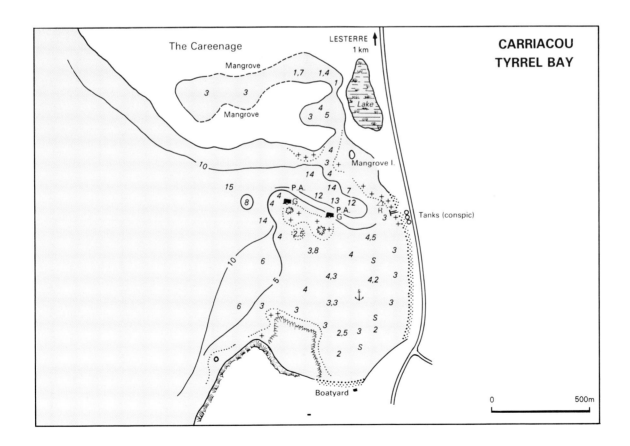

is said to be accessible to boats drawing less than 1·5m but this is doubtful and 1m may be closer to the mark; survey its very narrow entrance (12–13m) by dinghy. Once in, there is said to be 2–3·5m.

Facilities

Two supermarkets near the beach. Several bars and restaurants. A boatyard for yachts (under French management) is being set up in the southern part of the bay. The village of Lesterre is 1km.

Communications

Buses, Taxis.

Carriacou, Sandy Islet

12°29'·2N 61°29'·2W

Sandy Islet is a nature reserve 1·3M west of Hillsborough. It is a very white sandbank with two clumps of coconut palms. There is a pleasant anchorage near the south coast in extraordinarily clear water, protected from the northeasterly swell and generally very busy with day trips from Hillsborough and elsewhere.

Approach

Beware of shoals (3m) 0·4M east of the islet and of the reef extending 150m WNW.

Anchorage

Anchor in 3m on sand, about 100m from the south coast.

Carriacou, Hillsborough

12°29'N 61°27'·6W

Hillsborough, the unpretentious capital of the island, is situated in the centre of the wide Hillsborough Bay. It is the port for Carriacou but like Dominica it simply has a jetty, this one on piles, 60m long, opposite the centre of the village.

Approach

The easy passages are, from the south, seaward of Mabouya and Sandy islets and from the north, just west of Jack a Dan Rock on which there is a small light. There are inshore passages from both sides. Pass midway between Sandy Island and mangrove-covered Loriston Point and head for Hillsborough on

The long jetty at Hillsborough, Carriacou.
Anne Hammick

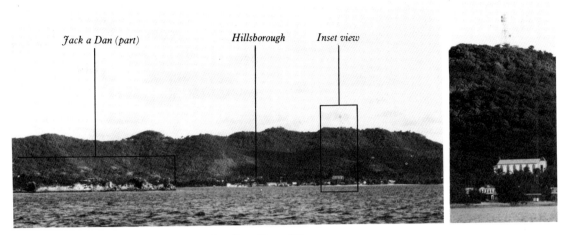

Jack a Dan (part)   Hillsborough   Inset view

Landing NW of Hillsborough. Inset: Leading line: Mont d'Or
mast and church on 145·5°

082°; a 4m patch can be avoided by eye if need be.
There are uncharted reefs stretching 500m east of
Loriston. Passing between Jack a Dan and Craigston,
keep in the western third of the channel; this is not
for deep draught boats.

Anchorage

Anchor in 4–5m on sand, about 100m north of the
jetty. There is a dinghy landing on the south side of
the jetty, subject to surge but better than landing on
the beach on the north side. The pier has 3m but
berthing against the piles is difficult. The northerly
swell often makes the anchorage uncomfortable.

Facilities

Customs and immigration on the jetty.
Supplies in the village. The market in Hillsborough
is better stocked than any other in the Grenadines.
Two hotels and a few simple restaurants.
Barclays Bank.
Carriacou Boatbuilders can haul out 100 tons with
2·75m draught. They claim to be able to do any
repairs.

Communications

Airport 3km.

Carriacou, Watering Bay

12°30'·5N 60°25'·6W

On the shores of Watering Bay, the picturesque hamlet of Windwards was the main boat building centre
on the island in the 19th century. It is a typical traditional, Antilles-style port with many local boats, a
large number of which move only under sail. Yachts
seldom put in here.

Approach

The approach through a wide channel between the
coastal reefs and the coral barrier further out to sea
presents no particular difficulty but is limited to vessels drawing less than 2·6m. The best landmark is
the long school building with a central facade and a
red roof on the southwest coast of the bay. A bearing
of 215° towards this building leaves to starboard the
reef which extends off the west coast and which is
cursorily marked in the south by a pole with a blue-
ish petrol can attached to it. Once past this mark
move to starboard towards the landing stage of
Windward.

School (conspicuous)   Pole with can   Reef
topmark

Carriacou. Watering Bay looking NNW

Carriacou. Watering Bay. Village and landing at Windward on 245°

Anchorage
Anchor near the landing stage in 2·5–3·5m on sand.
Facilities
None

Petite Martinique

12°31′N 61°23′W

This little island was colonised in the 17th century by Breton sailors and carpenters who developed their tradition of naval construction, fishing and smuggling. Continuity is assured by several old boatyards situated near the beach in the shade of coconut palms.

Petit Saint Vincent and Petite Martinique looking SE

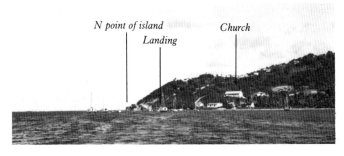

Petite Martinique anchorage looking

Approach
From the south, give Rapid Head a fair berth and beware the 7m shoal on its east side, the inshore and the offshore reefs of Carriacou's east coast and mind both Petit Tobago and Fota Rock. Pinese has shoals well to its southwest (see below). The current may well set hard against you in the channel. Despite the requirement to clear at Hillborough, the usual approach is from the north and those on Petite Martinique do not seem bothered; for details see Petit St Vincent (below).

Anchorage
Anchor in 5–8m, 100–150m WSW of the landing stage. Watch out for barely covered shoals which extend for about 130m from the shore 250m southwest of the landing stage and in front of the southern part of the beach.

Petit St Vincent

The contrast is striking between the luxury of Petit St Vincent and the extreme primitiveness of Petite Martinique only a few hundred metres away. Petit St Vincent is private hotel-island, green and edged with beaches of very white sand. On the south coast there is a pleasant anchorage in clear water well protected from the prevailing winds near the landing stage of the hotel where fuel and water can be obtained.

Approach
Arriving from the north, steer 150° towards the summit of Petite Martinique in order to pass between the two sandbanks of Pinese in the west and Mopion in the east. Do not enter this way unless you have identified these two banks. Pinese, meaning Bed Bug, is sandy, is difficult to see, is barely above water and indeed in 1984 went missing. Mopion is easier to identify because it is slightly higher and has a small thatched shelter on top of it (unless now removed by a hurricane). The channel between the two, which is about 250m wide with 7–13m, is unsafe near Mopion. When through alter course to the east towards the hotel landing stage which can be seen near the southeastern tip of the island.

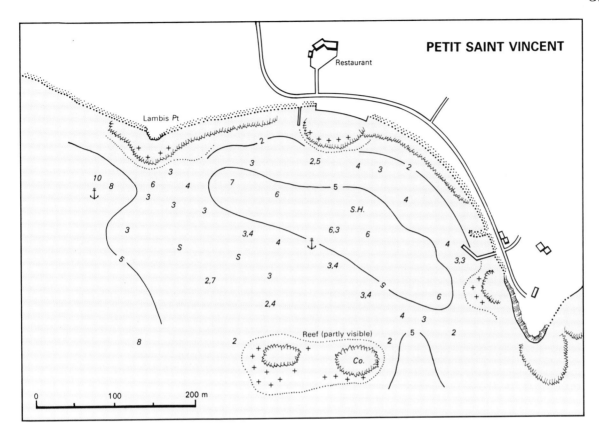

PETIT SAINT VINCENT

Anchorage

Anchor in 3–6m on sand to the west of the landing stage. Beware of a reef which is difficult to see just to the south of the anchorage; do not approach on the east side.

Vessels with a deep draught should anchor west of Lambis Point in 10–12m.

There is a fair anchorage inside the reefs on the north side. Eyeballing is necessary. There is a 2 knot current.

Facilities

Water and fuel at the hotel landing stage (3·2m) (the only pier-side fuel between Grenada and Bequia). Bar, bakery, restaurants, souvenir but no serious shops (contact VHF Ch 16).

Grenadines: The Union group

Charts
Imray-Iolaire *B31, B311*
Admiralty *2872*
SHOM *3206*
US *25482*

Coasts, dangers
- Palm Island, also known as Ile de la Prune, lies less than 1M ESE of Union Island. It is surrounded by reefs except on the west coast, where it is possible to anchor.
- Union Island, which is 307m high in the west, is characterised by a very steep hilly outline. The northwest, west and southwest coasts are comparatively safe whereas there are reefs off the south, east and northeast coasts. Near the eastern extremity, Red Islet (35m) is in fact brownish with a small lighthouse (Fl.R.10s6M) which for the past two years has not been working. In the south, Frigate Island, the southern side of which is perpendicular, is easy to identify from the southwest and the southeast.
- Mayreau, a small green island 100m or so high possesses only one hamlet. There are several islets, rocks and dangers in the northern approaches – from the northwest to the northeast: Catholic Rocks (21 and 11m); Catholic Islet (51m) and Dry Shingle (a few metres); Baline Rocks (low and jagged). A course in a direct line between the southwest point of Canouan and the northwest point of

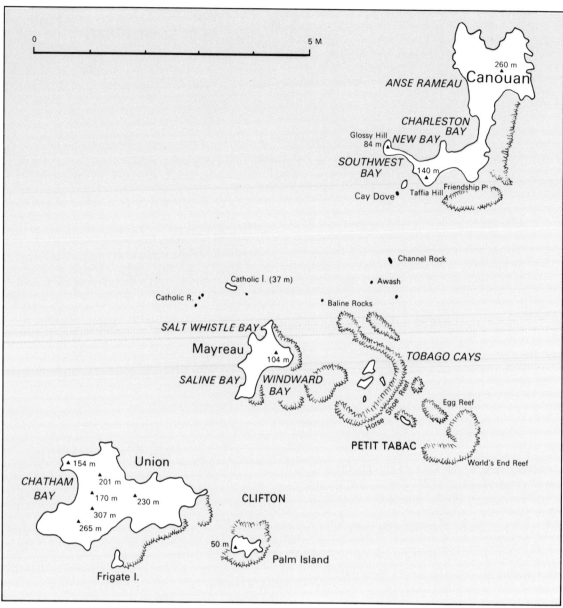

Mayreau avoids these dangers. Off the west coast of the island, there are shoals for 0·3M to the WSW off Pointe Grande Col which has a white buoy off it and a wreck with 3m over it 0·25M WNW of the same point.

- East of Mayreau a large group of coral reefs, only partially uncovering, extends for 4M. The biggest of these is Horseshoe Reef enclosing four green islets, the Tobago Cays; a fifth islet, Petit Tabac, lies approximately 0·6M south east of the group outside Horseshoe Reef. The channels and anchorages are described on pages 47–51.
- In the centre of the channel between the Tobago Cays and Canouan stand Channel Rocks which are very low but show clearly and are easy to recognise. South of them lies Break Rock awash and difficult to see when a fresh wind raises crests on the waves. The current is often strong in this channel.
- Canouan, the most northerly island in this group, is very arid and crossed by a steep range of hills with a peak 260m high in the north. The southwest of the island ends in a conspicuous conical hill.

The northwestern and southwestern extremities of the island are safe as is the northern part of the east coast. The southeast and south coasts have coral reefs 0·75M off, on which the sea always breaks.
- Finally, Petit Canouan (67m), steep and conical in shape, has a little lighthouse (but no light).

Palm Island (Prune Island)

12°35'·2N 61°24'·0W

Prune Island was renamed Palm Island by its only owner who, shortly after the second world war, was motivated to make a remarkable single-handed crossing of the Pacific. A hotel island, it is attractively laid out and popular for day visits; cruise liners call. Though flat and sandy it has three hills and reefs on all but the west side. The only anchorage is in front of the white beach with two small landing stages on the west coast.

Approach

Beware Grande de Coi reef in the southern approach; the sea does not always break on it and the buoy may be missing. Head for the northwestern sector of the most northerly of the two landing stages in front of which the seabed slopes very rapidly.

Anchorage

For yachts the better anchorage is between the small piers and the reef to the south. There is a 2m patch but this can be seen quite easily. The reef gives some shelter but swell can come over it; the anchorage is very uncomfortable in a northeasterly swell.

Facilities

Bar, restaurant and a small store

Union Island, Clifton

12°35′·5N 61°24′·9W

Clifton is the main village of Union Island with several hundred inhabitants. It is situated at the eastern extremity of the island in a bay well protected from the east by a coral barrier but which has a reef (Roundabout Reef) in the middle of it, a considerable obstruction to the anchorage. Many yachts put in and it can be difficult to find room during the tourist season. It owes its reputation as much to the atmosphere and the services provided by the Anchorage Yacht Club as to the beauty of the setting. It is also the most convenient port of entry and exit for yachts coming from or going to Grenada. Curiosity: the shark pool in Anchorage Yacht Club.

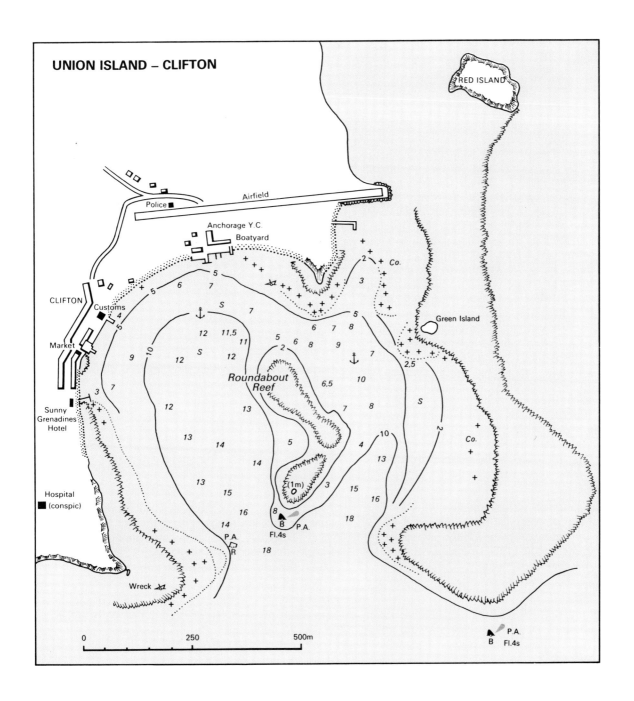

Union I. Clifton looking N.

Union I. Entrance to Clifton Harbour.

Approach

From the south, it is easy to be set westwards by the current and you must clear Lagoon reef which lies ¾M east of Frigate island. Beware the isolated reef Grande de Coi, which dries but on which the sea does not always break. It lies 0·5M west of Palm Island and about 0·6M SSW of Clifton Harbour; the once-red buoy marking its west side is hard to see if there.

On the north side, the current in the Mayreau Channel can also be strong. The anchored yachts can be plainly seen between Red Island and the mainland of Union. It is important not to head towards them or mistake Red Island, which is small and conical, for Palm Island. Red Island can only be passed to the East and Clifton can only be entered from the south. Clifton's protecting reef should be marked on its south side by two black buoys in poor condition; the southeastern of these was missing in 1990 and the south buoy does not mark the turning into the harbour which is still further west. Although there is supposed to be a light on Red Island it would be no aid to entering the harbour and a night approach is not recommended; it has to be eye-balled.

Entrance

The hospital, a square white building with a red roof standing on the western side of the entrance, is the best landmark for identifying Clifton. Roundabout reef is slap in the middle of the bay; pass either side.

Anchorage

The best anchorages are to the north and the east of the bay in 6–10m on sand.

The eastern pier is reserved for local charter yachts and the public pier, by the Administrative Building, is frequently used by local cargo boats.

Formalities

Customs at the post office 0800–1200 and 1300–1700 daily except Friday when it closes at 1500 for the weekend. When closed it may be possible to clear at the Anchorage. Immigration at the airfield, a short walk.

Facilities

Anchorage Yacht Club: Water (expensive and in the dry season, scarce), washing facilities, showers, restaurant, bar where mail can be collected . Two slips, one taking small island schooners. (contact VHF Ch 16 and 68).

In the village: diesel (by can), supplies (often a limited choice), restaurants, souvenir shops.

Communications

Airfield with daily services between the limits of Grenada and St Vincent.

Union Island, Frigate Island

12°34'·9N 61°26'·3 W

Frigate Island has a steep peak at its southern end tapering to a low stony spit on the north. There is a fairly deserted, unusually calm anchorage to the northwest of the island though some swell may creep round the corner and it can be gusty in the lee of the 77m peak.

Approach

Approach from the south and follow the west coast about 80–100m off. Depths decrease gradually to 3–4m with a sandy seabed NW of the peak. Beyond that it becomes shallow.

This small islet on the reef fringing Clifton Harbour, Union
Island, was 'home' to a local fisherman.
Anne Hammick

Anchorage

Anchor according to depth, sand with extensive
patches of weed. The holding on sand is good.

The bay towards Ashton is shallow though used by
small motor fishing boats. A shoal draught boat
might be able to creep in but once past the island
there is no shelter until very close in by the village.

Union Island, Chatham Bay

12°36′N 61°27′W

A good anchorage can be found on the west coast of
the island in this spacious and deserted bay, in front
of a sandy beach surrounded by volcanic cliffs covered in vegetation. There is often some slight swell
and there are gusts from the surrounding heights;
possibly for these reasons few yachts call here.

Approach

The bay is open. Beware an isolated shoal (2m) in the
middle near the beach.

Anchorage

The best anchorage is in the northeastern corner in
4–5m on sand, 100–150m from the beach.

The seabed is more uneven in the southern half of
the bay where fishermen frequently lay out their
nets, which are not easy to see.

The Tobago Cays

12°38′·0N 61°21′·5W

Left to themselves, the Tobago Cays would provide
some of the more beautiful anchorages in the
Antilles. They consist of four uninhabited islands
with very white beaches, shaded by coconut palms
and covered in vegetation. The opaline lagoon is enclosed by a large coral barrier on which the Atlantic
swell breaks constantly. Now, however, in the more
popular anchorages the noise of the surf is lost under
the beat of the radios – but it is a big area of semi-
sheltered water and it is still possible to find a place
of one's own.

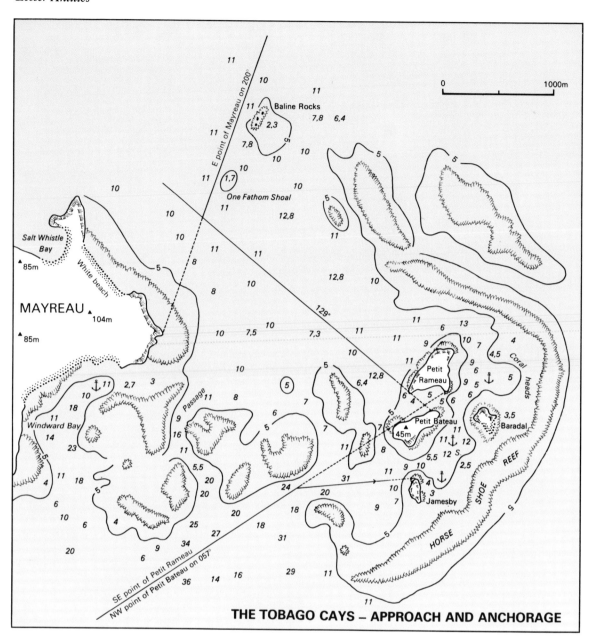

THE TOBAGO CAYS – APPROACH AND ANCHORAGE

Leading line for S entrance
Baradal open of Petit Bateau

Grenadines. The Tobago Cays looking NE. *Hugo du Plessis*

The Tobago Cays looking SE

The Tobago Cays. Views of leading line (129°)

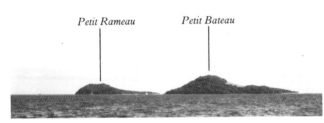

The Tobago Cays. S entrance. Leading line on 058°

There are a large number of reefs between Mayreau and the Tobago Cays as well as to seaward of them. Petit Tabac, a very low islet fringed with coconut palms, emerges from a reef on the seaward side. Deep channels make it possible to pass between the reefs but they are unmarked; currents are often strong and unpredictable and in the main channels outside, stronger though more predictable. A dinghy which breaks down in Mayreau Channel may be well on the way to Panama before it is reported missing. Care and attention is necessary; see page 6 and consider the position of the sun.

Approach and channels

Southern approach The southeastern point of Petite Rameau in line with the northwestern point of Petite Bateau on 057° leads about 100m south of the reefs which extend to the WSW off Petite Bateau and which are not easy to see. Take it cautiously. Alternatively the central of the three hills on Palm (Prune) Island in transit with High North on Carriacou leads one just clear of the southwestern end of Horseshoe Reef – particularly useful if entering under sail. When inside the reef turn towards the north

tip of Jamesby on 085°. If leaving by the south, when outside continue southwest and do not turn west, for instance to go to Chatham Bay or Mayreau, until the hospital at Clifton is well open of the top of Red Island or Monkey Point on Mayreau bears 287°. The passage is easy enough in good light but the shoals south of Mayreau are not so easy to see, particularly if departure is taken after noon.

Northern approach A course of 200° towards the eastern point of Mayreau leaves Baline Rocks, a group of blackish jagged rocks (3m), 200m to the east and a shoal with less than 2m situated 0·35M SSW of Baline Rocks 120m to the east. Look for the leading marks on 128°: a decapitated triangle with the shorter side at the top on the south point of Petit Rameau and the same with the shorter side at the bottom on the north point of Petit Bateau, about 20m high. The marks are supposed to be painted white; they are difficult to see and are quite easily confused with yacht masts.

The channel to the north of Petite Rameau is little used by yachts in spite of being relatively wide and free from isolated dangers. Coral outcrops run a short distance northwards from the island and southwards from Horseshoe Reef, but for the yacht wishing to enter or leave the Cays under sail this passage would be safer than that between Petite Rameau and Petite Bateau, which is considerably narrower and frequently obstructed by anchored yachts.

The north-south channel east of Mayreau can be followed quite easily by eye if the yacht can be positioned at the entrance. From the south head on 341° towards the east edge of Mayreau. From the north follow the reef round from L'Anse Bandeau. In both cases good light is advisable and be prepared to abort if the channel does not become clear.

Looking northeast towards Baradal Island from Jamesby, showing the deservedly popular anchorage.
Anne Hammick

Baradal Island in The Tobago Cays looking southwest. The islands visible are (left to right) Jamesby, Union and Petit Bateau.
Anne Hammick

Petit Rameau   *Baradal (in distance)*   *Petit Bateau*

Grenadines. The Tobago Cays. Anchorage between Petit Rameau and Petit Bateau. *Hugo du Plessis*

Anchorages

There are several anchorages around the islets on a sandy bottom with good holding. They are well sheltered from the swell by the reef but mostly very open to the trade winds which can be strong making the lagoon choppy and even rough. You must be properly dug in with proper scope particularly in the channel between Petite Bateau and Petite Rameau (3–4m, sandy bottom in the centre) which can have a strong reversing current; many charter yachts do not use chain but rope (often more than necessary) and tend to career around their anchors. The most popular anchorage is the area between Petite Bateau, Baradal, Jamesby and the exterior reef, 13m decreasing gradually towards the reef. There are extensive reefs to the east of Baradal, though in good light it is possible to pick a route between the isolated coral heads well towards the fringing reef. Particular care will be needed if intending to anchor overnight in such a location, as it will be impossible to retrace the route after sundown should the weather deteriorate. The beach on the eastern side of Jamesby has several coral heads off it for a distance of 80m but water south of this islet is safe (2·5–3m).

Outside anchorages

If careless this is a dangerous area. It is essential to keep a good look out, sail in good light and watch carefully for the set of the current which may not go as predicted. The anchorages are less protected than those in the Tobago Cays and should only be used in fine weather.

The small sandy lagoon on the northern edge of Petite Tabac Islet can be approached with caution from the west. Enter on a heading of 222° and keep close to the reef and to the sandy point which extends north and west from the islet. Beware of two barely covered coral heads about 60m from the beach. There is 3m in the entrance and 2–2·5m a little to the east of the two coral heads. Do not try this anchorage in a northeasterly trade wind.

There is a temporary anchorage inside Worlds End Reef which is good for fishing and underwater diving. Pass south of Petite Tabac taking a back bearing of 294° on its northeastern point and enter a bay in the reef. Continue about 300m leaving to port a large area of coral awash and to starboard several isolated coral heads. Anchor in 5m, sand and weed.

Mayreau, Windward Bay

12°38'·0N 61°23'·3W

Mayreau is an arid, spiky island, scrub-covered and very burnt-up in the dry season. Its concrete roads are without cars but watch for skate-boards and mobile soap-boxes. A certain level of prosperity is reflected by breeze block houses but the island, like others, is by no means rich.

The southeast coast of Mayreau forms a large bay protected from the prevailing swell by its own reefs as well as those out to sea beyond the Tobago Cays. The bay is bordered by a long deserted beach and is seldom visited by yachts.

Approach

A course of 340° towards the conical peak of Station Hill on which the village is situated leads into the bay. Leave the reefs off the southeast tip of the island (awash and quite easy to see) about 100m to port and continue up the coast about 300m off to the north of the bay.

Anchorage

Anchor opposite the only section of the beach clear of reef, in 6–7m, sand, about 100m from the shore.

Mayreau looking SW from 2M

Grenadines. Union I. from Mayreau. *Hugo du Plessis*

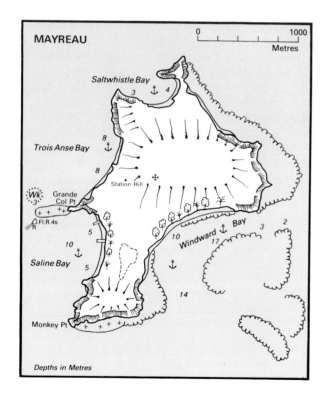

Mayreau, Saline Bay

12°38'·0N 61°23'·8W

Saline Bay is situated on the southwest coast of the island and provides a wide anchorage in front of a deserted white, sandy beach. Monkey Point at the south is reasonably clean but Grande Col Point at the north has a reef extending west from it for 400m marked by a white inflatable buoy and a wreck covered by 3m of water about 300m north of this. The current sets across this reef. The northern end of the beach has two landing stages and a road leads to the village lying on nearby high ground where there is a fine view over the Tobago Cays and towards the islands to the south. The Government steamer *Snapper* calls twice a week and throws out drums of water which are floated ashore by the pier. The beach is also used by P & O for a barbecue, with steel band and waiters, to entertain their cruise passengers. Nevertheless, the anchorage, which is subject to swell (sometimes from both ends), is less busy than Salt Whistle Bay.

Approach

When approaching from the north keep well out from Grande Col Point. Depths of 7–9m in the approach diminish steadily towards the beach.

Anchorage

There are two large mooring buoys well out in the bay and two yellow oil drum buoys of uncertain purpose off the cliff on the south side. Anchor in 5–6m on sand, 100–150m from the shore. For peace, it is best to keep away from the pier and as close to the southern side as possible. There is often too much surge to land in comfort; a stern anchor for the dinghy is useful.

If Saline Bay becomes too crowded, try the bay north of Grande Col Point though there is less protection from the swell if it is coming round from the north. The best anchorage is in the north corner.

Facilities

A few supplies in the village. Water is scarce. Bar and small restaurant.

Mayreau, Salt Whistle Bay

12°38′·8N 61°23′·5W

Salt Whistle Bay is between two rocky headlands and is bordered on the east by a white sandy beach in front of a plantation of coconut palms. The anchorage is generally crowded in the tourist season.

Approach

Keep well out when rounding the northern headland to avoid the shoals which extend from it. There is 6m in the entrance, decreasing gradually towards the beach.

Anchorage

The bottom is sand and weed and good holding. The anchorage is uncomfortable in a northeasterly swell; the best anchorage is as close to the eastern beach as possible.

Facilities

Hotel – chalets, bar, restaurant.

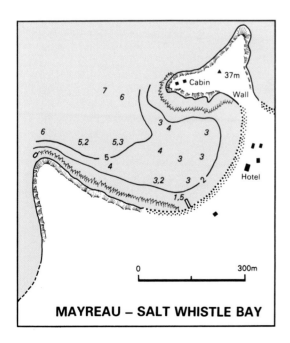

MAYREAU – SALT WHISTLE BAY

Canouan, Windward Bay

12°42′·0N 61°19′·2W

Canouan is regarded by most as an overnight stop but it is worth spending some days to explore it. It was once a plantation island, all one estate and prosperous as well, with some evidence that unlike so many West Indian plantations, the profits were ploughed back. There is a road round the island, designed for ox carts and good for walking. At the northern end of the island the road leads through a beautiful, deserted valley with a very English looking church with a low steeple above a really blue lagoon. A hurricane in the 1920s, coinciding with an agricultural slump, seems to have finished off the plantation. Canouan also had a whale fishery and a cotton gin. Now island life is centred on Charlestown which is moderately prosperous in Grenadine terms.

The southern half of the windward side of Canouan has a coral barrier which shelters one of the more beautiful lagoons in the archipelago with safe, unfrequented anchorages in a deserted setting. The approach, however, is tricky and a good recommendation is to anchor in Charlestown, walk over and look at it from the coastal road.

Approach

Do not approach this anchorage when wind and swell are strongly from the southeast. Good light is essential as reef dodging is necessary. From a point southeast of Canouan Baleine, off Dove Cay, head 045° to Friendship Point (the southeastern tip of Canouan) and go behind the reefs which lie to the south of the point. This course passes south of a 2m shoal off Taffia Hill. Round Friendship Point approximately 100m off. There is a conspicuous sandy islet northeast of the point, actually part of the reef. Close to a distance of 30–40m off shore at the level of the first inlet which offers little shelter. Northeast of this inlet there is a narrow channel (over 30m) with 6–7m between the steep coast and the reef which partially uncovers.

Anchorage

Anchor a little to the north of this channel in the opening to Riley Bay in 4m on sand. The current, which always sets towards the south, must be taken into account. There is 3–4m for another few hundred metres and yachts with a really shallow draught can get further.

Canouan in the Grenadines seen from the south. The change in colour indicating the northern fringe of Horseshoe Reef can just be seen.
Anne Hammick

Canouan, Southwest Bay

12°41'·8N 61°21'·0W

The south coast of the peninsula at the southwestern extremity of Canouan forms a large bay edged by a beach of extremely white sand where the low buildings with green roofs of a hotel and a small landing stage can be seen. In a northeasterly trade wind anchor in 4–5m, 100–150m from the beach in front of the hotel. However, the swell often makes this anchorage uncomfortable. Southeast of this anchorage, the channel between Dove Cay and Canouan has 3m and is reef-fringed. It should not be used.

Canouan, Charlestown Bay

12°42'·3N 61°19'·8W

This wide bay on the west coast is bordered in the south by a long deserted, sandy beach and in the east by a rocky coast. Lying back from the beach the small houses of the only village on the island are dotted over the hillside. This is often visited by

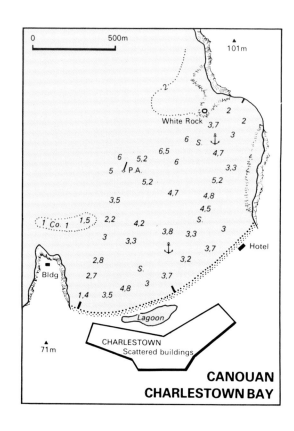

Pte Rameau   *Charlestown Bay*   *Taffia Hill*   *SW point of Canouan*   *Union I*

Canouan. Charlestown Bay looking SW

Canouan. Charlestown Bay buoy and hamlet looking SE

yachts but it is not calm. Swell can be bad and the wind gusts strongly over the ridge and down the valleys.

Approach

If coming from the south and beating in, beware the reef starting at Glossy Point and running west as far as Bachelors Hall Point, almost ½M offshore at the middle of the bay. From the north, Glossy Point looks like a separate island as the spit connecting it is low.

Entrance

Make up to the red buoy marking the centre of the entrance and turn in on 160°, taking care of the shoal (1m) northeast of Bachelors Hall Point and 0·5M SW of White Rock.

Anchorage

Anchor anywhere in front of the beach in 3–5m on sand but avoid the pier which is busy. The bay is shallow and it is possible to anchor well out. There is often a swell in this anchorage, particularly in a northeasterly trade wind in which case try Charles Bay, inside White Rock in the northeastern corner.

Neighbouring anchorages

Anse Rameau, 1M north of the buoy marking Charlestown Bay, open to the south, is bordered by a small beach of white sand with fishermen's huts. This is a pleasant anchorage; get well in to the northeast corner where there is deep water close-to, sand. Beware of the reefs extending 40m off the southwestern point of the inlet.

New Bay, immediately west of Charlestown Bay, is badly protected and only recommended for dinghies.

Facilities

A hotel-restaurant at the eastern end of the beach and some supplies in the village (very limited choice). Water is scarce.

Communications

Airfield. Inter-island shipping.

Mustique and adjacent islands looking SSE

Savan Islet and Savan Rock looking E

Grenadines: The Bequia group

Charts

Imray-Iolaire *B30*
Admiralty *791, 2872*
SHOM *3206*
US *25482*

General

This group consists of the islands, islets and rocks from Savan Rock, south of Mustique, to Bequia. The main island of the group, Bequia, has an interesting history. It was claimed by the French for the Compagnie des Iles d'Amérique but before any white settlements were established the slaver Pamir was wrecked on it. Survivors intermarried with the Caribs and by the time serious white settlement was attempted in 1763, when St Vincent was handed over to the British, their descendants, known as Black Caribs (as in Dominica) were firmly in control with their own king. They held out until 1796 when survivors were sent first to Battowia and subsequently to Rattan, Honduras, where earlier the Caribs of St Vincent had been banished. In the 18th century Scottish sailors settled and were joined later by whale hunters from New Bedford and by some French settlers who established themselves on the south coast at Paget. It is one of the last islands in the world where whale hunting took place and in 1986 the last harpooner retired. At the times of the migrations, lookouts posted on the heights alerted the whalers of a passing school and when a whale was killed it was taken to the whaling station at Petit Nevis. Crafts include models of whale boats (and all sailing boats on demand) and carving on whale bone.

Coasts, dangers

- There are several islets to the south and southwest of Mustique. Savan Rock (32m) has whitish-coloured shores fringed with reefs. Savan Islet (40m) is covered in grass and inhabited by a few fishermen. There are dangers off Petit Mustique for a distance of about 0·5M. In fine weather, it is possible to anchor temporarily to leeward of Petit Mustique or Savan Islet (5–8m depths) but approach with caution.
- Mustique is a green island with two peaks, one in the centre (121m) and one in the south (143m). On the first of these there is a large light-coloured hotel with arcades and a red roof which is conspicuous from the distance. A large building and a radio pylon are also easily visible on the headland (65m) at the northeastern end of the island.
- The approaches to Mustique are dangerous. The west coast of the island is fringed with reefs and the approach is obstructed (0·6M out) by the dangerous Montezuma Shoal, covered with very little water on which there is no longer any marker (1988), (see page 56). The north and northeast are particularly hazardous where there are reefs, rocks and islets. Currents are strong and their direction unpredictable. The most dangerous places are the shoals and reefs lying north and southwest of Double Rock; the rusted remains of the M.V. *Antilles* wrecked in 1973 begin to resemble the reef itself. It is unsafe to pass between the *Antilles* and the coast. The Pillories are surrounded by dangers and there is a drying rock and a breaking patch ¾M southeast of them. Further south, the east coast is open to the Atlantic swell and should not be approached.
- Some 4M northeast of Mustique are Battowia (206m) and Baliceaux (130m), two dry and rocky islets surrounded by rocks and reefs which should be approached with caution (see page 58).
- South of Bequia there is a group of four islets: Pigeon Islet (46m), steep; Ile Quatre (140m), steep in the northwest and the south and with several reefs to the east; Petit Nevis (98m) with rocks and reefs close to; Semples Cay (20m), steep. The channels between these islets are safe but currents can be strong.
- Bequia (268m), the largest of the group, lies less than 5M south of St Vincent. From the south, the west end of the island at first appears to be the Ships Stern, about a mile east of West Cay which is too low to be seen. West Cay and Big Cay lie off the western point of the island and there is a small light on the westernmost of these. The pass between Big Cay and Bequia is used by those with local knowledge but has a dangerous reef. The northwest coast is free of danger except in the entrance to Admiralty Bay (see page 60). Off the southeast coast there are several reefs and shallows.

Savan Rock, south of Mustique. Note the natural arch.
Anne Hammick

Petit Canouan looking ESE

Mustique, Grand Bay

12°52′·7N 61°11′·3W)

Mustique, meaning mosquito, is almost entirely a private island, the privileged holiday resort of various international celebrities with villas scattered amongst the green hills. It is the most expensive island in the Grenadines. There is only one, rolly, anchorage which tends to be crowded at night. The island is, however, worth exploring.

Approach

Because of its position arrivals are commonly from the southwest or northwest. The best landmark is the large light-coloured hotel with a pink roof which stands on a peak (123m) in the middle of the island. Montezuma Shoal (1m, 0·4M out from Grand Bay) is unmarked though plain to see in good light. If coming up from Petit Mustique do not cut the corner when entering Grand Bay – see below. An arrival from northeast or east of the island is more hazardous – see page 57.

Anchorage

The only anchorage is in Grand Bay (Britannia Bay to the Ordnance Survey) on the west coast, in front of a white beach edged with coconut palms, and is made uncomfortable by swell. The southern shore of the bay has reefs off it which continue out to sea southwest a third of a mile beyond the point. There are reefs off the north shore. Anchor in 5–8m on sand, 100–150m west of the landing stage, leaving it clear for the ferry. If this area is full, it is possible to anchor elsewhere on the dead coral of the shelf which begins about 250m offshore. Use two anchors, one a fisherman's.

The best dinghy landing is by the pier, where there can be bad surge, or on the beach by Basil's Bar.

Facilities

Fuel from a garage about ½M inland

There is a bar-restaurant on the beach and an expensive restaurant in the north of the island (Cotton House), advance booking essential (VHF Ch 16).

Communications

Airfield (Air Mustique to other islands).
Ferry.

Baliceaux and Battowia

12°57′N 61°08′W

These two steep-sided and barren islets have a few fishermens huts which are occupied in season but are otherwise inhabited by goats and a ginger cat.

Approach

The leeward sides are reefed and the windward sides unapproachable in safety.

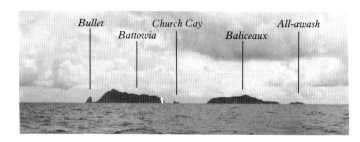

Battowia and Baliceaux looking SSE

Anchorage

The easiest and best protected anchorage is an inlet on the southwest coast of Baliceaux, just north of the southwest point. Start by passing about 200m east of this point heading 025° with the peak of Battowia in the dip behind the fishermen's shacks. To port, a deep reef with isolated rocks breaking the surface leads NNE to the northern point of the inlet and continues up the west coast. Anchor by eye in 4–5m, sand, about 150m off the beach – the bottom is stony inshore.

There is a second anchorage between the islands but it can only be visited safely in unusually good weather, which generally means in summer, not winter, by an experienced navigator. The approach is from windward, there are strong currents and there is no room for error. The channel between the two islands, 0·4–0·6M wide, has a reef in the middle but closer to Battowia than to Baliceaux. Church Cay (approximately 20m high) and several small rocks are at the southeast end. Enter from the southeast, north of Church Cay, anchor in 7–9m in the channel between Battowia and Church Cay.

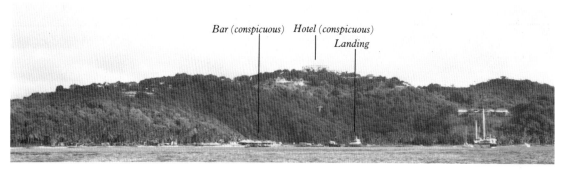

Mustique. Grand Bay looking ESE

Grenadines. Battowia from Baliceaux. *Hugo du Plessis*
(View distorted by wide angle lens)

The Grenadines (N group) looking SSE

Petit Nevis

12°58′·2N 61°14′·7W

The island is used as a picnic site and is a little seaside resort. The small whaling station, with its cauldrons and winch for hauling up the whales, still stands; Petit St Vincent is not a place for the squeamish when, occasionally, it operates.

Approach

There is a reef off the southwest point. Currents in the channels on both sides run strongly and the south channel breaks at times.

Anchorage

Anchor on the west coast, off the small pier in 4–6m, sand with chunks of coral and assorted debris. The shelf is about 300m wide and it pays to anchor well off to allow the day and charter boats to cram in to the shore. There is some swell but the anchorage is more sheltered than might appear. The fact that the place is advertised largely as a day resort helps make for a quiet night.

Bequia, Friendship Bay

12°59′·1N 61°14′·7W

A long beach fringed with coconut palms skirts this pretty bay on the south coast which lies in a setting of green hills. There is a secure and little-used anchorage here but it is often affected by a slight swell. A large white hotel with a landing stage is conspicuous on the northeast coast of the bay.

Entrance

There is a reef off the east point and the west side of the entrance is marked by St Elairs Cay, a large dark rock joined to Bequia by a line of reefs. A current sets across the entrance. Enter the bay heading north midway between the two and leaving this rock 100m to the west in order to avoid the shoals off the eastern point of the entrance. When approaching from the west by the channel between Bequia and Petit Nevis where the current is often strong, pass south of Semples Cay (steep).

Anchorage

There are depths of 6–7m in the centre of the bay which diminish gradually towards the beach. The seabed is sand and the holding is moderate. The swell seems least on the east side. Land at the hotel pier.

Facilities

Restaurants

Communications

Taxis. It is within walking distance of the town if exercise is needed.

Bequia, Admiralty Bay

Admiralty Bay cuts into almost the whole north coast of the island and serves the village of Port Elizabeth. It is a regular port of call for local craft from the islands and now for a large number of charter yachts which have over the years helped corrupt local standards. The harbour gets crowded over Easter when the regatta is held – this includes races for all yachts from the Bequia models to the biggest; it is more fun than the Antigua Race Week.

Approach

From West Cay there are no particular dangers. The northern limit of Admiralty Bay is a fairly high headland with Wash Rocks and Devils Table off it marked by a red buoy; keep 200m off the headland. Further in there are reefs or shoals on both sides within 100m of the shore (Belmont Reef on the south shore is marked by a black and white oil drum). The best landmark for Port Elizabeth is the conspicuous radio mast on the hill to the south of the village.

Anchorages

Anchor according to choice and draught but keep clear of the pier and its fairway; it is used by ferries, cargo vessels and quite large tankers. The centre of the bay has 12–16m with variable holding, patchy sand over coral; a little to the west of Bequia's defunct marina has 6–8m on sand. Alternatively try Princess Margaret Bay or Lower Bay; both can be affected by swell, the second worse than the first, and both beaches are used by cruise ships for barbecues.

Admiralty Bay, Bequia, seen from the north.
Elizabeth Hammick

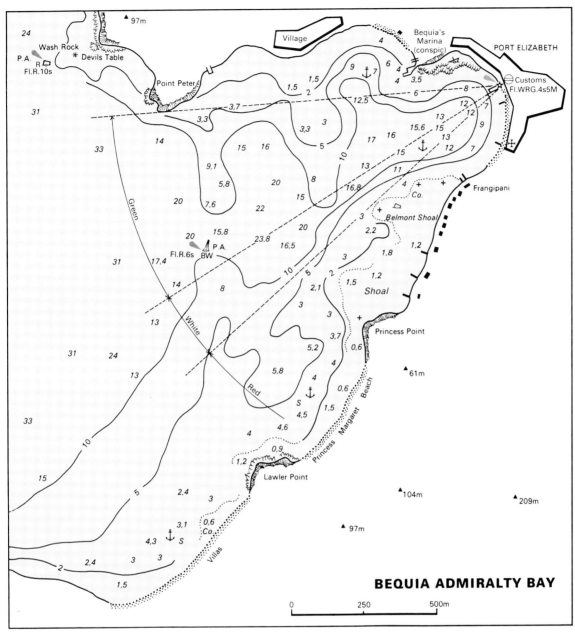

BEQUIA ADMIRALTY BAY

Bequia. Admiralty Bay entrance

Formalities

As a port of entry, the formalities are more easily handled than in Kingstown. Customs are in the post office 0800–1200 and 1300–1500 Monday to Friday. Immigration in the police station next door. There is a small charge for forms and a $10 capita tax on departure.

Facilities

Water from a tanker (expensive) and fuel from Bequia Marina (its only service). Well stocked chandleries in the town, sailmaker, supplies (shops and a small market – limited choice). Several restaurants and bars.

Barclays Bank 0800–1330 Monday to Thursday, 0800–1230 and 1400–1700 Friday. Post office.

Communications

Frangipani (hotel and travel agency) provides a Poste Restante service for yachts (P.O. Box 1, Bequia, St Vincent, Grenadines, West Indies – contact VHF Ch 68) and ☎ (809-458-3824), Telex 7587 Frangi VQ and Fax 809 458 3824. For some years all mail addressed to yachts c/o the Post Office has been passed on to the Frangipani, so it is worth checking at both.

An airport is under construction on the south coast of the island (1991).

Frequent ferries to St Vincent and thrice weekly to Union via most islands.

Coconut palm and colourful Pride of Barbados on Union Island in the Grenadines.
Anne Hammick

IV. St Vincent

Charts
Imray-Iolaire *B30*
Admiralty *791, 501*
US *25484, 25483*

General remarks

Geography

St Vincent is the main island of the independent state of St Vincent and the Grenadines which includes most of the Grenadines (see page 35). It has a backbone of volcanoes rising in the north to Soufrière, 1180m (the name Soufrière is common, with good reason, in the Lesser Antilles). St Vincent's Soufrière is active; a serious eruption coinciding with the Mount Pelée disaster of 1902 wiped out 1600 victims and its latest manifestation was in 1979. Almost half the island is forested with an equal area under temporary crops; only a small proportion is under permanent crops such as banana and other tropical fruits, root crops, coconut, nutmeg etc. Sugar production was closed in 1985 though some cane is still grown for rum. Kingstown has a fine, well maintained botanical garden, one of a series created by the British in their colonies to develop agriculture. Two specimens of interest are a scion of the breadfruit tree brought by Bligh to the West Indies in 1793 and the remarkable Cannonball Tree; trees are not labelled and it is worth visiting with a guide.

Like most of the islands there is little wind on the leeward side; but patience is rewarded by the most dramatic scenery anywhere in the Caribbean. High, very steep, higgeldy-piggeldy mountains culminating in the peak of Soufrière, usually hidden in clouds, covered in green jungle, scarred by lava flows with torrents and waterfalls catching the sun.

St Vincent became independent on 27 October 1979 and is governed by a House of Assembly consisting of 13 members elected for five years, the Attorney General, 4 senators appointed on the advice of the Prime Minister and two on the advice of the Leader of the Opposition. It is a member of the British Commonwealth.

The island is not well-off. Its income depends largely on bananas together with root crops such as tannias and sweet potato, grown on the coastal strip where most people live. Tourism plays only a small part. There is no road round the island.

History

St Vincent is said to have been discovered by Columbus. It was never occupied by the Spaniards and the Caribs resisted the attempts of the French and the British to conquer it until 1783 when the British established themselves. In 1797 the Caribs, with French aid, rebelled and, after a very tough resistance, the survivors were shipped off to Rattan Isle, Honduras; it remained a British possession until independence. It differs from others in the Lesser Antilles in that there are more traces of Carib settlement and as there was little French influence, so there is no French in the patois apart from the name and Roman Catholicism is not so well established.

Approach

From the Grenadines head for to Kingstown (page 66) or the anchorages behind Duvernette Islet, both easy to identify (and page 65).

The northern part of the island, which is dominated by the conical outline of Mount Soufrière (more often than not hidden in the clouds), has no special characteristics. Arriving from St Lucia, follow the northwest coast; Chateaubelair Island and Dark Head can be identified from a long way off.

Hurricane holes

One poor prospect, the Blue Lagoon.

Formalities

In St Vincent itself it is only possible to clear at Kingstown; this is tedious and unnecessary if you have cleared into St Vincent's islands in the Grenadines, for instance at Bequia.

Flag

Three vertical stripes of blue, yellow and green, with the yellow of double width and charged with three green diamonds.

Coasts, dangers

Duvernette Islet is a vertical rocky spur (60m) with a lighthouse (VQ(2)2s) (the very quick flash is so quick that the two seem one).

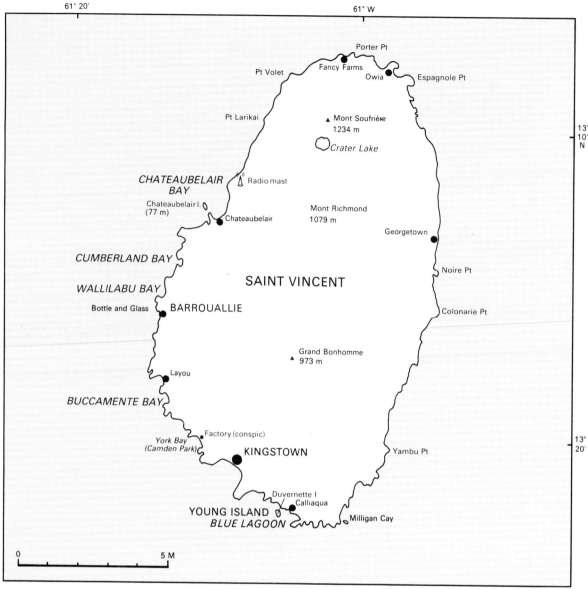

61° 20'   61° W

Porter Pt
Fancy Farms
Pt Volet
Owia
Espagnole Pt
Pt Larikai
▲ Mont Soufrière
1234 m
◯ *Crater Lake*
13°
10'
N
CHATEAUBELAIR
BAY
⚊ Radio mast
Chateaubelair I. ◯
(77 m)
● Chateaubelair
Mont Richmond
1079 m
● Georgetown
CUMBERLAND BAY
SAINT VINCENT
▎ Noire Pt
WALLILABU BAY
Bottle and Glass ▎ ● BARROUALLIE
▎ Colonarie Pt
Grand Bonhomme
▲ 973 m
● Layou
BUCCAMENTE BAY
Factory (conspic)
York Bay
(Camden Park)
● KINGSTOWN
Yambu Pt
13°
20'
Duvernette I
Calliaqua
YOUNG ISLAND ◯
BLUE LAGOON
◦ Milligan Cay

0   5 M

- South of Kingstown, the runway of the aerodrome, which is lit and slants towards the WSW, is very clearly visible from the southwest. Lying further back, a large radio pylon is conspicuous on a height.
- Between Kingstown and Chateaubelair islet there are a series of small bays, separated by rocky capes, most with fishing hamlets. The best landmarks are a large modern factory near a long wharf in Camden Park Bay, the wrecked trawler in Mount Wynne Bay, a disused sugar refinery with a chimney 0·6M south of Barrouallie, the dark rocks of Bottle and Glass in front of the village of Barrouallie, a radio mast on the southern point of Wallilabou Bay and Chateaubelair Islet (70m), dark and steep and very easy to identify.
- Between Chateaubelair and Porter Point, the northern tip of the island, which is not easy to identify, the coast is mainly unobstructed, steep and very green. Hiva Rock is about 100m off Larikai Point and 0·4M north, there are shallows of 3·4m approximately 200m from the land. There is a race off Baleine Point. The best landmarks are two red and white radio masts 1·4M northeast of Chateaubelair Islet and the large isolated buildings of Fancy Farms which lie west of Porter Point and are clearly visible from the north.
- The east coast is almost completely straight, has no protection to offer and few landmarks. Here and there are villages and hamlets; Georgetown is the most conspicuous and characterised by its square, black stone belfry.
- The southeast point of the island has an unreliable light with Milligan Cay lying off it.

Young Island, Blue Lagoon and Calliaquoa

13°07'·7N 61°12'·7W

These anchorages provide qualified shelter from the elements and from fellow yachtsmen.

Young Island

Young Island was named after Dr Young who founded the botanical garden. It is a very green islet with a luxurious and discreet hotel, separated from the south coast of St Vincent by a channel about 200m wide well protected from the prevailing winds. South of this islet, Duvernette Islet (60m), a steep rock with an old fort and a lighthouse on top of it, can be easily identified from all directions. The an-

chorage is in a reversing tide which runs up to 2 knots in the middle. It is cluttered with paying moorings of doubtful holding power and best avoided. If possible, anchor close to the beach; use two anchors if feasible.

A day trip to explore St Vincent by taxi can be made from here.

Approach

The easier approach is from the west. The eastern approach is through a channel edged by reefs which are difficult to see.

Anchorages

The best anchorages are to be found in the western entrance to the channel, either in the middle (7–9m) or in front of the beach along the northern shore (3–5m, 60–80m from the land). The eastern end has a high tension submarine cable. As stated the current is strong in the central part of the channel but it is much weaker near the north beach.

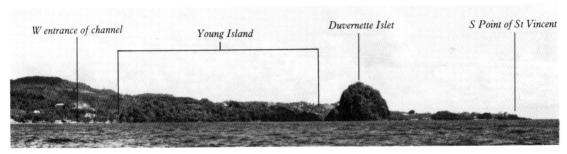

W approach to Young Island

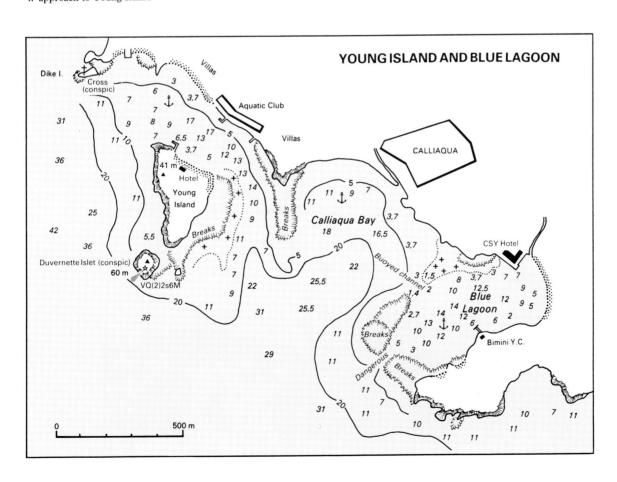

Facilities

Restaurants on the mainland shore. It may be possible to obtain water from the Aquatic Club.

Communications

Taxis, buses to Kingstown.

The Blue Lagoon

The Blue Lagoon is a bay 0·5M ESE of Young Island, enclosed by a coral barrier on which the swell breaks continuously; a lot of it comes over the reef so the anchorage is not calm.

As a hurricane hole it is a poor prospect especially for a visiting yacht; the best sites will be occupied by local charter yachts and in any case the reef will not keep out the swell.

Entrance

There are two channels. The northwest channel is 15m wide with a depth of 1·8m and is marked by white buoys and by poles. The southwest channel is unmarked, very narrow but has a depth of 2·7m; the reefs on either side barely cover and local knowledge is essential.

Anchorage

The lagoon is full of moorings and it may be difficult to find room to anchor. Caribbean Sailing Yachts (CSY) have two lines of moorings in the middle running southwest from their dock on the east shore and it is best to avoid anchoring nearby. Most of the heavy mooring chains lie in the middle of the harbour so if you have to anchor there, rig a trip line. If there is room it might be possible to tie up at the pontoon of Bimini Yachts (contact VHF Ch 87) but it is subject to swell.

Facilities

Fuel and water at CSY and Bimini, if there is room to get alongside. Some stores from CSY. Bar and restaurant at CSY.

Communications

Buses to Kingstown pass nearby.

Calliaquoa Bay, between Young Island and Blue Lagoon

Calliaquoa Bay is more subject to swell but is an alternative to Young Island and the Blue Lagoon. The centre of the bay has a new coastguard pier. Anchor north of the pier or midway between the pier and the reef on the south side, 2–3m or more according to choice, sand.

Facilities

Supplies in Calliaquoa.

Communications

Taxis in Calliaquoa, buses nearby.

Kingstown

13°09′·0N 61°14′·5W

The capital of St Vincent has about 30,000 inhabitants. Lying along the shores of a long bay open to the southwest, it has a unique colonnaded street and other relics which provide a curious example of colonial architecture, British and others, rather sadly dilapidated. In the southeastern part of the bay there are quays for cargo boats. The anchorage is often uncomfortable because of the swell.

Approach

The best landmarks are the ships in the deep water dock, a high-rise 'financial centre' near the docks, the towers of the two cathedrals, the tall lattice tower of the signal station, Fort Charlotte and the barracks on the top of Johnson Point.

Berthing, anchorage

To clear, yachts can berth temporarily at the north quay in the little harbour of the commercial port, if there is room. If not, they must anchor in front of the port in 10–13m. The customs offices are on the quay; the police, in the town, approximately 200m to the northwest of the customs.

Facilities

Supermarkets and a large choice of supplies in the town (there is a daily market). Restaurants, banks, souvenir shops. There are no facilities for yachts.

Bimini Yachts base

NW channel to Blue Lagoon

Belfry   Police building   Warehouse (Commercial port)

Kingstown looking NE

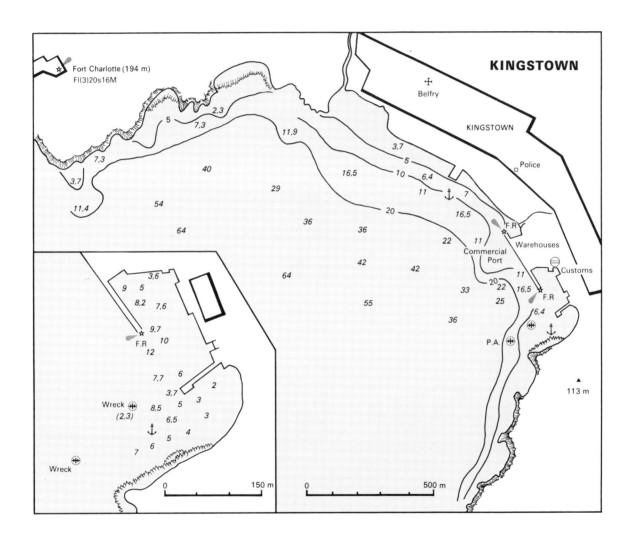

Fort Charlotte (194 m)
Fl(3)20s16M

KINGSTOWN

Belfry

KINGSTOWN

Police

Warehouses

Customs

Commercial Port

P.A.

F.R

F.R

F.R

Wreck
(2,3)

Wreck

113 m

0   150 m

0   500 m

Kingstown. Johnson Point looking N and Fort Charlotte

67

Communications

Airport 7km. There are daily connections with the main islands. The best links to Europe and the USA are via Air Mustique to Barbados or Air Martinique to Martinique. Leeward Island Air Transport (LIAT) provides a useful inter-island service but is known to some as leave island any time.

Ferry three times a day to Bequia and three times a week to Union Island calling at others en-route.

From Kingstown to Wallilabou Bay

Between Kingstown and Wallilabou Bay there are several bays, some of which are possible anchorages.

- The northern part of Buccament Bay is a rocky headland on which lies Lapaze Rock, about 20m high and covered in cactus. On the east coast, a small grey church with pink window frames which can be seen on the hillside surrounded by a few little houses, is a good landmark. It is preferable to anchor in the northeast corner of the bay in front of a small beach with coconut palms around it, in 3m, 50m from the shore where the seabed is sandy and regular. This is probably the best of these three anchorages.
- Layou is a village of shabby little houses lying along the southeastern part of a sandy bay, 2·5M south of Bottle and Glass rocks. A large white hangar can be seen in the north part of the bay, and a ruined landing stage near the village. The approach is safe. The seabed is level and sandy in the southern part of the bay, with 3–4m, approximately 100m SSW of the landing stage. To the north of this the seabed shelves steeply towards the open sea.
- Barrouallie, a picturesque fishing village, lies behind a beach trimmed with coconut palms and south of the rocky headland, off which lie the conspicuous rocks – Bottle and Glass. There is a good anchorage in front of the northern half of the beach (which is cut in half by a large blackish rock) in 6–8m on sand, 80m from the shore.

Wallilabou Bay

13°14'·7N 61°16'·7W

Wallilabou Bay and Cumberland Bay are the bays on the west coast best protected from the swell. Wallilabou Bay is surrounded by particularly luxuriant tropical vegetation but is being developed; much of the land has been cleared and a hotel built. Locals, anxious to earn five dollars by taking a line ashore at the appropriate moment, sometimes meet approaching yachts well offshore.

Approach

It is not easy to spot Wallilabou itself from the sea but its position is made unmistakable by the radio mast on the southern arm, known as Indian Gallows, and a less conspicuous arch-shaped rock to the north of the entrance.

Anchorage

The bay is deep apart from a 10m patch in the middle. Anchor in 10–18m in front of the beach. Have a line taken ashore – to do it yourself will cause an upset.

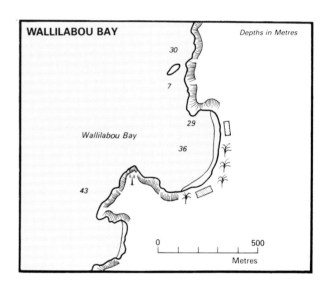

WALLILABOU BAY   Depths in Metres

Wallilabou Bay

30

7

29

36

43

0   500

Metres

New hotel   *Restaurant*   *Radio mast on Indian Gallows*

St Vincent Wallilabou Bay. *Hugo du Plessis*

Beach and anchorage

St Vincent. Cumberland Bay. *Hugo du Plessis*

Cumberland Bay

13°15'·7N 61°16'·0W

Cumberland Bay is enclosed by two, steep, rocky headlands; on the east side there is a beach in front of a large area of coconut palms. A mountain stream flows into the central part of the bay. There are a few thatched shelters on the shore. It is much quieter than Wallilabou and there is likely to be less hassle with beach boats.

Approach

The southern headland, below Petit Anse, has a rock off it. When entering, keep well off this point which has a dangerous shoal extending for 100m to the west and NNW and enter from north of west.

Anchorage

The centre of the bay is deep. Most yachts anchor off the south beach in 12–18m, 60–70m from land with a line ashore to a coconut palm (have a 60m hawser at the ready). Do not go into the northern corner of the bay where depths are less than 2m and the holding doubtful.

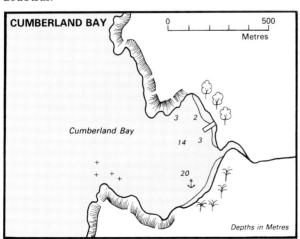

Chateaubelair Bay

13°17'·5N 61°14'.9W

This wide bay is open to the NNW and lies between Chateaubelair Islet and Richmond Point. Despite its beautiful setting, this anchorage has few visitors because the swell, which sweeps round the north of the islet, often makes it very uncomfortable.

Approach

Chateaubelair Islet (70m) is covered in dark vegetation and is easily identified. Richmond Point, which is hardly a headland, can be identified by two red and white radio masts. Behind Chateaubelair is a distinctive arrowhead of trees. Do not use the channel on the landward side of Chateaubelair Islet. It is very narrow (10–12m in the middle) and it would be embarrassing to get snarled by a fish trap float.

Anchorage

In the east of the anchorage there are cliffs with coconut palms growing on top of them and to the southeast a wide beach where, behind a landing stage, the town of Chateaubelair lies.

Depths in the centre of the bay are considerable. Go fairly close to the land in front of the northern part of the beach where the 5m depth contour runs approximately 100m from the shore, on sand and rocks.

It is also possible to anchor southeast of Chateaubelair Islet, in front of Petite Bordel. It is very steep-to (15m approximately 40m from the shore) and a line ashore is advisable.

69

Chateaubelair Bay looking S

St Vincent. Buccamente. *Hugo du Plessis*

Saint Vincent looking NNE

Saint Vincent looking S

V. St Lucia

Charts
Imray-Iolaire *B1*
Admiralty *1273, 197, 494*
SHOM *4985*
US *25521, 25528*

General remarks

Geography

St Lucia is a mountainous island with an area of 622 sq km and 135,000 inhabitants of whom 52,000 live in the capital, Castries, situated on the northwest coast. It is volcanic, covered with dense tropical forests particularly in its southern half where Mount Gimie rises to 958m, and is still active in certain areas; Soufrière was considered as a source of thermal energy. It has a wet season from May to August followed by a dry patch but most rain falls in November and December; depending upon the altitude, annual rainfall is between 1·5 and 3·45m.

St Lucia became an independent state on 22 February 1979 and is a member of the British Commonwealth. It has an elected House of Assembly with 17 members and an 11 seat Senate appointed by the Governor-General, 6 on the advice of the prime minister, 3 of the leader of the opposition and 2 after consultations with other significant groups.

Tourism and bananas are essential to the island's economy but coconut is also significant and soap, coconut meal, rum and clothing are manufactured.

Because of poor planning, the tourist industry tends to be intrusive and ugly.

History

Supposed to have been discovered by Christopher Columbus during his third voyage (1498), the island was continually the object of Anglo-French rivalry and changed hands 20 times in two centuries before being captured by the British in 1803 and formally ceded to them on Napoleon's downfall in 1814. The legacy of the French presence remains today. Over 90% of the population is Roman Catholic; the place names are almost exclusively French – the capital is named after the Marquis de Castries who was minister for the colonies under Louis XVI; most St Lucians speak a form of French (though knowledge of the original language may give no advantage).

Tourism

St Lucia is generally warmly hospitable and has some of the most spectacular ports of call in the Antilles. The single road which circles the island may not have been repaired since independence but having left behind the concrete grid of Castries, the western route serpentines through forests and plantations, up the mountainside beyond Baie du Marigot to Soufrière, where sulphur springs bubble, and on to the dramatic Deux Pitons with magnificent vistas on the way. The Atlantic coast is less interesting.

Bilharzia has been reported in the interior. Do not paddle in streams and standing fresh water.

Arrival

The highest peaks are almost always covered in cloud but there are no particular problems in making a landfall on St Lucia.

From the south, the headland of Cape Moule-à-Chique which stands out clearly from the hinterland and from the southwest the conspicuous conical peaks ('Dracula's Fangs') of the Pitons can be identified from a distance.

Arriving from the north the best landfall is on Pigeon Island which is the easiest place to identify on the coast (see page 73).

Formalities

Clear at Vieux Fort, Marigot, Castries or Rodney Bay.
Flag
Blue with a design of a black triangle edged in white, bearing a smaller yellow triangle, in the centre.

Maintenance

Castries, Rodney Bay.

Communications

International airport at Hewannora at the southern end of the island with European and U.S. connections. Airfield at Castries with international connections within the Caribbean.

Hurricane holes

Two prospects, Marigot and Rodney.

The west coast from Cape Moule-à-Chique

Dangers

- The southern tip of St Lucia is the conspicuous headland of Cape Moule-à-Chique (181m) whose southern face is sheer. 1·8M north of this Cape is a conspicuous conical hill (90m) with a mast with aerial warning lights (Fl.WG.5s) and between them, the international airport, Hewannora.

- From the open sea long white buildings on the southwestern slopes of Mount Tourney can be seen. Between Moule-à-Chique and Gros Piton there are a number of reefs extending off the coast for 0·3M. Anchoring is possible in Vieux Fort Bay (see page 74) where there is a banana boat pontoon and Laborie Bay (see page 74). Anse de Pitons is flanked by Gros and Petit Pitons which are conspicuous volcanic peaks (750 and 798m) identifiable from a distance.

- There are several rocks off Grande Caille Point which is the northern arm of Baie de la Soufrière, sheltering Soufrière village (see page 75).

- The coast between Grande Caille and Point Marigot Harbour is steep-to and has a number of fishing villages placed at the mouths of narrow valleys. Pointe de la Ville, which is the most prominent headland in this area, is not conspicuous from a distance. Marigot Harbour is a very well protected anchorage (see page 77).

- Grand Cul-de-Sac Bay has been developed as a tanker port and the large green oil reservoirs are conspicuous from the northeast.

- Castries, in a deep indentation south of Vigié Pointe, is the capital and principal port of the island (detailed description see page 78). Vigié Pointe is a steep headland (67m) with lighthouse (white tower with a red top, 11m, Fl(2)10s).

- Anse du Choc, between Pointe Vigié and Fourreur Island, has wide shallows and the passage between Fourreur and the mainland is full of fishing floats. It is possible to anchor but the bay is open to the northeasterly swell. Fourreur Island is a clearly visible rock (5m) on which there is a light (Fl2).

Cap Moule-à-Chique looking NE

Grande Cul-de-Sac Bay oil terminal looking SSE

Pitons looking SE

- Further on, Pigeon Island, 104m high and joined to St Lucia by a causeway, can be identified by its two peaks. There is a marina in Rodney Bay, south of this island, described on page 79.

- Burgot Rocks (11m) are clearly visible and should be passed to seaward. Pointe du Cap, the northern tip of the island, is free from danger and dominated by green hills. There is a large hotel with a brown roof 0·4M SSW, near a beach.

Saint Lucia looking N

Mt Gimie (958m) (obscured)

Saint Lucia looking S

The east coast from Pointe du Cap

- This coast is indented by a number of inlets and small bays in which there are dangers. They are used by local fishing boats who are familiar with the area but do not provide enough shelter for yachts. It is advisable to stay at least 1M off this coast. There are not many landmarks; the most conspicuous are described below.
- Cape Marquis, 4M from the northeastern point of the island, has a small lighthouse on it and is dominated by Mount Gaiac (261m), a conical shaped hill which is conspicuous from all directions.
- 8·5M further south the village of Dennery situated at the head of a small inlet partially protected by an islet (45m) can be identified by a large church by the shore and a hospital with several low-lying yellow buildings with grey roofs lying back a little on rising ground. The church is obscured by the islet from the east and ESE and should not be confused with Micoud church (yellow with brown roof), 5·2M further south. 1·8M north of Cape Moule-à-Chique, a conspicuous conical hill (90m) has a clearly visible mast with aerial warning lights (Fl.WG.5s).
- Maria Islet (100m) which is very steep, is also very clearly seen on the edge of the coastal shelf. The international airport, Hewannora, is immediately behind.

Point Sable

13°43'·5N 60°56'·5W

This wide bay provides a pleasant temporary anchorage in fine weather and with a moderate swell. It is obstructed by reefs and partly protected by Maria Islet which is steep-to and 100m high. Enter from south of the islet and keep about 100m off the very obvious reef off the south and southwest coast of it on a bearing of 335 degrees. Keep well out when rounding the western edge of the reef and anchor in 3m depths on sand approximately 100m WNW of a beach.

Vieux Fort

13°43'·6N 60°57'·5W

Vieux Fort, a port of entry and the main commercial centre in the south of the island, is a lively town situated to the north of a wide bay which is well protected from the trade winds by Moule-à-Chique promontory. In the northeast corner of this bay there is a long landing stage for cargo boats near large sheds and oil tanks.

Approach

Moule-à-Chique promontory is identifiable from a distance from all directions.

Anchorage

Anchor either south of the cargo jetty in 5–7m depths on sand, 150m from the east coast of the bay, or in 3–4m depths on sand 100–150m south of the ruined landing stage of the village.

Facilities

Supplies and several restaurants in the village.

Communications

Hewannora international airport, 2km.

Laborie

13°45'N 61°00'W

Laborie, one of the most delightful fishing villages on the island, lies in the shade of coconut palms near a long sandy beach where boats are hauled out over wooden rollers. In front of the village, a small bay rarely visited by yachts provides a well protected anchorage from the east or northeast trade winds.

Approach

The best landmark for identifying Laborie is a large grey church with a triangular facade and red roof, seen through coconut palms in the western half of the village.

A bearing of 035° on this church leads between the reefs extending 0·4M out to sea in the western part of the bay and those off the eastern headland which is rocky and has a reef extending 40m to its west; it is a tight fit.

Anchorage

Once round the eastern headland and its reef, alter course to starboard and anchor in 3–4m on sand 150m southwest of the piles of an old landing stage near which there is a square yellow building.

Facilities

Supplies from a little market and in the village shops (limited choice). Fish and crayfish from the returning fishermen. Two or three simple restaurants.

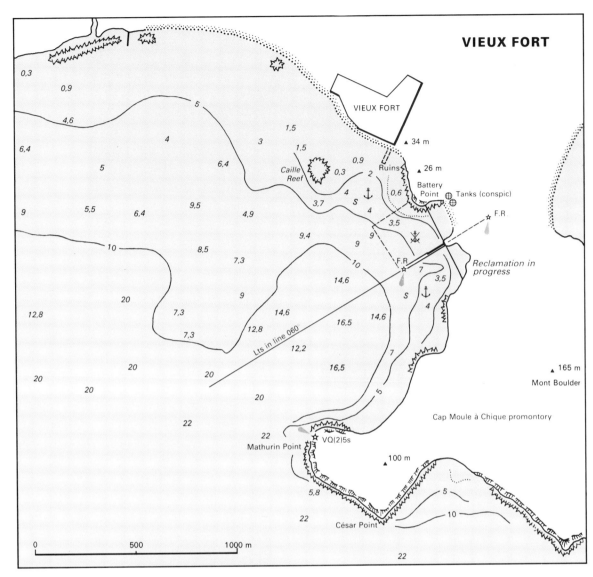

VIEUX FORT

0,3

0,9

4,6

5

6,4

5

4

3

1,5

1,5

6,4

6,4

Caille Reef

0,9

0,3

0,6

▲ 34 m

Ruins

▲ 26 m

Battery Point

⊕ Tanks (conspic)

9

5,5

6,4

4,9

3,7

S

2

4

4

3,5

9

9

☆ F.R.

10

8,5

7,3

9,4

10

14,6

9

☆ F.R.

7

3,5

S

Reclamation in progress

12,8

7,3

12,8

14,6

16,5

14,6

4

7

20

7,3

Lts in line 060°

12,2

20

20

20

16,5

5

20

20

20

22

22

☆ VQ(2)5s

Mathurin Point

▲ 165 m

Mont Boulder

Cap Moule à Chique promontory

▲ 100 m

22

5,8

César Point

5

10

22

22

0   500   1000 m

Village

Commercial port

Cap Moule-à-Chique

W approach to Vieux Fort. Cap Moule-à-Chique on 120°

Anse des Pitons and Baie de la Soufrière

13°50′N 61°04′W

The luxuriant landscape of these two anchorages dominated by the vertiginous heights of the Pitons is undoubtedly the most spectacular of the Lesser Antilles. In Anse des Pitons the coconut palms which grew up a gentle slope behind a beach of black sand now give way to development of an intrusive kind. Baie de la Soufrière is wide and has a picturesque vil-

Anse des Pitons looking NNE

Baie de la Soufrière looking E

Laborie looking NNE. Church on 017°

lage with a landing stage. The steep shelf in both these bays makes it necessary to anchor close in with a line ashore. Local youths in their boats help in this manoeuvre – for a remuneration.

Approach

The Pitons make it easy to identify both these anchorages from a distance.

Anchorages

In Anse des Pitons there is 20m approximately 40m from the beach. Anchor in 20–23m and take a line ashore if you can still find a coconut palm.

In Baie de la Soufrière, the 50m contour runs about 120m from the shore. The best anchorage is in the northern part of the bay, edged with coconut palms, between the short pontoon belonging to Hummingbird Hotel and a group of small but bright oil tanks. Anchor in 15–20m on sand, 50–70m from the beach and take a line from the stern to the coconut palms. The sea-bed is uneven so take care to remain a good 20m from the shore.

Facilities

Restaurants at the Hummingbird Hotel and in the village. Limited supplies.

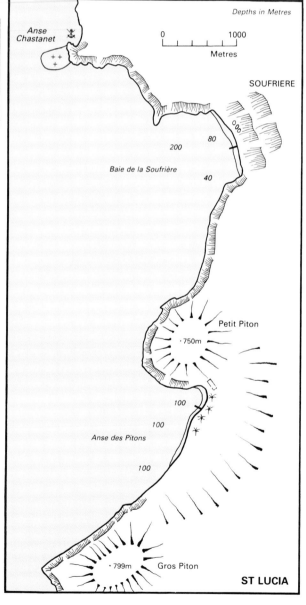

From Soufrière Bay to Marigot Harbour

There are several inlets in this section of the coast, two of which provide pleasant anchorages which are unfrequented but often affected by the northeasterly swell.

- Anse Cochon is the first good anchorage north of Soufrière. It has a deserted beach and thick vegetation with a stream flowing into the southeastern corner. There are 12m in the entrance, decreasing steadily towards the beach. Anchor in 5m on sand, approximately 80m from the beach. Keep 100m off the north and south shores which are foul with rocks.
- Anse de la Raye, with Pointe d'Orange as its northern point, is bordered by a pretty fishing hamlet and near a beach with coconut palms on which multi-coloured boats are hauled out. There is a short landing stage (1·5m) near a grey church with triangular facade. Anchor in 3–4m on sand in the northern half of the inlet, halfway between the landing stage and the rocks off Pointe d'Orange.
- The other inlets, particularly Anse des Canaries, are unsafe close to the shore and are more open to swell.

Marigot Harbour

13°58′N 61°02′W

This is a well protected bay at the foot of hills covered in vegetation and bordered by coconut palms and mangrove. It is one of the more famous anchorages of the Windward Islands and is often very full; The Moorings Ltd, a charter company, has its base here and has built quays and a hotel-restaurant – one of the better designed developments. It is difficult to recognise from the sea and is said to have been used as a hiding place by Rodney dodging the French fleet (Rodney's base was Gros Islet, now called Rodney Bay). The anchorage is made somewhat airless by the surrounding high hills and can be buggy; there is quite good bird-watching to be had. It is a good hurricane hole (the principle danger is from other yachts) and the best place from which to start a day's outing to the spectacular southwest.

If during the hurricane season when yachting is at its maximum the marina has a berth available this is one of the better places to be when it blows.

Approach

The entrance is between two steep bluffs covered in vegetation and can best be seen from a distance of at least ½M off shore. From the north, there is a yellowish cliff on the south side of Anse Roseau with a

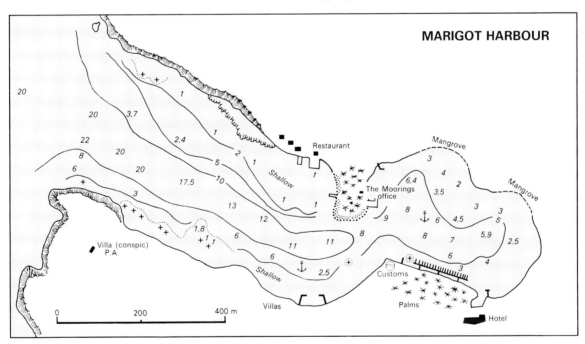

Marigot Harbour

Marigot Harbour looking ESE

quarry, visible from the northern side of the Anse, and a villa with a red roof on the bluff at the entrance. From the south, the Hess oil transhipment installation in Grand Cul-de-Sac Bay stands out – at night its lights are unmistakable. Enter, keeping a little to the south of the centre of the bay to avoid the dangerous coastal reefs off the Doolittle Hotel, then, to reach the inner lagoon, keep close to the spit with coconut palms on it which is safer than the southern side.

Anchorage

Anchor in 5–9m in the lagoon on a muddy bottom with poor holding.

If the lagoon is full anchor outside near the private pontoons (very shoal) on the south coast; this shelves quite steeply and has coral heads inshore.

Facilities

Restaurants, some supplies in the neighbouring hamlet (500m). Small expensive supermarket aimed at the charter trade (otherwise take a taxi to Castries). Fuel and water from the dock next to customs and Immigration on the south side near the harbour entrance (the water shoals from 5 to 1·5m).

Communications.

Taxis can be hired by the day. Buses from the main road a mile away over a steep hill. Telephone at the Hurricane Hole Hotel.

Grand Cul-de-Sac Bay
13°55′N 61°01′W

This deep inlet, used in their time by the invasion fleets of both sides, has been developed as an oil transhipment port for very large tankers debarred by their draught from entering the ports on the east and south coasts of the USA. It has little attraction for a yacht but may provide a welcome escape from other yachts. The only feasible anchorage is off the beach at the head of the bay.

Castries
14°01′N 61°00′W

Castries, the capital of the island, was twice completely destroyed by terrible fires, in 1927 and 1948. It is now a very lively modern town but without architectural style (though its pavements are level). It is a commercial harbour with little consideration for yachts and though a good port of call for technical purposes is otherwise of limited interest; it may be better to come from Rodney Bay or Marigot by bus or taxi. It has a well protected commercial port at the head of a deep bay.

Although a port of entry, it is more convenient for a yacht to clear at Marigot or Rodney Bay. However, if a yacht is to be left in St Lucia, a visit to customs here is necessary to fill the forms and provide an inventory.

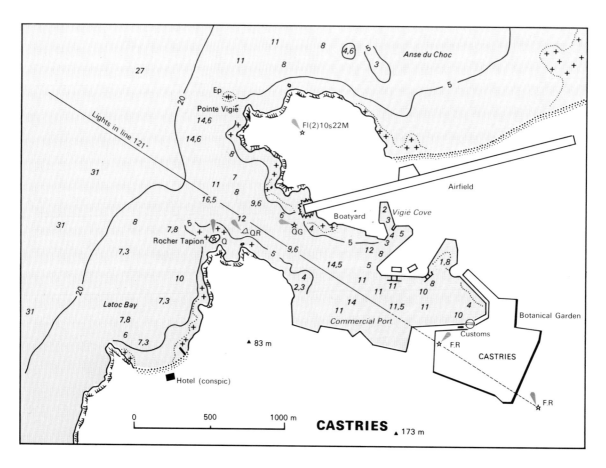

CASTRIES ▲ 173 m

Pointe Vigié lighthouse

Entrance

Castries looking SE

Approach

The lighthouse on Pointe Vigié to the north of the trance can be easily seen but the entrance is not obvious until it is opened up. From the south mind Tapion shoal, off the southern headland, marked by a red oil drum. The leading marks (two white triangles with a vertical red line) can be disregarded by yachts and in any case are not easy to see in daylight – the inner one may be concealed by a cargo boat at the quay. The lateral buoyage is adequate.

Berthing and anchorage

To clear, go alongside the north quay of the commercial port, in front of the customs house, a yellowish gable-end building mid-way along the quay. Do not leave a boat unattended as something bigger such as a cruise liner may come along outside.

Anchor in Vigié Cove in 5–20m between the entrance and the bend. The inside of the bend is shoal and is occupied by a new coastguard pier.

The marina at the head of Vigié Cove sometimes has berths free.

Facilities

Supplies and the usual facilities of a capital town of the Antilles.

Water and fuel at the pontoon (2·5m) of Vigié Cove.

Castries Yacht Services on reclaimed land west of Vigié Cove has a 35-tonne travel-lift. It has a ring fence with good security and it is a good place to leave a yacht.

Stores for yachts in transit are duty free but it pays to employ an agent to clear them.

Communications

Inter-island airport.

Geest banana boats call weekly, about 10–14 days from Barry, South Wales, United Kingdom. This is useful for shipping anything heavy – minimum load one cubic metre.

Rodney Bay

14°04'·5N 60°58'·5W

Rodney Bay has two distinct sections, the bay itself and the lagoon which is described below.

In the late 18th century the bay was used by Rodney as his base; he had to recapture it every time it was handed back to the French following a peace treaty. His headquarters on Pigeon Island, then a genuine island, was also a U.S. flying boat base in the second world war and is now a museum. The east coast of the bay is a long sandy beach. Gros Ilet, near the entrance to the lagoon, is one of the oldest villages on the island which usually has a splendid and noisy jump-up on Friday night.

Approach

Coming from the south, beware fish trap floats between Fourreur and the mainland. Otherwise the approach is open.

Anchorage

Rodney Bay is well protected from the prevailing winds but an Atlantic storm can produce a big swell. Most boats anchor off the beach on the southeast side, within dinghy reach of the lagoon and marina, but this can be noisy at night when the discos are going. An alternative is the anchorage on the north side of the bay but the bottom, and the holding, is irregular with patches of sand, coral, flat sheets of rock and sand over coral. If the light is good, pick sand. The coast north of the village is shoal and the northeast corner shallow. Water-skiing takes place off the northern beach and paragliders are launched from a platform off the hotel beach; keep clear of the latter.

Rodney Bay: the lagoon

A channel dug across the beach by Gros Islet leads to the lagoon which is less clean and cool than the bay. Rodney Bay Marina, the best yacht harbour south of the Virgin Islands, is in the lagoon. Although murky and unattractive for swimming the water has beautiful phosphorescence at night.

Holding tanks will be required after 1992, possibly earlier.

The lagoon is a good hurricane shelter but it quickly fills up in storm conditions.

Rodney Bay looking ESE

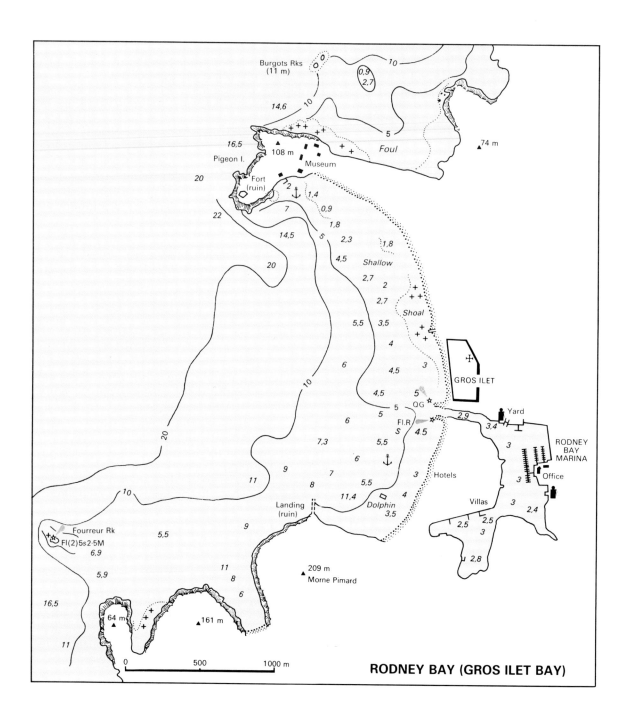

RODNEY BAY (GROS ILET BAY)

Rodney Bay. Entrance channel to the marina

Entrance

The entrance is difficult to make out until it is opposite. There are two rubble breakwaters resembling rocky outcrops, the north one close to a faded yellow building which looks like and is a public loo, itself 100m south of a red roofed restaurant on stilts and the south breakwater is 100m north of a conspicuous hotel. The leading lights, Fl.1s front, Oc.4s rear, lead very close to rocks where, due to damage, the end of the north breakwater hooks round. The breakwaters are lit, Q.Fl.G on the north and a lower light Fl.R.2s on the south side. Do not go north of the leading line and as soon as the lagoon opens up bear away to starboard. There is a ruined pier just south of the entrance. The green breakwater light is pale and might be mistaken for a the front leading light; do not confuse the flashing red aircraft warning lights on the hill behind with the breakwater light.

There are about 3m in the entrance and between 2 and 4m in the lagoon itself which is slowly silting up.

Formalities

Free mooring whilst clearing at reserved berths near the south end, marked by a yellow pile now rather difficult to identify. Customs and immigration are in the same office, open 0800–1800 but sometimes closed at midday, no charge except after 1630 and at weekends. Yachts staying up to three days need to clear inwards only; after a longer stay yachts must clear outwards as well.

Berthing and anchorage

Contact the marina on VHF Ch 16 for a berth.

Alternatively anchor south of the marina in mud with variable holding; an anchor may drag after holding for weeks. The inner lagoon has better holding than the northern part.

Facilities

The facilities are extensive but a bit pricey.

Complete services in the marina: electricity, water, showers, W.C., laundry. Barclays Bank (Monday to Thursday 0900–1200, Friday 0900–1200 and 1400–1530). Restaurant.

Well-equipped boatyard (50-tonne travel-hoist). Owners are allowed to work on their boats; labour and services available but not to a high standard.

Small supermarket specialising in French stores, bakery, wine merchant and many other shops.

Water (minimum 100 gallons) and fuel at the boatyard quay on the north of the lagoon where is a service charge of EC$13 ($5US). If going north, note that fuel in the French islands is more expensive and there is no convenient fuelling berth in Dominica; the next economical filling station is in Antigua.

Lots of restaurants in the Rodney Bay area.

Communications

Car hire. Buses for Castries pass the Marina gates. Telecommunications but faxes are expensive.

VI. Martinique

Charts
Imray-Iolaire *A30, A301*
Admiralty *371, 494*
SHOM *6738, 7041, 7087, 7088, 7089*
US *25524, 25525, 25527*

General remarks

Geography

Martinique is situated in the centre of the Lesser Antilles arc, just south of the 15th parallel which traditionally marks the line between The Windward Islands in the south and the Leeward Islands in the north. This distinction is almost forgotten today in publications written in French but is still remembered by the British. The island is rich and largely cultivated. It possesses a most varied terrain, ranging from the very dense tropical forests of the mountainous centre to the petrified desert, Savane des Pétrifications, in the south and from the beaches of black sand in the northwest to the intensely white ones of the east and the south. Its mountainous landscape is dominated by Pelée (1350m), an active volcano which erupted in 1902 wiping out the ancient capital of the island, Saint-Pierre. The present capital is Fort de France. Many anchorages are accessible to yachts and, a rarity in the Antilles, the windward coast provides some secure shelter under the protection of wide coral reefs.

On 1 January 1947 Martinique was transformed from a colony to an overseas *département* of France equal in status to those of metropolitan France. It has a population of 360,000 inhabitants and an area of 1080 sq km.

The island is several generations ahead of the islands of the British Commonwealth. Fort de France is the largest and most sophisticated city in the Caribbean with a good deal of industry and well developed docks. The island has good roads, even a motorway. It is prosperous and there is a lot of agricultural land producing bananas which take up the greatest area, sugar, of which more than half is converted to rum, and pineapples. There are quite large numbers of domesticated animals. Over half its exports go to France and a third to Guadeloupe.

History

Martinique, discovered in 1502 by Christopher Columbus during his third expedition, is one of the few islands not renamed by the great navigator. Its name derived from the Carib name, Matinino, the island of women, or Madinina, the island of flowers. It was only colonised by the French in 1635 by Belain d'Esnanbuc under Richelieu's Compagnie des Iles d'Amerique. With the exception of the mishaps lasting several months in 1762 and the period of eight years (1794–1802) when the colonials, rebelling against The Convention and the abolition of slavery decreed in it, called in the English, it has remained French ever since. In the Second World War it sided with Vichy and the navy, with little else to do, spent much time in survey which helps explain the superiority of the French charts of the area.

The event most vividly imprinted on the island's memory is the terrible eruption of the Mont Pelée on the 8th May 1902, when, in a few seconds the capital Saint-Pierre, its 30,000 inhabitants and all the vessels at anchor were wiped out, burned to death under a scorching cloud which spared only one single prisoner who was miraculously protected by the thick walls of the municipal jail.

Approach

A particular warning, which applies to all French islands, is to keep a good look-out for fish floats. They are to be found almost anywhere in soundings, even well off shore. They are frequently found in groups. They are small and difficult to see, especially up sun, when there is a sea running or in rain and impossible to see at night. They can disable a yacht by fouling her rudder or her propeller.

Approached from the south, Martinique appears as two islands because of the low land separating the hills. Morne Larcher (477m), the southwestern tip of the island can be easily identified as far as 15M away but Diamond Rock (176m) blends in to the high land behind; in hazy weather, though, the white Hotel Diamant, just west of Marigot de Diamant, stands out. The town of Sainte-Luce, white against a background of hills, can easily be seen from a distance of 10M. Further inland, the Montagne du Vauclin (505m) conical in shape, is the most conspicuous peak. The peaks in the northern part of the island are only visible in very clear weather. Ilet Cabrits off the

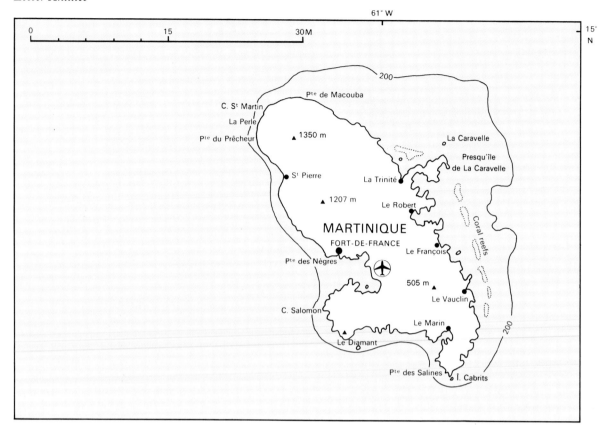

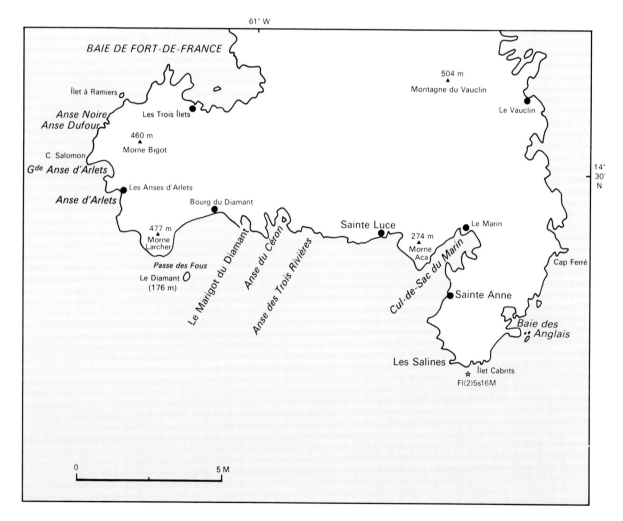

southern tip of Martinique is difficult to pick out but its lighthouse (Fl.R.5s16M) is helpful when approaching by night.

When approached from the north Martinique has the appearance of a very broadly based cone dominated by Mont Pelée (1350m) which is almost always capped in cloud. To the east, the Presqu'île de la Caravelle appears to be separated from the island. The best landfall is at Pointe du Prêcheur (see page 101) on which there is a lighthouse (Fl.R.10s19M) which makes a night arrival possible. As with Dominica, strong gusts are likely when approaching the northern tip of the island and to leeward of it.

Tourism

The French say Martinique is as much a part of France as Normandy and they are almost right. The stamps and coins are French, the Gendarmerie appears French and the taxi drivers think they are in Paris. Tourism is well developed and an important source of revenue. The most spectacular excursion is via the Route de la Trace leading from Fort de France to the Mont Pelée. The climb takes 3 hours on foot from where the road ends and is reserved for trained walkers. A tour of the island by sea with numerous and very varied ports of call, is equally rewarding with a week's pleasant cruising (approximately 95M) included.

The more serious student of local culture should visit the Schoëlcher library.

Formalities

Ports of entry. Marin, Fort de France, La Trinité. Outward clearance has to be done in Fort de France but it is not necessary to take the boat there for that purpose.

Flag

The tricolour of three vertical stripes of blue, white, red.

Maintenance

Fort de France.

Communications

International airport. Car hire. Bus services.
VHF and SSB shore station

Hurricane holes

Martinique has some good hurricane holes listed in the Appendix and a reputation for bold sailing and poor anchoring. The east coast shelters in particular require reconnaissance and their approaches are hazardous even in good conditions.

The south coast of Martinique from Cap Ferré to Ilet à Ramiers

Coasts, dangers

- Cap Ferré, a small hillock joined to the coast by a low isthmus, is not very conspicuous. In this area it is advisable to keep outside the 20m line and to be on the watch for the many fish traps anchored with floating lines. Baie des Anglais, which is very well protected, is difficult to reach (see page 86)
- On the barren Ilet Cabrits (17m) there is a lighthouse with a red pylon 27m high (Fl.R.5s16M) next to two light-coloured buildings. There are reefs to the west, southwest and east of this islet. The coast between Ilet Cabrits and Cap Ferré is open to the swell and the east wind, and off it are reefs and banks of coral with several low-lying islands.
- Between the southern tip of the island and Cul-de-Sac du Marin (see page 87) there is a wide coastal shelf with very little water over it. The village of Sainte-Luce, identifiable by the white, square belfry of its church and a large road-bridge to the east, is the best landmark in the area. 1·3M ESE, Morne Aca has a remarkable TV tower reaching a height of 305m.
- Between Cul-de-Sac du Marin and Pointe du Diamant, 9·5M to the west, the coast is low-lying and has a coastal shelf 0·4–1M wide with less than 10m depths and frequent sandbanks. There are several well protected anchorages here but they are difficult to reach.
- Pointe du Diamant, which is steep, is dominated by Morne Larcher (477m), also steep and easily recognizable from the distance. 1M to the southeast, Le Diamant (176m), a very steep and grey-sided rock, stands out prominently; this, of course, is Diamond Rock, the scene of a famous British landing in the Napoleonic Wars when guns were hauled to the top of the rock, an amazing feat, and it was formally commissioned as HMS *Diamond Rock*.
- Between Pointe du Diamant and Ilet à Ramiers (39m), 5·5M to the north, the coast is safe, high and with several inlets offering good anchorages. Inland, green bluffs dominate the landscape, among which is Morne Bigot (460m) on which stands a TV mast which is conspicuous from the sea. On the coast the white church with a grey spire of Anse d'Arlets is a good landmark. Ilet à Ramiers is rounded and has a small fort standing on top of it which is not easy to see amongst the vegetation.

Baie des Anglais

14°25′N 60°51′W

Baie des Anglais is one of the most attractive anchorages on Martinique. There is plenty of room in this completely protected bay between mangrove shores where beautiful white egrets and many other species of birds make their nests. Small rounded hillocks arise inland where the occasional building can be seen. It is also one of the more alarming places to get in to. Baie des Anglais itself is only accessible to vessels drawing less than 2m.

Note From observations made in this area (1977) it appears that the magnetic variation is greater than is shown on the charts.

Approach

The channel which leads to the lagoon which forms the Baie des Anglais passes between Ile Hardy (14m) to the north and the group of islets called Perce (6m), Burgaux (7m) and Tois Roux (8m) in the south. When the swell is heavy it flows into the channel making it dangerous. In any case the entrance to the channel calls for the skipper's whole attention and a good light is necessary (sun in the east). The peninsula inshore of Ile Tois Roux is steep and connected to the mainland by a low spit; it looks like an island. It is important to identify all these islets ac-

curately, then Ilets à Egrets, which is very low and green (sometimes difficult to spot) and Pointe de la Vierge des Marins, on which stands a small square chapel. Enter the channel heading 290° towards the northern edge of Ilets à Egrets, leaving to port immediately after the entrance the reefs WNW of Ilet Perce on which the sea sometimes breaks and a sand spit close to starboard. Vessels drawing more than 2m can anchor between these two reefs and Ilet à Egrets in 4m depths on sand. The swell makes itself felt here.

Entrance

To enter, alter course to 319° toward the old mill (grey truncated tower) of the dwelling of the Anglais des Grottes, 0·5m inland; this appears slightly to the left of Ilet de Paletuviers which forms the northern side of the entrance to the bay (the mill mentioned here is not the one shown on chart SHOM 6738).

Anchorage

In the bay anchor either in 2m on mud, north of Ilet de Paletuviers or in 3—3·5m depths WNW of Pointe de la Vierge des Marins.

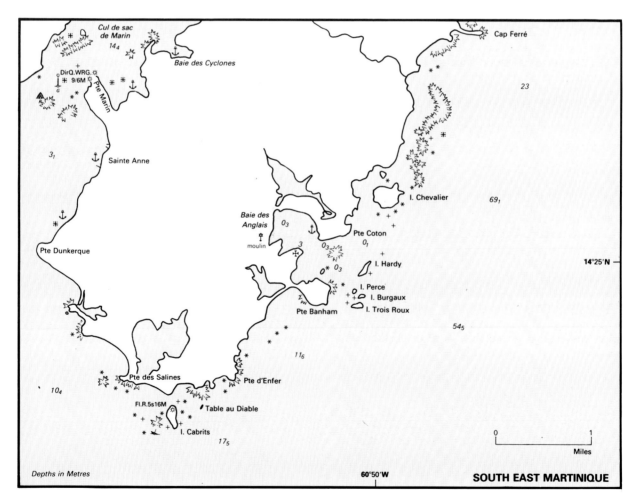

Sainte-Anne and anchorages to the south

14°26'·0N 60°53'·2W

Sainte-Anne, a pleasant small holiday town rather than a delightful fishing village, lies along the shores of a very open bay which is nevertheless well protected from the trade winds. The water is of exceptional clarity with depths of 3–5m over sand. The Club Mediterranée has a base here which maintains exclusive rights to its portion of the beach.

Approach

The landmarks of Sainte-Anne are, from south to north, a shrine on the hill, the large light-coloured roof of the new market, a short TV aerial behind the village and the grey, square belfry of the church.

Entrance

There are no difficulties in the approach from the south. Coming from Cul-de-Sac du Marin, it is possible to pass between Banc des Trois Cayes and Banc de la Crique but inshore, southwest of Pointe Marin, is shoal.

Anchorage

Anchor either in front of the beach in 2·5–4m depths 250–300m from the shore, or in front of the village in 3m depths, 150m WSW of the landing stage (1·7m at the end).

Facilities

Supplies (market and shops), restaurants.

Anchorages to the south

2M south of Sainte-Anne, the beautiful beach of Salines, a long ribbon of white sand edged with coconut palms, provides a pleasant anchorage well-protected by Pointe des Salines and the reefs which extend from it. The best anchorage is in the eastern part of the bay in 2·4m depths halfway between the beach and with Pointe des Salines on a SSE bearing.

Cul-de-Sac du Marin

14°28'N 60°53'W

Cul-de-Sac du Marin is a large well-protected bay at the head of which Bourg du Marin, a port of entry (though attendance by officials can be irregular), is situated. It is the base for one of the largest French charter companies. A number of shoals obstruct the entrance and the interior of the bay but excellent markers make the approach easy. The indented coast, which is mostly deserted, provides good natural shelter from hurricanes; it has half a dozen good mangrove coves but access to some of them would require prior reconnaissance. The place becomes crowded when a hurricane threatens.

Approach

Enter Cul-de-Sac du Marin through Passe du Marin on a bearing of 073° towards the leading light on Pointe Marin, a white column with a green top 150m north of a large white tower with a conical roof which is conspicuous amongst the buildings of the Club Meditérranée. Once the Banc du Singe has been cleared, steer northeast towards the channel between Banc Major and Banc du Milieu, marked by lit buoys along both sides.

Anchorages and berthing

Anchor 200m from the shore, south of the church of Marin in 3–4m depths on mud.

The harbour situated SSW of the church has quays with 2·5–3m depths where one can go alongside.

Yacht club A number of moorings managed by the club are anchored northeast of the Banc de la Douane. A charge is made for their use.

A quay for pleasure boats, 120m long, has been built southeast of the yacht club. It is partly managed by the yacht club, partly by a company which rents out sailing boats, and it is always full. The approach to it is difficult as there is little depth.

Ilet Baude The inlet in the southeast of this islet, deserted and bordered by mangroves, provides a totally protected anchorage in 4–6m depths. The approach through a winding channel between shoals with very little water covering them should only be made in a very good light.

Baie des Cyclones There are 4–6m depths in the centre of this bay which is deserted and green. In the approach keep well away from the shoals off Pointe Cayot (Pointe Cailloux).

Steeple   Mast   New market

Sainte-Anne looking ESE

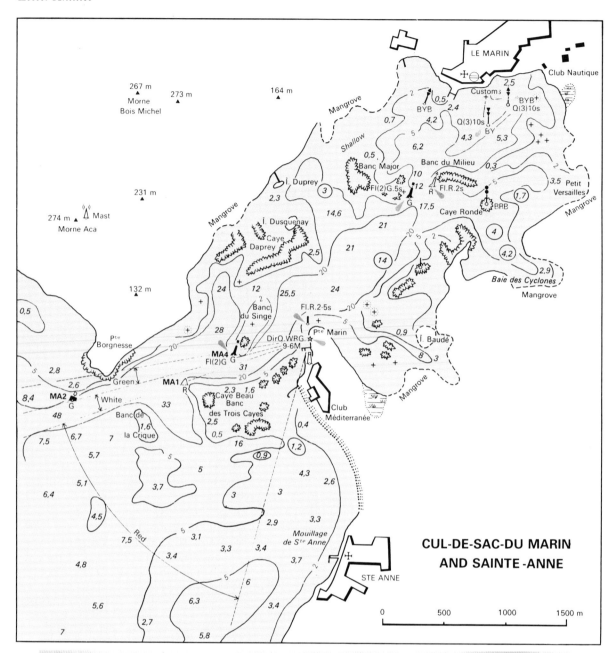

Map labels

267 m ▲
Morne
Bois Michel

273 m ▲

164 m ▲

LE MARIN

Club Nautique

Mangrove

2   0,5
BYB   2,4
0,7   4,2
5   6,2

Customs   2,5

Q(3)10s
BY   BYB
4,3   Q(3)10s
5,3

0,3

Shallow

0,5
231 m ▲

Banc Major

Banc du Milieu

2

3,5 Petit
Versailles

Î. Duprey
2,3   3

10
Fl(2)G.5s
12
R   Fl.R.2s

17,5
G

274 m ▲ Mast
Morne Aca

Mangrove

Î. Dusquenay
Caye
Daprey

14,6

21

Caye Ronde

BRB   1,7

4

Mangrove

2,5

21

20   5

4,2

132 m ▲

24   12

25,5

24

14

2,9
Baie des Cyclones

2
Banc
du Singe

20

Mangrove

28

20

Fl.R.2·5s

0,5

Pte
Borgnesse

20

DirQ.WRG.
9·6M

MA4
Fl(2)G G   31

Pte Marin

0,9

Î. Baudé

8   3

2,8

Green
2,6

MA1
R

20

5

Mangrove

8,4   MA2
G

White

33

Caye Beau
Banc
des Trois Cayes

2,3 1,6

R

0,4

Club
Méditerranée

48

Banc de
la Crique   1,6

2,5   0,5

16

0,9

1,2

7,5   6,7   7

5,7

5

5

4,3

2,6

6,4

5,1

3,7

3

3

3,3

4,5

2,9

Mouillage
de Ste Anne

3,3

7,5   Red

5

3,1

3,3   3,4

3,7

2

**CUL-DE-SAC-DU MARIN
AND SAINTE-ANNE**

4,8

3,4

6

STE ANNE

5,6

6,3

3,4

0   500   1000   1500 m

7

2,7

5,8

Basin   *Club Nautique*   *Yacht quay*

Le Marin looking NNE, inner passage

Facilities

There are water and electricity points on the pleasure boat quay as well as on the northern quay of the harbour. Showers and toilets in the yacht club. Limited technical assistance.

Supplies and several restaurants in the village.

Rivière-Pilote and Sainte-Luce

14°27'·9N 60°55'·5W

The anchorages of Rivière-Pilote and Sainte-Luce are of little interest to yachtsmen and are often uncomfortable because of the swell.

Rivière-Pilote The mouth of the river is silted up and the depths diminish rapidly within the 10m depth contour. In calm weather there is a more attractive anchorage in Anse Figuiers in 3m depths 100m from the beach bordered by coconut palms. Beware of the shoals off the south and southeastern coasts of this inlet.

Sainte-Luce The square white belfry of the church and a road bridge east of the village are typical landmarks. Keep well clear of Grande Cay which is difficult to identify before turning on a bearing of 350° towards the belfry, then to the NNW towards the village landing stage which is covered with a tiled roof. Anchor in 12–15m depths on mud southeast of this landing stage.

Anse des Trois Rivières

14°21'·1N 60°58'·3W

Anse des Trois Rivières is not as pretty as the next two described. In the ENE of the inlet there is a hamlet rising in terraces up a hillside. This fairly unfrequented anchorage is protected from the swell by a reef which uncovers in places.

Approach

The anchorage can be reached through a narrow fault in the coastal shelf. Align a square white villa which can be seen on a tree-covered height inland with the chimney of a distillery which stands out white and isolated in the landscape. This alignment on a bearing of 018° leads first along the western side of the fault in 6m depths, then through the centre which is deep. When 7m depths are reached, turn onto a bearing of 054° towards a large grey building with a metal roof, conspicuous in the upper part of the hamlet.

Anchorage

Anchor in 3–4m depths on mud, 250m WSW of the hamlet.

Anse du Céron

14°28'N 60°59'W

Anse du Céron is a very twisted inlet, deserted and surrounded by a green and valleyed landscape. There are some anchorages which are little frequented because the approach is obstructed by shoals.

Approach

The approach must be made with extreme caution and should only be undertaken when the sun is high so that the shoals can easily be picked out. A bearing of 036° towards a reddish water tower standing about 1M back from the shore leads through a deep fault in the coastal shelf as far as Caye Oli, awash, the south and east of which is safe. This is joined by shoals to Pointe Giraud on which stands a small white oratory next to a cabin.

The best anchorage is in the eastern arm of the inlet between Pointe Giraud and Ilet du Céron. To reach it go round the eastern side of Caye Oli at approximately 100m and continue on a bearing of 345° watching out for the shoals which lie off Ilet du Céron towards the SSW and the west; they are difficult to see because the water is not clear.

Water tower on 037°

Entrance to Anse du Céron

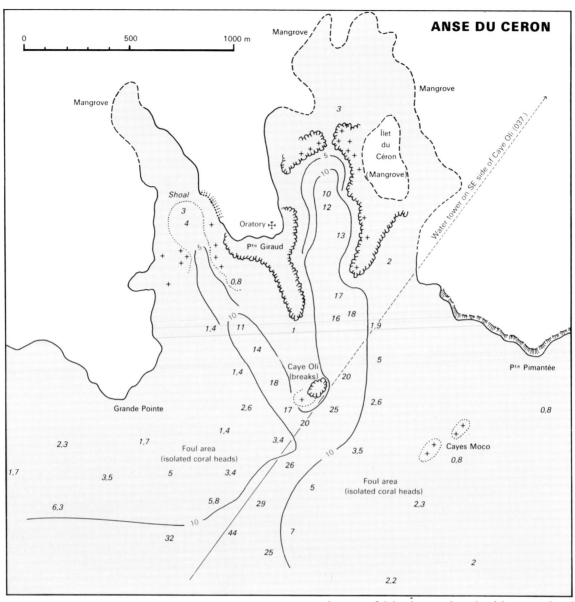

ANSE DU CERON

Anchorage

Anchor in 10–12m depths on mud along a line between Pointe Giraud and the northwestern tip of the islet. This anchorage is bounded to the north by a series of shoals through which a narrow winding channel leads to a perfectly protected stretch of water with depths of 3m, northwest of the islet.

The northwestern arm of the inlet where there is a minute anchorage with 4m depths is less attractive. To reach it, pass to the west of Caye Oli then steer with caution towards the entrance (NNW), avoiding the shoals off Pointe Grimaud and the western shore.

Le Marigot du Diamant

14°28'·3N 61°00'·5W

Marigot du Diamant is a well-sheltered inlet whose shores are fertile to the west and more arid to the east. There is a hotel on Pointe du Marigot which forms the southwestern arm of the inlet. This anchorage, fairly deserted and with exceptionally clear water, is very pleasant but can become uncomfortable in a swell.

Approach

The approach should only be made in a good light when the variations in the colour of the water over the shoals can be easily seen. The depth sounder should be in constant use. Marigot du Diamant can be identified from the following landmarks: Morne Cabrits (217m), conical in shape, which can be clearly seen northeast of the anchorage, a yellow warehouse on the north coast of the inlet and, finally, the light-coloured buildings, 2 storeys high, of the hotel.

Entrance

The entrance to Marigot is through a deep fault in the coastal shelf on a bearing of 028° towards the summit of Morne Cabrits. Then on 348° towards the northwestern tip of the pontoon which is marked by a white column. Round Pointe du Marigot, off which there are shoals, at a distance of approximately 100m.

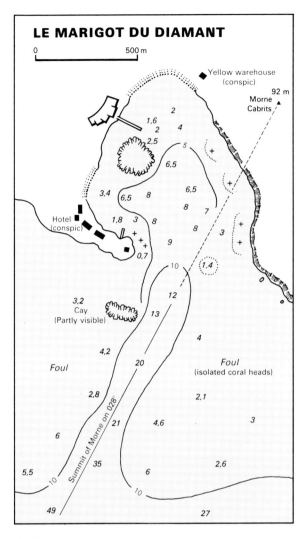

LE MARIGOT DU DIAMANT

0   500 m

Yellow warehouse (conspic)

92 m
Morne Cabrits ▲

Hotel (conspic)

3,2 Cay (Partly visible)

Foul

Foul (isolated coral heads)

Summit of Morne on 028°

Anchorage

After rounding the headland, anchor between it and the reef to the north (just south of the northwestern pontoon) and to the east of the beach with the hotel, in 4–7m on sand.

Anse d'Arlets

14°30'·0N 61°05'·5W

Both Grande and Petite Anse d'Arlets are wide and easily accessible anchorages.

Grande Anse d'Arlets is edged by a long white beach fringed with coconut palms. Amongst the greenery is a hamlet and some villas.

Petite Anse d'Arlets contains the village of Les Anse d'Arlets, one of the smartest of the island, which is identifiable by its white church opposite the landing stage. The swell is greater here than in Grande Anse.

Approach

The approaches are quite safe and the seabed is level sand. The central part of the beach should be avoided as there is a coral reef extending approximately 100m out to sea in front of a conspicuous restaurant with a green roof. The southern half of the inlet offers better protection from the swell which comes round the southern half of the island.

Anchorage

In Grande Anse d'Arlets anchor in 3–4m depths, 150–200m from the land. Do not anchor between two yellow buoys in the middle area which are used for seine netting. A landing stage in 1·7m depths makes it possible to go ashore.

In Petite Anse d'Arlets anchor in 3–4m depths on light sand, approximately 150m WSW of the landing stage at the end of which there are 2m depths. An uncovering cay lies approximately 100m WNW of the landing stage.

0·6M further south lies Anse Chaudière which is in effect the south side of Petit Arlets bay. It shelves gradually one may anchor in 3–4m depths on sand, 80–100m from the shore. It is used by day boats and divers but is quiet by night.

Anse Dufour and Anse Noire

14°31'·5N 61°05'·5W

These two adjacent inlets offer attractive anchorages which are easy to reach but are often uncomfortable or untenable because of the swell.

The first has white sand and the second is edged by black sand at the mouth of a very luxuriant ravine where there are several small huts, one of which is a restaurant. The contrast, within so short a distance, of the two types of sand is a remarkable sight. In Anse Dufour, which is the less attractive of the two, a fishing hamlet is situated close to the beach of white sand on which the gommiers are hauled out.

Approach

There are no off-lying dangers and the inlets are free from reefs. Both bays are popular spots for the big day charter yachts.

Anchorage

In Anse Dufour, anchor in 5–7m depths on sand in the middle of the inlet.

There is a small restaurant in the hamlet.

In Anse Noir, anchor in 4–6m on sand 100–120m from the beach where the metal landing stage is used by day trip boats.

Hotel   Pte du Marigot   Warehouse   Morne Cabrits

Le Marigot du Diamant looking NNE

The northwest coast of Martinique from Ilet à Ramiers to Macouba Point

Coasts, dangers

L'Ilet à Ramiers (39m) which marks the southern end of the Rade de Fort de France, is rounded and covered with dark vegetation. There is a small old fort on top of it which is not easy to see.

- The Rade de Fort de France which opens between L'Ilet à Ramiers and Pointe des Negres, is one of the largest and best protected of the Lesser Antilles. The town of Fort de France (100,000 inhabitants) extends along the north coast of the bay and over the hills behind. From the sea the most conspicuous landmarks are a group of white buildings in the Schoëlcher quarter (west of the town) and, on a hill 2·6M north of the town, the white

basilica of Balata, which is a replica of the Sacre Coeur in Paris and is very clearly visible set against the green background (see page 94).

- The interior of the bay and the town of Fort de France are described in paragraphs on pages 96 to 99.
- Pointe des Negres, which marks the northern entrance of the Rade, is prominent but low-lying and has a lighthouse on a mast (Fl.5s25M). Northeast of it is a conspicuous grey building 12 storeys high (photograph page 99). Between Pointe des Negres and Saint-Pierre there are several fishing villages along the coast which has no off-lying dangers. The port of Case Pilote is described in paragraph on page 99.

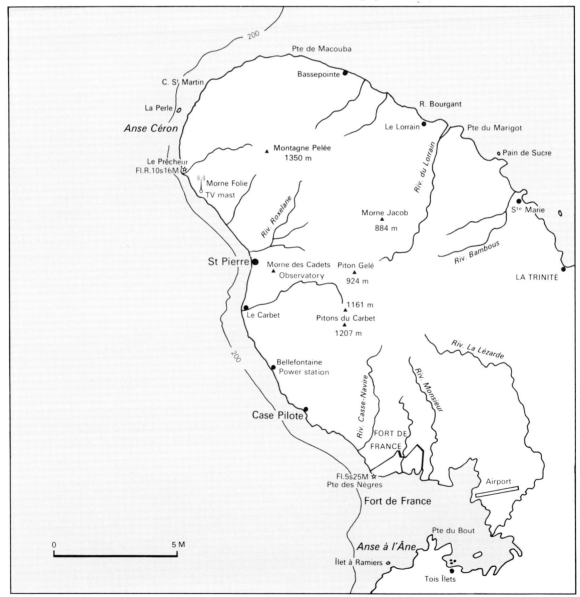

Martinique looking SSE

- Between Rade de Saint-Pierre and Macouba Point, the northern tip of the island, the coast is mostly sheer and dominated by the steep foothills of Mont Pelée. The power station (14°40′N 61°05′·7W) south of Belle-Fontaine is the best landmark on this coast. Le Carbet (2M south of Saint-Pierre) can be identified by its church with a slender steeple near a large white building. The conspic-uous Volcanological Observatory on Morne des Cadets (405m) is a good landmark. 1M to the SSE of Le Bourg du Prêcheur there is a conspicuous mast of a TV relay station on Morne Folie (101m). Le Bourg du Prêcheur itself can be identified by the lighthouse (Fl.R.10s16M) on the headland of the same name and by a radio mast to the east of it. There is also a church with two towers and a large grey, square tower with a red roof set back from the village. La Perle, a steep rock (27m) with vegetation on it is difficult to pick out from a distance against the coastal background. The channel on the landward side is unsafe near the coast.

Anse à l'Ane

14°32′·5N 61°04′·3W

Anse à l'Ane, 0·7M east of Ilet à Ramiers, provides an anchorage which is much less busy than the one at Anse Mitan, and is near a beautiful beach edged with coconut palms among which several villas can be seen. A landing stage 40m long in 1·3m depths stands in the northern part of the beach; the E side of this pier is reserved for ferries.

Anse Mitan. Bakoua pier

Approach

From Ilet à Ramiers the approach is open but there is an unmarked crystalline rock (0·7m) in the middle of the bay between the headlands; favour either side of the bay until the conspicuous Hotel Meridien in Anse Mitan is hidden by Pointe d'Alet. It is then safe to anchor anywhere. From Anse Mitan, do not cut the corner round Pointe d'Alet which has a reef (0·9m) off it.

Anchoring

The seabed is of fine sand and depths decrease gently towards the beach. Anchor inside the shoal patch in 3m depths about 200m from the beach.

Facilities

Restaurants, a supermarket.

Communications

Frequent ferries to Fort de France and Anse Mitan.

Anse Mitan

14°33′N 61°03′·5W

Anse Mitan is a popular anchorage. It is large, with a reasonable depth sheltered from the prevailing east wind though in strong west winds it is exposed to the swell and dangerous. Ashore is a high class resort known as Pointe du Bout with big hotels, lots of restaurants and boutiques, all laid out in a Mediterranean style. It is extremely busy in the tourist season.

Approach

From the east, there are reefs off Pointe d'Alet to be avoided. In the bay, Cay de l'Anse Mitan, outside the line of the headlands and marked by a small buoy (conical surmounted by two black spheres), has 0·9m over it.

Anchorage

Anchoring is prohibited near the beach inside a line of yellow buoys (if there) and near the south pier, which is used by ferries. If near the pier, rig an anchor light in the proper place where it can be seen; do not use the masthead light for this purpose. Anchor where it suits. Holding is patchy in the south part of the bay which is noisy on disco nights close to the beach. The sewer outfall is at the southwest end of the beach. There are a few berths at Hotel de Bakoua's pier but this is in bad repair and swell may make it difficult; it may be possible to lie bows-to with a stern anchor.

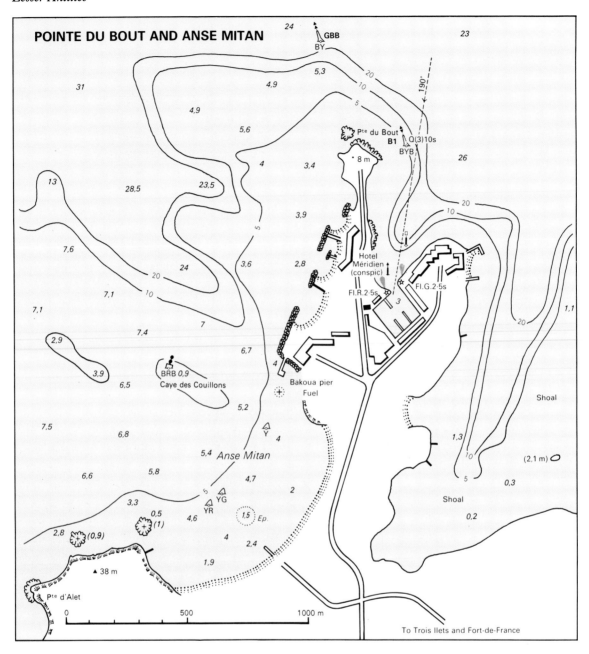

POINTE DU BOUT AND ANSE MITAN

Land at Bakoua pier or on the west side of the south pier, leaving the east side for the ferries.

Facilities

Water, fuel and gas at Bakoua pier.

Chandleries, supermarket, shops, all closing midday, restaurants, hotels.

Credit Agricole unreliably open 0800–1245 and 1400–1630 Tuesday through Friday and Saturday mornings.

Communications

Car hire. Fast ferries to Fort de France

Phone box convenient to the south pier. Hotel Caribe Auberge may help with fax.

Rade de Fort de France southeast: Trois Ilets

SHOM chart *6892* should be used.

The southeastern part of the bay of Fort de France has one crowded, small marina and several almost deserted anchorages which are well protected and pleasant despite the fact that the water is usually murky.

Marina de la Pointe du Bout

14°33'·4N 6°1 03'·3W

A small marina surrounded by a residential and hotel complex. It is always very full and it is best to negotiate a berth before arrival, possibly by anchoring

Pointe du Bout looking E

Entrance to Pointe du Bout marina looking S

nearby and doing the job in person. Once accepted, it is a secure place in which to leave a yacht.

Approach

Hotel Meridien is the best landmark on Pointe du Bout which ends in a small wooded hillock. Two cardinal markers, north and east, indicate the dangers off this headland. The approach is then by buoyed channel.

Berthing

There are 3m in the harbour but it tends to silt up. Visitors should tie up to the pontoon and quays to the southeast where there are moorings, as instructed by the harbour master.

Facilities

Water and electricity at the marina quay, supplies from the marina supermarket.

Petite Ilet

14°32′·09N 61°00′·04W

The approach to this anchorage is obstructed by an unmarked sandbank (1·5m) north of Gros Ilet. Steer from the buoy at Cay à Vache towards the one at Cay Sobbé, then from the latter steer 112° to reach the anchorage south of Petite Ilet which is low and covered in vegetation. If the buoys are not there (and they were missing in May 1990) both SHOM chart 6892 and expert navigation are essential. Anchor about 100m out from the wooden landing stage (5m depths, mud).

Gros Ilet

14°32′·07N 61°01′·03N

West of this green islet (67m) lies an anchorage which is well protected from the trade winds and waves they stir up in the bay. Round the buoy off Pointe de la Rose, steer 143° towards a conspicuous large parabolic aerial inland and then turn east towards the summit of Gros Ilet. Anchor on this axis in 7–10m on mud approximately 150m from the islet. The edges of the bank are steep.

Pointe Angboeuf

14°33′N 61°02′·04W

0·3M southwest of this point there is an anchorage surrounded by greenery in 6m, light mud. In a fresh easterly wind there is considerable wash here. This anchorage is reached by rounding the headland and keeping about 100m off the coast. Depths decrease rapidly within the 5m line and there is 0·5m patch in the middle, about 150m WNW of the first island.

Bourg de Trois-Ilets

14°32′·03N 61°02′·03W

It was on an estate near this pretty town with its smart little houses that Empress Josephine was born (née Marie-Joseph Rose Tascher de la Pagerie). In the inlet where the town is situated there is a quiet anchorage but it must be approached with great care. Go very slowly and watch the depths. After rounding Pointe de la Rose north cardinal buoy, head for the east end of the village with its conspicuous church spire. Continue until the west end of the golf course, a noticeably smooth green area, is between the two

Island   *Church*   *Pier in line with dip in hills*   *Island*

Martinique. Trois Ilets. *Hugo du Plessis*

west islands and the TV mast on the hill behind is one third on the south side of the gap. Alter course onto this heading until the short pier, which usually has two or three yachts on it, is in line with the dip between two close-spaced peaks behind. Then keep close on this line and proceed with caution up to the harbour. Go inside, if there is room, 2m or anchor in 3–4m depths in the inlet and land at the pier or ashore the beach nearby. There are several restaurants and shops in the village.

Eastern part of the Rade de Fort de France: Cohe du Lamentin

Cohe du Lamentin is normally of no interest to a yachtsmen. There are industrial installations, including a large oil refinery on the west and northern shores and the eastern shore is bordered by mangroves. A narrow neck of water leads through the mangroves in the southeastern part of Cohe du Lamentin to the scanty installations of the private marina of Port Cohe which is the best hurricane shelter in the bay and has 2–2·5m depths. The entrance, situated north of Pointe de la Vierge, can be identified from the wreck of a boat on the north coast. Head ESE towards this entrance where there are depths of about 2m. Caretakers and maintenance work at the marina. Local yachts anchor or moor in the bay of Cohe du Lamentin.

Fort de France

14°36′·0N 61°04′·0W

Fort de France, the capital of Martinique, has 100,000 inhabitants and is one of the busiest ports of the Antilles. Compared to Fort de France, all the other island capitals are villages. The old centre, between Rivière Madame and Fort St Louis, forms a chequer board of narrow streets buzzing with activity during the day and is next to a large shady garden, Place de la Savane, which opens out toward the sea. The importance of the city compares poorly with arrangements for visiting yachts. Only the Yacht Club de la Martinique in the Baie du Carenage has a few pontoons and they are all taken up by local boats. Yachts therefore anchor in Baie des Flamands, necessary for those needing to carry out formalities, where there is very often an uncomfortable lop and a lot of noise. The alternatives are to go to the marina or the anchorages of Pointe du Bout and go by ferry to clear customs – many shoppers commute from Anse Mitan by ferry.

Approach

The approach is well buoyed and presents no difficulty by day or night. In the approaches to the bay the best landmarks are a large group of white buildings in the west of the town, Pointe des Negres which has a lighthouse on a 28m pylon (Fl.5s25M) and a conspicuous grey building 750m to the northeast, and the white basilica of Balata clearly visible on a hill 2·6M north of the town. The shallows outside the port (Banc Mitan and Banc du Gros Ilet) are marked and present no danger to yachts.

In the centre of the town the slender steeple of the cathedral is easily recognised, and to the east the grey walls of Fort St Louis on which there is a lighthouse (F.WRG.13-10M). Finally, east of Fort St Louis, the cranes in the harbour of Baie des Tourelles and the warehouses and silos on Point des Carriers are conspicuous.

By night the lighthouse on Pointe des Negres is clearly visible but the other lights are difficult to distinguish from the lights of the town.

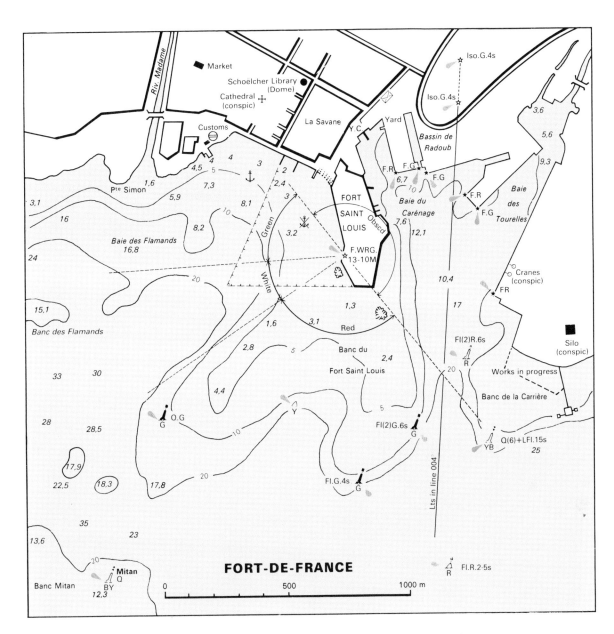

FORT-DE-FRANCE

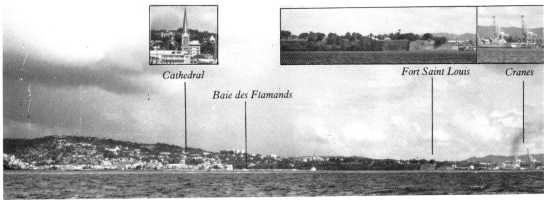

Cathedral

Baie des Flamands

Fort Saint Louis

Cranes

Fort de France looking NE

Pointe des Negres lighthouse marking the entrance to Fort de France, Martinique. The anchorage can be seen at far right.
Anne Hammick

Mont Pelée, which erupted in 1902 destroying the town of Saint-Pierre.
Anne Hammick

Pointe des Negres lighthouse and conspicuous building looking NNW

Anchorage

Anchor in the west part of the Baie des Flamands, in 3–6m depths on mud, about 150–200m from the shore taking care not to obstruct either the approach channel to the fuel quay or the approach and turning area for the frequent ferries which use the middle of the three piers shown (the west one is used by pilot boats which have their own moorings to its west, the east one is rubble). The anchorage tends to be crowded with yachts unnecessarily using the full scope of their nylon warps; it is often possible to find space quite close inshore, near the esplanade, or towards the southwest part. Go ashore at the Abri Côtier dock on the west side or at the end of the pilots' pier.

The approach to Baie du Carenage and Baie des Tourelles, where services for yachts are to be found, is made by rounding the dangerous Banc du Fort St Louis whose southwestern, southern and eastern limits are marked by green buoys *0*, *2* and *4*.

There is an area for seaplanes in the southern part of Fort de France bay. Yachts must take care not to obstruct their taking off or landing.

Facilities

Fuel, water, gas and refuse bins at the Abri Cotier dock – book in, VHF Ch 9 or ☎ (602354). Customs and immigration are nearby, 0800–1100 and 1500–1800 daily, no charge.

All the facilities of a large town. Information from the tourism office. Getting cash from banks using *Visa* (Banque National de Paris) *Access* or *Eurocheques* (Credit Agricole) may be tiresome; for cash without hassle change US dollar travellers cheques at the *bureau de change* on the esplanade or try the Roger Albert store. The main chandleries are near to the fuel quay (Ship-Shop, SCIM) and in Baie du Carenage. The main boatyards for yachts are in the Baie du Carenage (Ship-Shop Careenage, 50-tonne travel-hoist and various yacht services including an electronics specialist) with numerous other services close at hand and in Baie des Tourelles (Grant Boatyard). Dry dock for larger vessels.

Tourism

The centre of the town has a definite charm and includes a number of interesting buildings, amongst them the Schoëlcher Library, a rococo masterpiece which was shown at the international exhibition in Paris in 1889 before being reconstructed here, and the cathedral which is remarkable architecturally for its earthquake-proof mixture of cast-iron framework and stone.

Communications

Telephone. All boxes use cards to be bought from the *Poste* facing La Savanne (Telecoms office round the corner). The international exchange code is 19 to be followed by the country and local codes. For collect calls dial 10; a recorded message will tell you to wait and when it has been repeated for the ninety-ninth time the operator will come on.

Poste restante can be bureaucratic; use Ship Shop, 6 rue Joseph Compère, where mail will be held indefinitely.

International airport. Car hire

Case-Pilote

14°38'·5N 61°08'·5W

Case-Pilote, a small fishing village clustered around a square is one of the oldest established villages of the island. It took the name 'Pilote' from a Caribbean chief who was in favour of the installation of the French in the area in the 17th century. The peace of the village, the brightly coloured gommiers on the beach in the shade of the coconut palms, the delightful 18th century church, all make this a very pleasant port of call outside the normal tourist route. A small harbour has been built in the south of the inlet where the village lies which can take vessels up to 12m.

Approach

Case-Pilote can be easily identified by the high cliff with a white cross on top of it which dominates the port and a white building at the foot of the cliff. Approach due east towards this building until the outer breakwater is identified as well as the small red buoy anchored about 20m north of the head of the breakwater. This buoy marks the extent of the remains of the old jetty which was destroyed by hurricane *David* in 1979 together with most of the boats inside.

Berthing

Depths are 3·5m in the entrance and 2·5–3m in the middle of the harbour. Tie up the bows to the northern half of the breakwater if there is room. It is also possible to anchor in 3–5m depths on sand, 100m from the beach.

Case-Pilote

Case-Pilote looking E

Saint-Pierre

14°44′N 61°11′W

Saint-Pierre, a small town of 5000 inhabitants which lies sleepily at the head of a large bay open to the west, has never recovered from the catastrophe of 1902 when Monte Pelée exploded and destroyed it completely. It then had 30,000 inhabitants, was the capital of the island and the principal trading centre of the archipelago. There were often over 50 ships at anchor there and the boats sunk in the catastrophe are now a hazard to anchoring. The intense commercial and cultural life which went on there won it the nicknames of 'Little Paris' and 'Queen of the Antilles'.

Today it is a quiet port of call where only passing yachts come to anchor but a small museum traces the history of the town and the catastrophe of 1902 by means of documents (explanatory panels, photographs, writings of the time) and of objects dug from the ruins, as unusual as they are moving. The ruins of the most important buildings can still be seen – the old Fort Church (the most impressive), the theatre (a replica on a smaller scale of the one in Bordeaux), the dungeon of Cyparis and the school.

There is good walking and it is possible to climb Monte Pelèe; the plantation producing sugar for St Jacques rum is here. A curious feature is rain falling from a clear sky; the rain clouds evaporate in the lee of the mountains before the rain reaches the ground.

Approach

The Rade de Saint-Pierre and its approaches are free of all danger but there are often strong gusts here. The town can be easily identified by its large grey cathedral with two towers. The other landmarks are the town hall which is light yellow and has a pointed clock tower, the statue of the 'Vierge des Marins' which is blue on a white pedestal and stands on a height (60m) south of the town, the red and white pylon of a TV station in the northern part of the town, finally, further back, the white building of the Morne des Cadets observatory (405m) which is conspicuous from the sea.

Anchorage

Anchor in 5–8m depths on sand, either north or south of two dilapidated landing stages in the centre of the town at about 100m from the shore. There is always a slight swell in this anchorage.

Facilities

There is a diesel pump on the south side of the northern landing stage where it is possible to go alongside if the swell is not too heavy. There is a wide choice of fresh supplies in the market and the neighbouring shops. Bank. Post office.

Communications

Bus to Fort de France.

Saint Pierre looking ESE

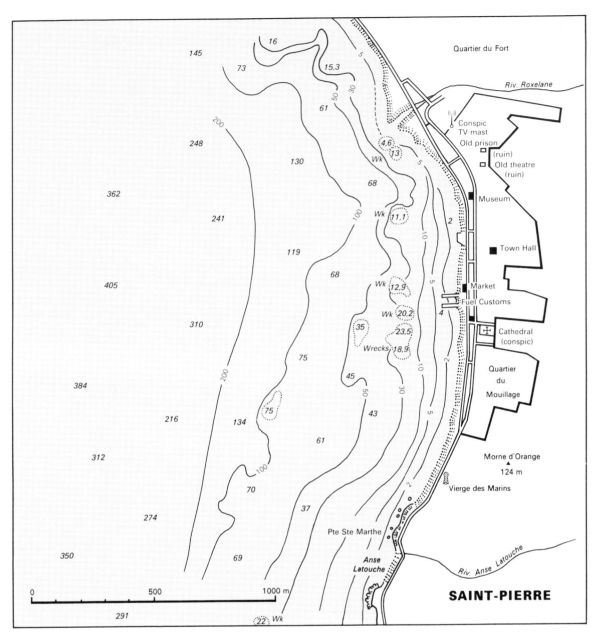

SAINT-PIERRE

Anchorages to the north of Saint-Pierre

Along the section of coast between the headlands of Le Prêcheur and St Martin there are three small unspoilt bays (Anse Céron, Anse Couleuvre and Anse à Voile) edged with beaches of black sand and magnificent tropical vegetation. The approach is safe but it is rarely possible to anchor there because of the swell.

Anchor in front of the village of Le Prêcheur in 6·8m depths about 100m from the shore. 1000m south of the village its landing stage 30m long has 4·2m depths at the end and it is possible to berth off its southern side.

Le Prêcheur looking ENE

East coast of Martinique from Pointe de Macouba to Cap Ferré

Coasts, dangers, channels

Along the windward coast of Martinique there are banks and coral reefs almost everywhere extending in places as far as 3M out to sea. Although the reefs are a serious danger to coastal traffic, they act as a break-water to an inshore area which has attractive anchorages, and several good hurricane holes, among its islets and indented coastline. However, sailing within these reefs, which are mostly unmarked and poorly charted, requires the navigator's full and constant attention and generally must be done with the assistance of a keen eye observing from as high a point as possible. Seaward of the reefs are the numerous fish trap floats which deserve a particular mention as they are more numerous and a greater menace here than elsewhere. A swell makes it difficult to see even a well marked float until it is almost underfoot and it is even more difficult when looking up-sun. The current, wind and waves set on-shore and to be disabled by fouling a trap near a reef could be worse than embarrassing.

- From the sea this coast has few landmarks. The villages of the extreme north, Le Lorraine and Basse-Pointe have little to identify them. Rocher Pain de Sucre (14°48′·5N 61°00′·7W) is conspicuous and beyond it the large white church of Sainte-Marie, with a red roof and a facade with two towers is a good landmark but it is obscured from the northeast by Ilet Sainte-Marie. 3M SSE Bourg de la Trinité, which lies at the head of the bay of the same name, is clearly visible from the north.
- The Presqu'île de la Caravelle, which runs 5M ENE, is identifiable from a distance. It is dominated by hills; the highest (226m) in the centre has a TV mast on it visible from all directions. A lighthouse (Fl(3)15s16M) on the cliffs (129m) lies back from the end of the peninsula and has a meteorological station below it.
- Loup-Garou (14°40′·7N 60°51′W), an islet of very white sand with some shrubs growing on it is a good landmark off Le Robert. Inland, Pointe de la Rose and Ilet Ramville stand on either side of the entrance to Havre du Robert at the head of which Bourg du Robert shows clearly from the east as a light-coloured patch. The next village south, Bourg du François, can only be seen from the ENE and shows up in light colour (see page 109).
- Ilet Thiery (32m, 14°37′·5N 60°51′W) has a conspicuous large white house on its northeastern tip next to a wind pump. A large grotto can be clearly seen on the southeastern coast.
- 3·7M south, Pointe du Vauclin (66m) juts out from the coast in a headland which is conspicuous from positions between N and NNE and E and SSE. 3½M inland, Montagne du Vauclin (504m) is the most conspicuous peak in the southeast of the island. Bourg du Vauclin has a large church with a green roof and a grey, pointed belfry identifiable from the distance when the sun shines on it.

Channels leading to the east coast

Several channels, some of which are marked, make it possible to cross the line of reefs and shoals which run parallel to the coast, 1–1·5M out to sea. These channels are described here from north to south.

Passe de Caracoli This wide, deep channel leads along the southeast of the cape of the same name at the end of Presqu'île de la Caravelle.

Passe de Loup-Garou This narrow channel between the shoals of Loup-Garou and those of Caye Mitan can be found on a bearing of 272° with the church at Le Robert and the northern edge of Ilet Boisseau (du Chardon) in line. This alignment is not easy to see from a distance. Loup-Garou – a very white sandy islet with a group of shrubs growing on it is a good landmark 0·7M northwest of the channel.

Passe de Caye Mitan to Passe du François Passe de Caye Mitan itself is wide and has minimum depths of 11m. From the north, round buoy *F1* (red) and enter the channel on 246° towards Pointe Dégras light, a white turret which is not easy to see by day (if the light is on this will be in the white sector). This course leads to the entrance of the Passe du François (see page 109) which is marked. Coming from the south enter the channel with Pointe de la Rose (91m) bearing between 300° and 277° (the belfry of the church at Le Robert in line with Pointe de la Rose is 282°) and turn on to Dégras light when it bears 246°.

Passe de Caye Mitan to the southern inshore passage From the north, when past buoy *F1* (red) go southwest towards a conspicuous house on Ilet Thiery and then pass ½M east of the island. From the south, enter as described above and turn south to pass Ilet Thiery as described. If continuing south, watch out for Caye Petite Pinsonnelle.

Passe de Caye Pinsonnelle The rusty remains of a wreck on the southern edge of Caye Pinsonnelle make a good landmark for identifying this channel. Head 235° towards Montagne du Vauclin passing 600m south of the wreck. When the wreck is due north turn on to 215° to ensure you clear Caye Petite Pinsonnelle, which is dangerous.

Passe NE du Vauclin The south side this channel is marked by a green buoy, *V2*, which is halfway across the bank and difficult to identify from the sea. It is almost in line with Montagne du Vauclin and Pointe du Vauclin on a bearing of 260° but to reach it on this bearing means crossing the bank at 7–8m where heavy swell will break. The correct approach is on 232° towards Vauclin light but this run must be started at least ½M away from the buoy which must be passed close to port. This is in the white sector of the Vauclin light but a night approach is not recommended without local knowledge.

Passe Sud du Vauclin This is the safest and the best marked of all the channels. Approaching from the south, steer 330° towards Pointe du Vauclin until the red buoy *PA*, which marks the southern limit of

Sainte-Marie looking WSW

Morne Pavilion TV station looking N

Presqu'ile de la Caravelle looking SE

Passe de Loup Garou. Le Robert church on N side of Ilet
Boisseau on 272° (the leading line is obscured in this view)

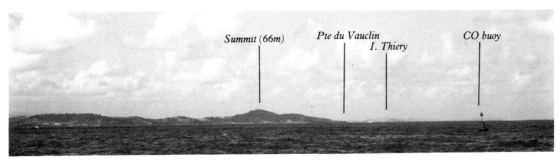

Vauclin pass from *CO* buoy

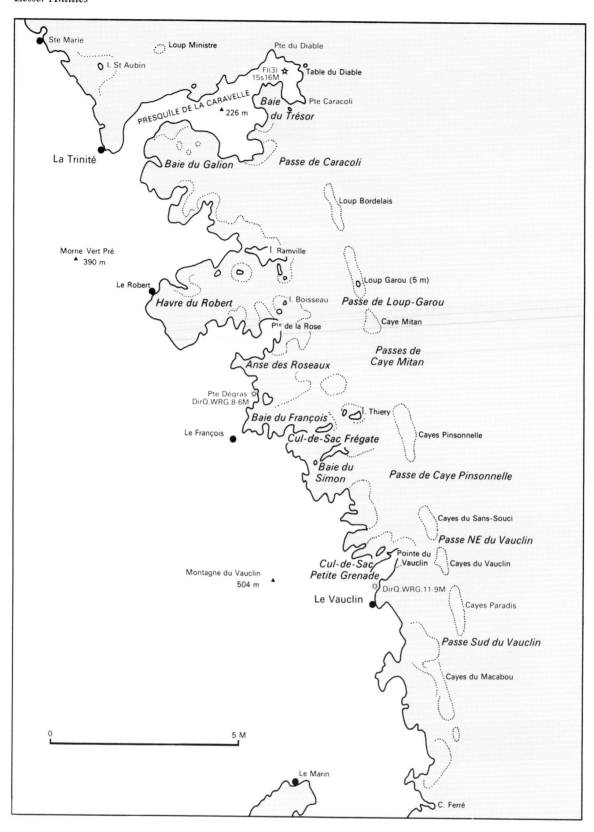

Ste Marie

Loup Ministre

Pte du Diable

I. St Aubin

Fl(3)
15s16M ☆ ● Table du Diable

Pte Caracoli

*Baie
du Trésor*

PRESQU'ÎLE DE LA CARAVELLE   ▲ 226 m

La Trinité

Baie du Galion   *Passe de Caracoli*

Loup Bordelais

Morne Vert Pré
▲ 390 m

I. Ramville

Loup Garou (5 m)

Le Robert

Havre du Robert   I. Boisseau

Pte de la Rose   *Passe de Loup-Garou*

Caye Mitan

Anse des Roseaux   *Passes de
Caye Mitan*

Pte Dégras ☼
DirQ.WRG.8-6M

I. Thiery

Baie du François

Le François   *Cul-de-Sac Frégate*   Cayes Pinsonnelle

*Baie du
Simon*   *Passe de Caye Pinsonnelle*

Cayes du Sans-Souci

Passe NE du Vauclin

Pointe du
Vauclin   Cayes du Vauclin

*Cul-de-Sac
Petite Grenade*

Montagne du Vauclin
504 m   ▲

☼ DirQ.WRG.11-9M

Le Vauclin ●   Cayes Paradis

Passe Sud du Vauclin

Cayes du Macabou

0   5 M

Le Marin ●

C. Ferré

Cayes du Pariadis, is reached. Continue to the next the buoy, Caye Coq (*CO* red) which should be passed to starboard sufficiently close to clear another unmarked caye situated 200m to the west. From this buoy turn towards the summit of Pointe du Vauclin on 325°, passing west of Cayes Sautées.

La Trinité

14°45′1N 60°57′7W

La Trinité, one of the oldest towns in Martinique, is situated at the head of a large bay well protected from the prevailing winds but open to the swell from the northeast. A visit here is of little interest but the town does provide the best opportunity on the east coast of taking stores on board.

Approach.

The approach from the northwest through the marked Loup de Sainte Marie channel presents no difficulties. From the east, however, the unmarked Loup Ministre (2·5m), 1·5M northeast of the en-

La Trinité approach on 247°

trance, is dangerous. Having rounded Pointe Diable and Rocher de la Caravelle (28m) avoid these shallows by heading towards Pointe du Marigot. When the conically shaped Morne Moco (689) is in line with the north coast of Ilet Saint-Aubin on 247° turn on to that heading. Loup Ministre is cleared when the TV mast on Morne Vert Pré (390m) and a large white building (hospital) in La Trinité in line bear 200·5°. Follow that heading as far as the entrance to Havre de la Trinité where the interior dangers are all marked.

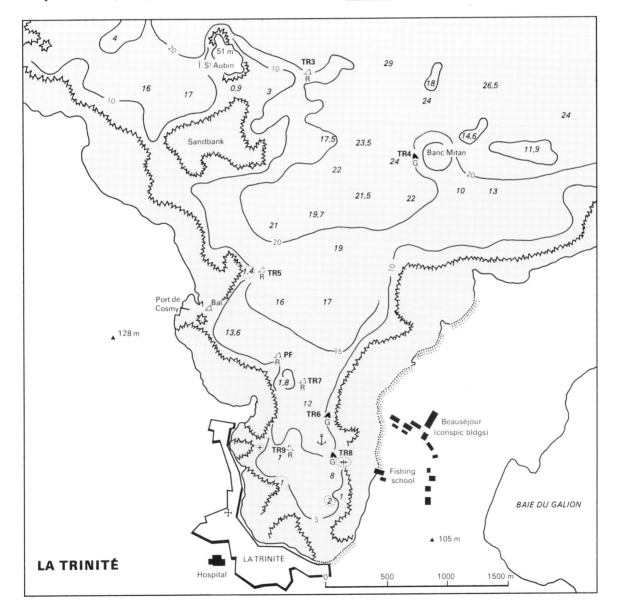

LA TRINITÉ

La Trinité approach on 200·5°

Anchorage

The best anchorage is to be found in 5–8m on muddy sand, 150m south of the buoy *TR8* which is situated west of the fishing school (conspicuous building with three arches). Otherwise anchor in 6–7m, 100m east of the landing stage north of the town.

Facilities

Supplies (markets and supermarkets), restaurants, post office, bank.

Baie du Trésor
14°45'·5N 60°53'·5W

Baie du Trésor provides some of the best shelter on Martinique in a wild and deserted setting between coasts edged by dense mangroves and a few little beaches. Perched on one of the hills which surround the bay, the ruins of Château du Dubuc (1740) still overlook the entrance to this erstwhile haunt of pirates, now almost deserted.

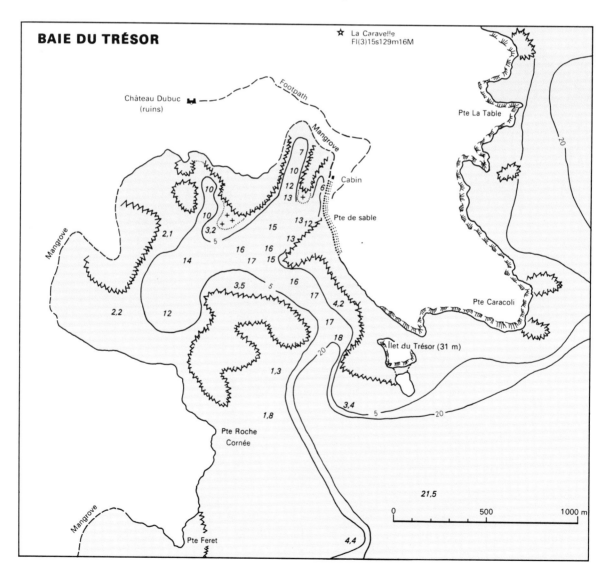

Château Dubuc   La Caravelle lighthouse   Ilet du Trésor

Reefs W of Ilet du Trésor

Entrance to Baie du Trésor

Approach

The entrance and the interior of the bay are obstructed by reefs between which a deep channel leads to the anchorage, but to reach it requires good light and the careful attention of the navigator.

Approach on a heading of 355° towards Caravelle lighthouse to avoid the shoals east of Pointe Roche Cornée (over which the swell can break dangerously) and identify Ilet du Trésor (31m) which is difficult to distinguish from the background. Then steer 335° towards Château Dubuc until the entrance to the channel is reached. The entrance lies between the reefs west of Ilet du Trésor, which are easy to identify because the sea almost always breaks over them, and the reef which lies in the middle which is more difficult to see. Enter the channel heading 005° towards the lighthouse, then continue steering by sight between the reef in the middle and those which lie off the east coast.

Anchorage

The best anchorage is in the northeast of the bay in front of a narrow beach just north of Pointe Sable in 10–13m, muddy sand, 500m from the shore. By taking a line ashore it is possible to get very close to the beach (there are several metres of water a few metres from the shore). Alternatively anchor under the ruins of Château Dubuc, 80m offshore in 10–11m.

Tourism

The peninsula of La Caravelle is a nature reserve, with footpaths leading to the lighthouse (1861) and to Château Dubuc where there is a small museum.

Baie du Galion

14°44'N 60°55'W

The shore of this wide bay is shoal and there are reefs between Pointe à Chaux and Ile de Galion. It is less attractive than Baie de Trésor but it has two unfrequented anchorages.

Pointe à Chaux The anchorage is 0·5M NNW of the point near Blin, an old distillery which can be identified by its chimney. Anchor in 4–5m on muddy sand, 200m from the coast which is bordered by shoals.

Baie Petit Galion This pretty bay between Pointe Jean-Claude and Pointe Banane makes a well protected anchorage bordered by mangroves. Loup Banane (2·3m) lies in the entrance and another shoal (2·3m) 0·4M north of the point of the same name.

Both have reefs off for some 300m. Anchor in a large indentation in the reefs on the west side of the point in 6·7m, 150m from the land. There is a shoal (3·3m) in the middle of this indentation.

Havre du Robert

14°40'N 60°55'W

Havre du Robert is a deep bay with many anchorages in its indented inner coastline, fringed with islets. At the head of the bay, Le Robert is a lively and smart little village and there is a small private marina in the southwestern part of the bay which is the only place on the east coast where diesel can be got on the quay.

Approach

The entrance lies between Petit Piton, which is clear on its south side, and the reefs off Pointe de la Rose which extend from 1M west to 0·75M north of it, beyond Ilet des Chardons. Within the harbour the islands on the north side are surrounded by reefs as are the headlands on the south though these are not so far off-shore. Pointe Fort also has a reef extending 0·5M ESE.

Anchorages

Ilet Duchamp A few houses have been built on this islet. When approaching, stay within 50m of the west coast in order to anchor in 5–10m, if necessary taking a line ashore. Only a short distance further out, depths increase to 15m over a level seabed of muddy sand.

Ilet Petite Martinique A very good anchorage can be found west of this pretty little wooded islet in 5–8m on muddy sand, approximately 100m north of three small pontoons (privately owned) and 60m from the shore.

Le Robert The extensive reefs which cover the whole of the head of the bay make the approach to the village very difficult. A course of 281° on the church of Le Robert (conspicuous) from a position north of Pointe Royale leads less than 100m from the southern edge of Banc de la Pointe Fort. This is marked by a pole, not always easy to see. Continue until Pointe Fort bears 050° and then go on to 305°. Leave to starboard the post which marks the SSW extent of the shoals off Pointe Lynch and to port another post on a bearing of 100° from the landing stage. Round this last marker at a good distance and go towards the landing stage. Go alongside the landing stage, 1·7m at its end, or anchor in 2·5m, 100m from it.

Entrance

Marina du Robert. Entrance on 185°

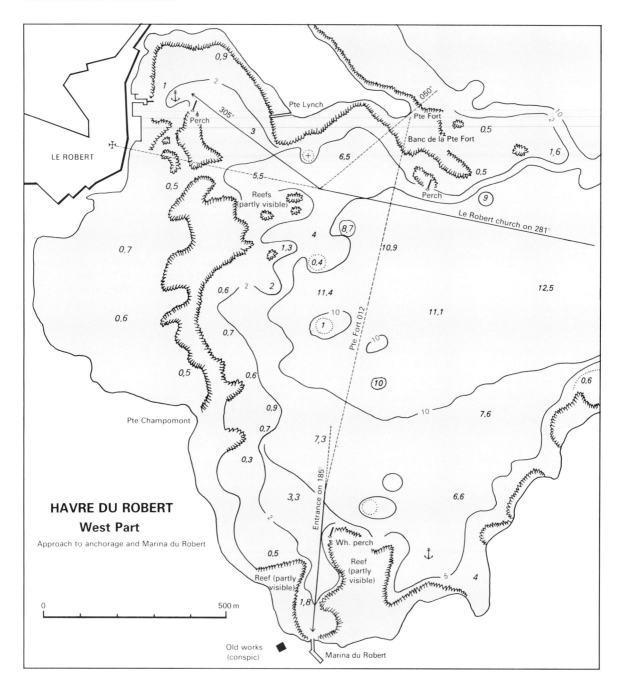

HAVRE DU ROBERT
West Part

Approach to anchorage and Marina du Robert

Entrance

Le Robert approach

Marina du Robert This minute marina is situated on the site of the old sugar refinery of Robert. All that remains are ruined buildings and a rusty metal framework which is easy to identify. The minuteness of the harbour means that only yachts less than 11 or 12m in length can get in. The approach through a scantily marked channel calls for caution. Approach first of all on a back bearing of 012° from Pointe Fort then steer 185° towards the entrance of the marina which is marked on the left by a TEXACO sign (red star on a white background). Follow this course, watching the depths carefully, and leaving 15–20m to port a white pole which marks the outer edge of a reef. The entrance of the marina, 10m wide with a depth of 1·8m, is formed by a short concrete mole to the east and the wreck of a barge to the west. There is 1·7–2m in the basin.

Baie de la Pointe Royale This provides excellent shelter in a pleasant setting where a few houses can be seen among the vegetation. The best anchorage is in the entrance to the southeastern arm in 5m on mud.

Baie de la Pointe Hyacinthe This bay has depths of 6–7m in the centre. Watch out for Banc Guillotine (1·9m) 300m north of the entrance, and for the sandbanks off the headlands which surround the bay.

Baie de Saintpée This pretty bay, surrounded by wooded hills and bordered by mangroves in the southeast, provides secure shelter and is little frequented. A few villas can be seen on the hillsides in the west and southwest. Enter midway between Banc Guillotine and Banc de la Rose (northwest of Pointe de la Rose) and go east of south into the bay. The shores are the least encumbered of the harbour. Anchor near the entrance in 6–7m, 100m from the east coast in front of a group of coconut palms near a private landing stage. Alternatively go into the southeastern arm of the bay where there is 6–7m on mud.

Ilet Madame There is a beautiful anchorage near the southwest coast of the islet protected from the sea by reefs which join it to Pointe de la Rose. The entrance is on a bearing of 145° between the dangerous reef which extends over 600m NNW of the islet and Banc de la Rose, with Pointe de la Rose in line with the southwest cape of Ilet Bouchard. Anchor in 9–13m, sand, 100–150m southwest of a landing stage near some small beaches and several coconut palms. Depths decrease very suddenly in the channel south of the islet.

Cul-de-Sac des Roseaux

14°38'·7N 60°54'·0W

Cul-de-Sac des Roseaux lies south of Pointe de la Rose off which reefs extend 1M out to sea. The interior of Cul-de-Sac des Roseaux is unsafe but on the south side of Pointe de la Rose there are two picturesque and well-protected anchorages, Anse des Roseaux, around which there are a few fishermen's huts and Anse de Coco. Starting from a point north of *F2*, at the northern end of the Passe du François, go towards a massive and jutting headland on the northern shore of the cul-de-sac. The inlet is on the starboard hand on an axis of 340° with an islet of mangroves at its entrance. This course avoids the shoals south of the entrance, west of Pointe Cigaraille. Anchor in the middle of the inlet in 4–5m, mud.

The entrance to the outer part of Anse Coco lies 1M at 322° from *F2* and there is about 600m between the reefs. Then the reefs give shelter to the west entrance to the Anse itself (about 200m). Both these anchorages have to be approached by eye.

Le François

14°37'N 60°64'W

The village of Le François lies some distance back from the coast at the head of a large bay to which it has given its name. Baie du François is accessible day and night through a buoyed channel between the reefs which protect it completely from the swell. There are several anchorages in this bay and a rudimentary 'marina' (Club Nautique du François) close to which a little port is being built.

Approach
The usual approach is through the north channel which is marked. See above, Passe du Caye Mitan, for the approach to the first buoy, *F2*. Go southerly down the channel and pass between *F3* and *F4* where channel turns to the WSW.

By night approach on 246·4° in the white sector of Pointe Dégras light (Q.WRG.8·6M) until buoy *F2* has been identified.

When the light is good it is also possible to reach Baie du François through the east channel which is unmarked. Steer a course of 220° towards the western side of Ilet Anonyme, then alter course to 280° to reach buoy *F3* leaving Caye Ronde and buoy *F4* to port.

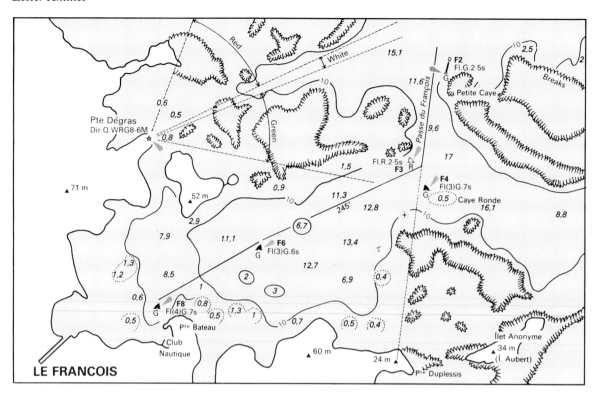

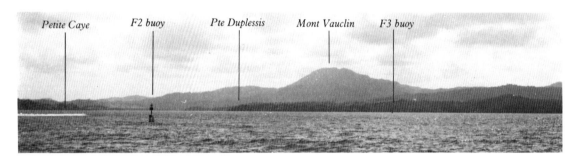

Passe du François from F2 buoy

Le François looking WSW from buoy F3

Ilet Thiery looking WNW

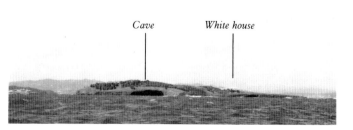

In order to reach the inlet where the yacht club is situated leave the last green buoy (*F8*) to starboard by about 150m after having passed Pointe Bateau. The yacht club stands on the eastern bank of the inlet.

Berthing

The yacht club has a few small wooden pontoons in 2–3m. On the west side of the inlet, quays and a pontoon with 2–3·5m are being completed.

Anchorages

There is a pleasant anchorage in 8–13m 150m WSW of the southwestern tip of Ilet Bouchard (also known as Ilet Oscar) though the swell can be felt here. The anchorage west of Ilet Lavigne in 5–9m provides total protection in a wild and austere landscape.

Facilities

Water points and a petrol pump in the yacht club. Restaurant on the shore nearby. Supplies, post office and bank in the village (2km).

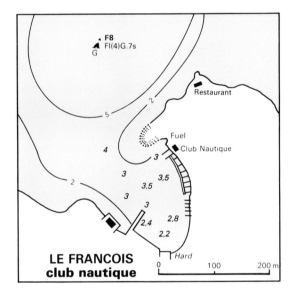

Cul-de-Sac Frégate

14°36'·6N 60°52'·2W

There are several quiet and well protected anchorages in Cul-de-Sac Frégate, near islets on which there are only a few houses built.

Approach

On the north side of the entrance, Ilet Thiery can be identified by a large white house and a wind pump on its northeastern cape and a large grotto at sea level on its southeast coast (see photo page 110). South of the entrance, Ilet Perle (11m), which lies ENE of Ilet Long, is a bare rock with a house and a coconut palm on it. Dangerous reefs and shoals extend 0·5M east and north from it. Enter the cul-de-sac heading WSW, skirting the reefs south of Ilet Thiery, which uncover and are straight-sided, at a distance of 100m.

Anchorages

Ilet Thiery. Anchor southwest of this islet in 3–6m on sand 150m from the shore. Watch out for an isolated coral head covered by a metre of water which obstructs the centre of the anchorage.

Between Thiery and Bouchard Ilets The magnificent turquoise lagoon which can be seen between Ilet Thiery and Ilet Bouchard is only accessible to vessels drawing less than 1·5m. It is approached through a very narrow and tortuous channel west and south of Ilet Bouchard.

Ilet Long An inlet on the northwest of this islet, where there is a villa and a landing stage (privately owned) provides a very peaceful anchorage in 8–10m on muddy sand, 70m WNW of the landing stage. When approaching this anchorage be careful of unmarked reefs which extend for 350m off the south coast of Ilet Anonyme and keep well off the northeastern headland of the islet which is unsafe.

Ilet Frégate There is a good anchorage in 4–6m, 60m from the north west coast of the islet, WSW of a small landing stage. In the approach keep well clear of the dangerous cay which extends 150m northwest of the channel between Ilet Long and Ilet Frégate and watch out for a little cay about 200m WNW of the landing stage which is difficult to see.

Baie du Simon and Pointe Cerisier

14°36'·0N 60°51'·3W

Baie du Simon is a wide bay, well protected from swell by a barrier of coral which extends from Pointe Cerisier to the seaward side of Ilet Long. There are good anchorages here of which the most attractive is the lagoon east of Pointe Cerisier.

Approach

To enter the bay there are two safe channels, unmarked, surrounded by steep reefs on which the sea breaks. Grande Passe lies on a bearing of 267° from the northern edge of Ilet Frégate (17m) where there is a group of trees and a small white house with a red roof. Petite Passe lies on a bearing of 290° from the peak of this islet.

Anchorage

Anchor in 10–12m behind the coral barrier, watching out for an isolated cay, awash.

East of Pointe Cerisier This anchorage, accessible only to vessels with a maximum draught of 1·8m, is airy, calm and in limpid water. Steer 150° towards Pointe Cerisier with the head of Pointe du Vauclin well detached from it to the left. This course skirts a cay marked by two poles, 40m to the east, and there are minimum depths of 1·9m. Keep 50m out when rounding Pointe Cerisier and anchor in 3–4m on sand, 200m southeast of this point.

Ilet Long It is possible to anchor between this islet and a line of cays which lie off it to the south leaving three channels which should only be entered with caution keeping a careful lookout, and in a very good light. The eastern channel is 25m wide and winds but

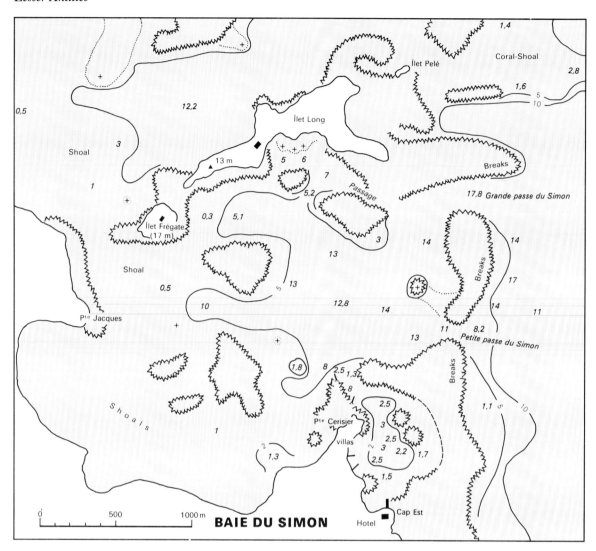

BAIE DU SIMON

Entrance to lagoon E of Pte Cerisier

it is deep and edged by reefs covered with very little water and easy to see. The entrance is to be found on a bearing of 298° from a white house with a red roof standing on the south coast of the western half of the islet. The central channel, which is wider (100m), is 5–9m deep and passes between cays which are difficult to identify and have ill-defined edges. Anchor in the middle of the bay, south of the island in 5–6m on sand. Be careful of coral heads close to the island. The whole western part of Baie du Simon is obstructed by a number of reefs which are difficult to see, some of which are marked by poles. It is not advisable to go in here without the help of someone with local knowledge.

Cul-de-Sac Petite Grenade

14°33'·8N 60°50'·5W

Cul-de-Sac Petite Grenade is a deserted bay surrounded by mangrove and green hills. It provides good shelter from hurricanes and is not much visited by yachts. This anchorage is very attractive but only accessible to vessels drawing less than 2m.

Approach

The entrance through a narrow channel (60m) between reefs which are awash, lies 0·5M northwest of Pointe du Vauclin. It is essential to enter in the morning when the sun is high to be able to see the

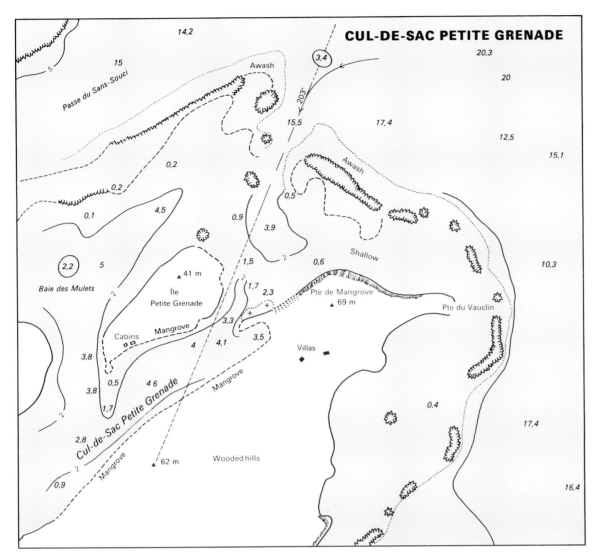

Entrance to Cul-de-Sac Petite Grenade

reefs and careful manouevring is called for. Enter the channel on a course of 203·5° towards the south-eastern side of Ile Petite Grenade, then having passed the reef which is on the east, turn slightly (15°) to port to clear the shoals east of Ile Petite Grenade, passing over the 2·2m shelf beyond which depths increase to 3·5–4·5m.

Anchorage

Anchor in the bay formed by the spit running out southwest from Pointe du Vauclin opposite the southeast side of Petite Grenade. The shore is steep-to but is a booby trap: sand on mud.

From the Cul-de-Sac Petite Grenade it is possible to reach Baie des Mulets, entirely surrounded on the seaward side by an uncovering reef.

Le Vauclin

14°33′N 60°50′W

Le Vauclin is a lively fishing centre which has a small harbour accessible only to vessels with a shallow draught. It is next to a village of little interest to tourists.

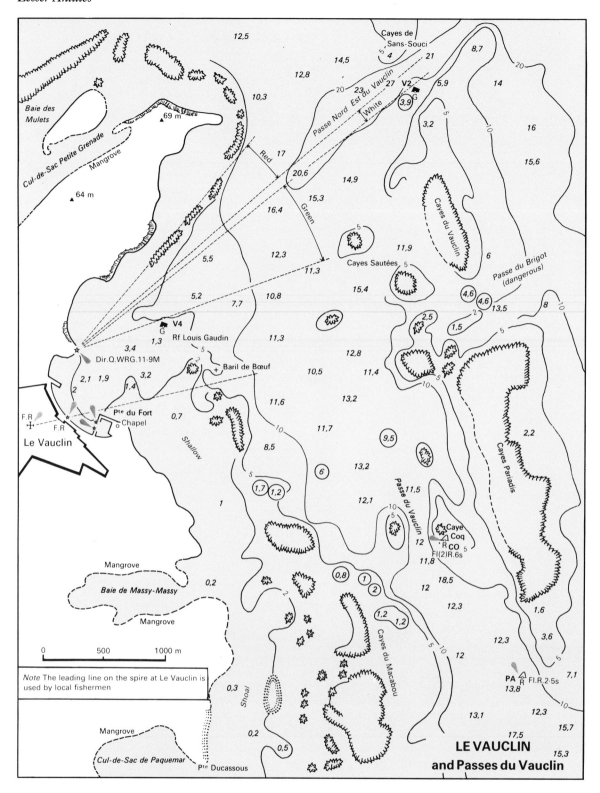

LE VAUCLIN
and Passes du Vauclin

Note The leading line on the spire at Le Vauclin is used by local fishermen

Approach

The conspicuous church of Le Vauclin is a good landmark. The channels northeast and south of Le Vauclin which cross the line of reefs from the seaward side are described on page 102. Leave to the south the green buoy *V4*, then steer towards the church on 233° and afterwards towards the entrance to the port on 180°. A small white chapel east of the port makes a good landmark. There are depths of 1·7m in the harbour entrance, less in the inner part. The anchorage outside the harbour in 2–2·5m is almost always disturbed by an uncomfortable wash.

Facilities

Water point in the port, tax-free diesel and petrol, supplies in the village, several restaurants, post office.

Le Vauclin looking SW, from V4 buoy

Vauclin and Montagne du Vauclin looking W

VII. Dominica

Charts
Imray-Iolaire *A26*
Admiralty *697, 728*
SHOM *3775*
US *25561, 25562*

General remarks

Geography

Dominica, the windward of the Leeward islands, is an independent state within the British Commonwealth with some 80,000 inhabitants living in 790 sq km. It is volcanic and dominated by a steep mountain range whose main peaks are Diablotin (1446m, the highest in the east Caribbean) and Trois Pitons. The topography is very rugged. Annual rainfall is heavy, between 1·75m on the coast and 6·25m in the mountains. The resulting forests are dense and have numerous streams and torrents. It is the wildest of the Lesser Antilles.

Following a turbulent history Dominica became an associated state of the United Kingdom in 1967 and an independent republic as the Commonwealth of Dominica in 1978. It is governed by a House of Assembly with 29 elected and 9 nominated members and is a member of the British Commonwealth.

It is not rich. Agriculture and tourism are the main sources of wealth and both are difficult to develop because of the nature of the land. The island's agricultural products are common to the area – bananas, coconuts, fruit and fruit preparations, essential oils, alcohol – but are in competition with products of other islands working on a better infra-structure.

The road system allows some exploration of the extraordinarily luxuriant tropical forest. The most spectacular trips are those to the giddy heights of the Cascades of Trafalgar, to the Emerald Pool and to the Boiling Lake – evidence of the igneous activity of the island. The best starting point is Roseau (see page 119), the capital of the island. A visit to the Indian River and its magnificent mangroves, near to Portsmouth (see page 123), is also worthwhile.

History

Dominica takes its name from its discovery by Christopher Columbus on a Sunday in November 1493 during his second voyage. Columbus himself did not land but sent a reconnaissance party who were immediately thrown off by the Caribs. For the next three centuries this pattern with different players repeated itself; of all the Antilles, Dominica was the one which stood out the longest against colonisation. The Caribs, the only people able to move about easily in the forest which covered the whole mountainous island, defended their territory so vigorously that after several abortive attempts at colonisation, in 1748 the French and the British agreed to leave this hostile territory to its own fate. The truce did not last long and the Franco-British battle for the conquest of the island soon resumed. In the 18th century control alternated between France and Britain with Carib interjections, ending in 1805 with Britain nominally in charge. But it was only in 1903 that the Caribs accepted an agreement with the British crown which allowed them an area of 1800 hectares on the east coast. The last remaining representatives of a race which has been largely wiped out in the rest of the Antilles still live there today.

Arrival

Approaching from the south, landfall will be Cape Cachacrou (Scots Head), a small steep headland (70m) joined to the coast by a low isthmus. East of it are several very steep bluffs among which Morne Fous (331m), conical in shape, is easy to recognise. There is a dangerous shoal off the west coast of Cape Cachacrou, the exact position of which is uncertain (see page 118).

From the north, the island appears like a broadly-based cone, rising more steeply in the west than in the east. The summit is more often than not lost in cloud. The best place to arrive is Prince Rupert Bay, which has the best anchorage on the island and easily identified approaches. From a distance, Pointe Ronde (Rollo Point) and the two peaks of Morne du Prince Rupert are easily recognised. Beware of strong gusts when approaching Cape Melville and to leeward of it. It is best not to approach by night; orthodox navigational lights are almost non-existent.

Formalities

Clear at the commercial port north of Roseau (can be reached by sea or land) or at Portsmouth.

Flag

Green, with a cross overall of yellow, black, and white pieces, and in the centre a disc charged with a Sisserou parrot in natural colours within a ring of 10 green yellow-bordered stars.

Maintenance

Nil.

Communications

Car hire.

Hurricane holes

None.

Coasts, dangers

- The northeast, east and southeast coasts of the island are exposed to the wind and to the swell and they have no secure anchorage. The current flows alternately to the north or to the northeast at a speed of 1–2 knots, then to the south or southeast at a negligible speed. When passing the island to windward it is advisable to stand off a good distance. Strong gusts are common near the northern tip of the island and to leeward of it.
- The west coast, which is safe close-to almost everywhere, consists alternately of small cliffs and beaches at the end of narrow valleys. It is everywhere dominated by steep hills covered in vegetation with here and there hamlets or fishing villages. The current is variable. The best landmarks on this coast are described below, south to north.
- Cape Cachacrou (Scot Head), the southwestern tip of the island, is a peninsula, not very high but steep, joined to the land by a low isthmus. West of this headland there is a dangerous shoal with less than 2m over it whose position is markedly further out (300m) than is shown on the charts (about 160m). The current can be very strong near this point – there is a race off the end.
- 2·5M south of Roseau on Pointe Michelle there is a church with a grey and light blue facade and a central, square clock tower next to a small cemetery near the shore.
- Woodbridge Bay, with Roseau, the capital of the island and its commercial port. The bay stretches for several kilometres south of the port on either side of the Roseau River (see page 119).
- Morne Daniel (150m) has several white parabolic aerials which are clearly visible.
- 0·6M north, silos and light-coloured oil tanks situated at the mouth of the Boery River are clearly visible from the distance.
- A little further north, the large light-coloured church of Massacre with its square tower, is conspicuous on the side of the hill (70m).
- 4M NNW the village of St Joseph can be identified by a large light-coloured church on the shore and a very tall radio mast on a height to the ESE.
- 2·8M further north Grande Savan is a gently sloping headland edged with cliffs.

- 5M further north Barbers Block is a large rounded bluff, easily identifiable both from the north and from the south, on whose peak (376m) there is a radio mast. 0·6M NNW is Pointe Ronde (Rollo Head).
- Finally, Prince Rupert Bluff is a prominent peninsula joined to the land by a low isthmus which separates Douglas Bay from Prince Rupert Bay. It can be identified from its double summit (207m). Prince Rupert Bay provides the best anchorage on the island.

Dominica. Cape Cachacrou

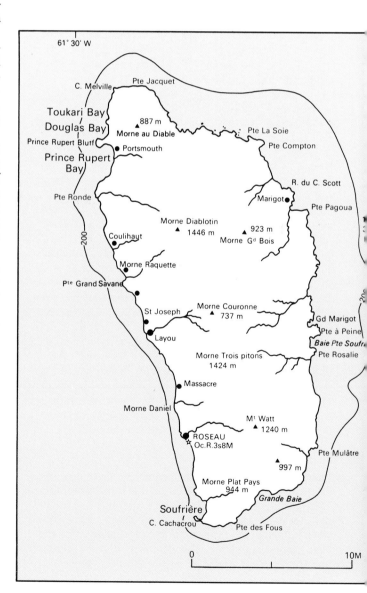

Cape Cachacrou looking N

Conspicuous silos and tanks at River Boery

Massacre church and village looking E

Church of St Joseph and radio mast looking ESE

Pte Grande Savan looking SSE

Soufrière Bay and Scot Head

15°13′N 61°22′·5W

Soufrière Bay, with a village of the same name in its northeastern corner, is the centre of an imposing semi-circular mountain range. A dangerous reef, Grande Maison, lies approximately 100m off the north coast of the bay to the west of the village. One may anchor in front of this, less than 100m from the beach taking a line ashore.

In the southern part of the bay anchor near the western end of the village where the seabed slopes less than elsewhere. There are 7–8m on sand about 50m from the shore. A line ashore is indispensable. These two anchorages should only be used in fine weather as sudden squalls can develop here in stormy weather.

Roseau

15°18′N 61°24′W

Roseau, the capital of Dominica, is a lively little town of 20,000 inhabitants. It is particularly of interest because it is a good starting point for excursions into the interior.

The commercial port north of the town consists of a flat area of land with high quays which are difficult for yachts to come alongside.

Approach

The town is open to the sea and easily seen; the most significant marks are the parabolic aerials of Morne Daniel, a mile north of Roseau River. There is no difficulty in the approach.

Anchorage

The most popular yacht anchorage is near the conspicuous, white-roofed Anchorage Hotel about a mile south of Roseau. The coastal shelf here falls off very steeply. It is usual to drop anchor 50–80m offshore in 12–18m over large stones, and accept the offer of one of the local lads to take a stern line in to a palm tree (a service costing the equivalent of about US$2). Dinghies can be landed on the beach or at the hotel jetty. There is usually some swell, which can make the anchorage uncomfortable.

Facilities

Supplies (market and shops), restaurants, banks. Dominica is noted for the quality and low price of its citrus fruits.

Communication

Car hire; frequent minibuses pass the Anchorage Hotel.

Tourism

Recommended trips: Trafalgar Falls – not to be missed, Emerald Pool and the Indian reserve of Salyvia. Because of the state of the roads and the absence of any road signs, it may be preferable to hire a taxi.

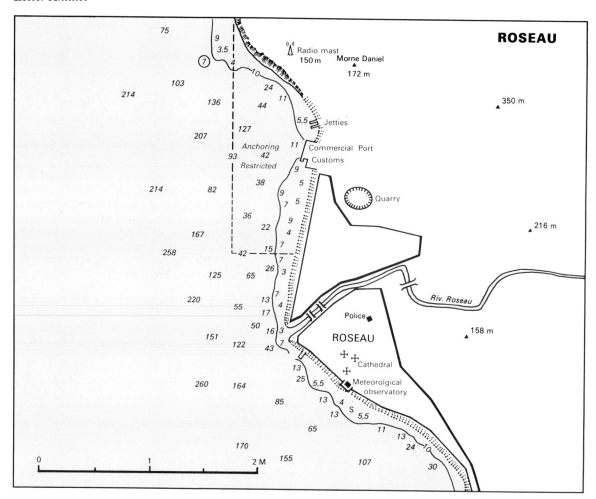

ROSEAU

75

9

3.5

⑦

4

10

214

103

24

11

136

44

5,5   Jetties

207

127

11   Commercial Port

Anchoring   42   Customs

93   *Restricted*

9

214   82   38   5

9   5

36   22   9

167   4

258   42 — 15   7

26   7

125   65   3

220   13   7

55   17   4

50   16   3

151   43   7

122

13

260   164   25   5,5

85   13   4   S

13   5,5

65   11

170   155   107

Radio mast
150 m   Morne Daniel
172 m

▲ 350 m

▲ 216 m

Quarry

Riv. Roseau

Police ▪

ROSEAU   ▲ 158 m

✝ ✝
✝   Cathedral
✝
▪ Meteorolgical
observatory

13   24

30

0   1   2 M

Cathedral   Meteorological observatory

Roseau. Town centre looking ENE

Roseau. Commercial port looking ESE

Roseau. Morne Daniel dish aerials

The Anchorage Hotel south of Roseau, Dominica, with two yachts lying stern-to the beach. *Anne Hammick*

Prince Rupert Bay and the town of Portsmouth, seen from Cabrits Fort on Prince Rupert Bluff. The new cruise ship jetty lies in the foreground. *Anne Hammick*

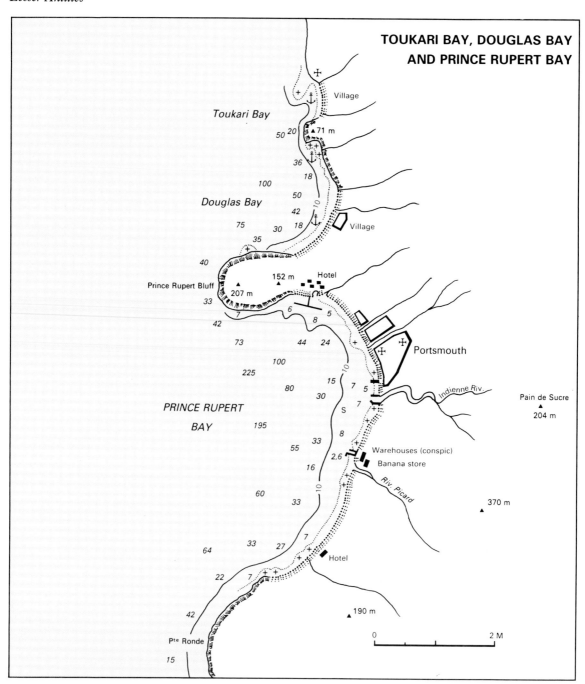

TOUKARI BAY, DOUGLAS BAY AND PRINCE RUPERT BAY

Toukari Bay

Douglas Bay

Prince Rupert Bluff

PRINCE RUPERT BAY

Hotel

Portsmouth

Indienne Riv.

Pain de Sucre
▲ 204 m

Warehouses (conspic)

Banana store

Riv. Picard

▲ 370 m

▲ 190 m

Hotel

P^te Ronde

0   2 M

Church   Customs building

Portsmouth looking ESE

From Roseau to Prince Rupert Bay

The west coast of the island has very few anchorages because of the steep inshore shelf almost everywhere and because one is almost always aware of the swell which flows round the island.

There is a good anchorage in front of the village of Layou where the 10m contour extends 300m from the coast. There are 4–5m 120m from the land in front of the northern part of the village. Do not approach the mouth of the river as there is a sand bank with very little water. This anchorage can be reached at night thanks to the excellent landmark provided by the radio mast of St Joseph which is marked by three superimposed fixed red lights. Approach heading northeast towards the radio mast watching the depth and anchor in 5–6m.

Southwest of Grande Savan a coastal shelf with less than 10m extends more than 300m from the land. Anchor here on sand with here and there areas of coral.

Prince Rupert Bay (Portsmouth)

15°34'·5N 61°28'·1W

Prince Rupert Bay, of which the bluff of the same name forms the northern limit, is the best anchorage on the island though the wind is often strong and gusty in the bay. On the east coast of the bay the picturesque village of Portsmouth is the second largest built-up area on the island. Entry and exit formalities can be carried out here – the authorities are to be found near the village landing stage.

Approach

The approach is free of danger, though there are frequently one or more ships at anchor in the centre of the bay. Prince Rupert Bluff and Barbers Block are excellent landmarks. From the entrance to the bay the following can be identified from south to north: a small hotel and chalet development in the southern part of the bay, off which yachts may be anchored; the light-coloured warehouses of the banana traders with their two jetties 50–70m long, (2·7m at the end); 0·75M to the north, the village with the pointed red tower of Portsmouth church in the centre and the building belonging to the authorities in front of which there are wrecks of two small cargo boats; and on the north coast, a group of white bungalows with red roofs. At the foot of Prince Rupert Bluff a T-shaped jetty and visitors' reception centre has recently been constructed for cruise ships. The staging is too high for a yacht to lie alongside.

Anchorage

Anchor in 4–7m on sand 150–200m off the village. Be careful of a reef off the coast, north of the church. It is also possible to anchor in the north part of the bay in 4–6m 200m from the land. Swell may sometimes enter the bay. It is possible to land anywhere on the long grey-sand beach.

Facilities

There are stand-pipes at intervals along the main street, which parallels the beach. Fresh fruit, vegetables and bread available, but limited canned and frozen supplies. Several restaurants.

Tourism

The Indienne River, which flows into the bay south of the village is one of the curiosities of the island. A yacht will usually be approached in the bay on arrival – often before the anchor is even down – by a local person wanting to sell his services as guide. To catch the full atmosphere of the Indienne River it is worth engaging a boatman willing to row up the river rather than one who relies on a large and noisy outboard. The ruins of Cabrits Fort which stand above the new jetty on Prince Rupert Bluff are in surprisingly good repair and well worth exploring.

Douglas Bay

15°35'·9N 61°28'·5W

The north cliffs of Douglas Bay are covered with vegetation and to the east there is a beach in front of a low coast with a hamlet. Prince Rupert Bluff forms the southern arm of this bay.

Approach

The approach is safe but when entering the bay look out for the floats of fish traps which are often made from broken bits of bamboo and are not easy to see.

Morne du Prince Rupert and Pointe Ronde looking S

Anchorage

Anchor either in the northern part of the bay, about 100m from the cliffs and in 6–7m, sand. There are coral heads with very little water over them. Alternatively, go to the eastern part of the bay and anchor about 120m from the beach in 5–6m, sand and weed.

Toukari Bay

15°36'·6N 61°28'·5W

Toukari Bay, the most attractive anchorage on the island, lies just north of Douglas Point. It is surrounded by steep bluffs covered with magnificent tropical vegetation and edged by a sandy beach lined with coconut palms. Small boats and fishermen's huts can be seen as well as a church near the north shore.

Approach

There is a coral reef which is difficult to see and covered with very little water extending from the north coast for about 150m towards the southwest. To avoid this danger keep well to the southern half of the bay when entering.

Anchorage

Anchor in 5–7m on sand about 120m from the beach. The swell, rounding Cape Melville, can sometimes make this anchorage extremely uncomfortable.

The atmospheric Indienne River near Portsmouth, Dominica
Anne Hammick

VIII. Guadeloupe and neighbouring islands

Charts
Imray-Iolaire *A28*
Admiralty *885, 804, 491*
SHOM *3423*
US *25563*
Detailed charts are mentioned in the relevant section.

General remarks

Geography

Guadeloupe is the largest (1702 sq km) and the most densely populated island (360,000 inhabitants) of the Lesser Antilles. It consists in fact of two islands, Basse-Terre and Grande-Terre, separated by a narrow, winding strait called La Rivière Salée.

The two parts of the island are curiously named. Basse-Terre, on the western side, is volcanic and mountainous dominated in the south by La Soufrière, an active volcano, 1484m high. With a high rainfall, it is mostly covered in a dense vegetation. On the eastern side, Grande-Terre, the smaller part, is a broad plateau of limestone formation with only two groups of hills in the north and the south. It is much drier than Basse-Terre.

Pointe-à-Pitre on the south coast is the largest town on the island but Basse-Terre on the west coast is the administrative capital.

Guadeloupe is surrounded by several islands which are dependencies: Les Saintes, Marie-Galante, and La Désirade.

On 1 Jan 1947 the island was transformed from a colony into a *département* of France equal to the others in terms of local government. It has a council of 42 elected members and a regional council of 39, both councils elected for 6 years. It returns two senators and four deputies to the National Assembly.

The economy is based on tourism and agriculture – mainly bananas and sugar of which a large proportion is converted to rum. Almost two thirds of its exports go to metropolitan France and a quarter to Martinique. Raizet airport is the sixth busiest of France.

History, tourism

Karukera 'the island of beautiful water' of the Caribs, was discovered on the 4th November 1493 by Christopher Columbus who named it after the famous Spanish sanctuary Santa Maria de Guadalupe de Estremadura, later shortened to Guadalupe. After several attempts to establish themselves the Spaniards, harassed by the Caribs, gave up the attempt to take possession of the island. In 1635 the French, under the authority of the Compagnie des Iles de Richelieu and sheltered by the umbrella provided by the Dutch who then dominated the Spanish at sea, landed in force and took over the island (the British took the same advantage elsewhere). It changed hands several times between the French and British during the late 18th century and though in 1813 it was almost transferred to Sweden, it was finally handed back to France after the Napoleonic Wars and the name established as Guadeloupe.

Guadeloupe has its hero; Del Gres, a one-time slave who, refusing to give himself up to the Bonapartist general Richepance, was blown up in Matouba on 28th May 1802 with 300 fellow partisans.

For the tourist, Guadeloupe has a varied countryside, both near the coast and in the interior where interesting excursions can be made. La Soufrière, Carbet Falls and the Route des Deux Mamelles are recommended among others. Pointe-à-Pitre (see page 137) is the best point of departure for visiting the island.

Arrival

When approaching from the south it is usual to pass between Marie-Galante and Les Saintes (see pages 127 and 150).

From the north, the most usual landfall is the northwest of Basse-Terre whose high and massive silhouette is easily identifiable at a distance.

Arriving from the east at the end of a trans-Atlantic crossing the high plateau of La Désirade (see page 148) is usually the first land to be identified, then Marie-Galante and Pointe des Châteaux (see page 143), the eastern tip of the island. The lights of La Désirade and Petite-Terre are helpful when approaching by night. The current bearing northwest in the approaches to La Désirade is often strong and must be taken into account.

When not in cloud, which is fairly rare, La Soufrière can be picked out.

Formalities

Clear at one of the following ports. Guadeloupe: Pointe-à-Pitre, Basse-Terre, Deshaies, Saint-François. Marie-Galante: Grand Bourg.

Flag

The tricolour, vertical stripes blue, white, red.

Maintenance

Pointe-à-Pitre.

Communications

Raizet airport at Pointe-à-Pitre, Basse-Terre, has international connections. Airfields at Marie-Galante and Iles des Saintes handle local flights.

VHF and SSB shore stations (Destrellan Radio Ch 25)

Hurricane holes

Blue Lagoon, Rivière Salée.

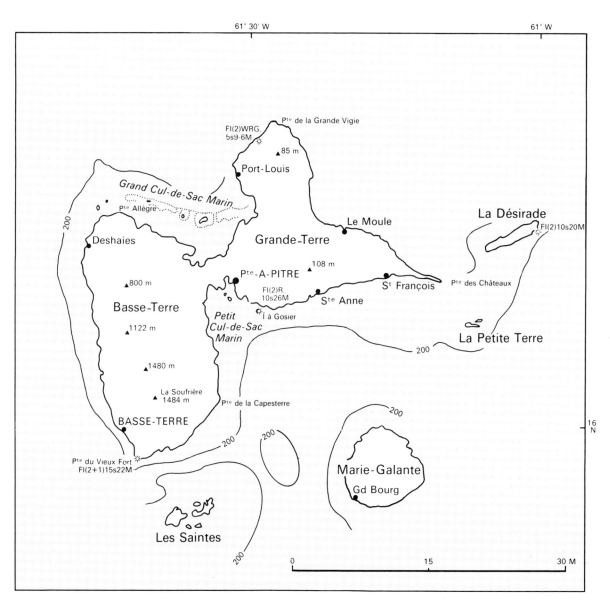

Les Saintes

Charts

Imray-Iolaire *A28, A281*
Admiralty *885, 491*
SHOM *7101*
US *25564*

General remarks. Approach

This small archipelago consisting of several islands and islets with a rugged landscape provides some of the most attractive ports of call in the Antilles. They have a life of their own with the unusual characteristic of a population which is 80% white, directly descended from a group of Breton and Norman fishermen who landed here in the 17th century.

Although tourism is rapidly becoming the main activity, the inhabitants of Les Saintes nevertheless remain the best fishermen in the Antilles. The model of their fast boats has been copied by all the fishermen of Guadeloupe as well as by a large number of yachtsmen. Most of the population is grouped around Bourg de Terre-de-Haut whose beautifully kept, flower-covered little houses lie along a magnificent shore.

Approach

From the south, any of the passes can be used. Passe Grand Ilet can be rough with current rips. The direct passage between Grand Ilet and La Coche has reefs on either side and it is necessary to keep to the centre. Grand Ilet blends with the higher land behind but the southeast end has a conspicuous triangular-shaped cliff. The current often sets anticlockwise round these islands and is east-going on the south side. Watch out for fishing buoys.

From the north, the Saintes Channel, which separates these islands from Guadeloupe, is 5M wide. The wind always tends to strengthen in the channel and the current, which flows westward most of the time, can be very strong. The sea is almost always choppy.

There are no unmarked dangers more than 0·15M off the coast of Les Saintes.

In all the anchorages the wind can be fluky and in unsettled weather can get up quite quickly from an unwelcome direction. It may be necessary to dodge round an island to escape it.

Rade des Saintes

15°52'·3N 61°34'·8W

Le Rade des Saintes, also known as Passe du Pain de Sucre, is surrounded by the steep bluffs of Terre-de-Haut and by Ilet à Cabrit and is well protected from the trade winds. There are secure and pleasant anchorages here but they are always very busy at the weekend.

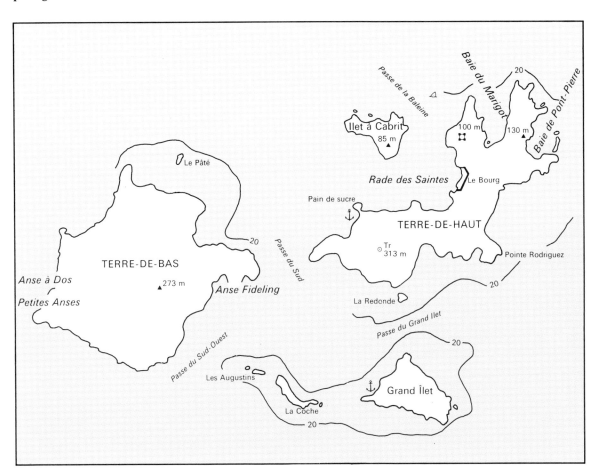

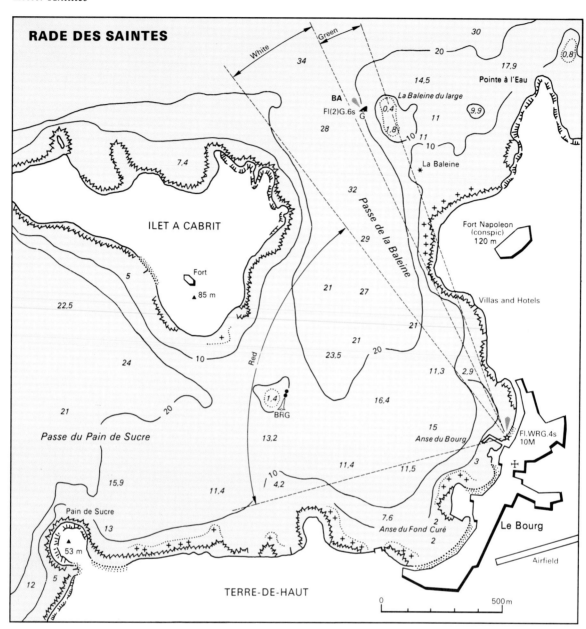

RADE DES SAINTES

ILET A CABRIT

Fort
▲ 85 m

Passe de la Baleine

BA
Fl(2)G.6s

La Baleine du large

Pointe à l'Eau

La Baleine

Fort Napoleon
(conspic)
120 m

Villas and Hotels

Passe du Pain de Sucre

BRG

Anse du Bourg

Fl.WRG.4s
10M

Le Bourg

Pain de Sucre
▲ 53 m

Anse du Fond Curé

TERRE-DE-HAUT

Airfield

0   500 m

Buoy BA   313m
Town and anchorage

Terre-de-Haut from Passe de la Baleine

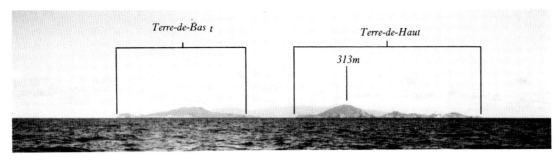

Les Saintes looking NNW. Guadeloupe in the background

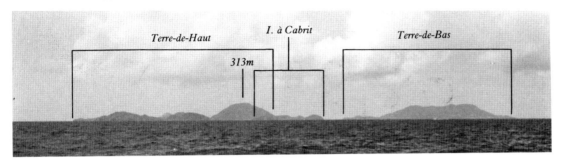

Les Saintes looking SSW

Approach

From the south, keep 300m off Pointe de Boisjoli and be careful of shallows in the middle of the western approach with a buoy marking an isolated danger.

From the northeast, the approach most often used is through Passe de la Baleine. There are two hazards in this entrance. The northern one, La Baleine du Large, which breaks, is marked by a buoy most conveniently passed to starboard. Southeast of this is La Baleine which shows slightly above the water but which is otherwise unmarked.

When under sail, keep as close as possible to the wind towards Bourg des Saintes as soon as La Baleine has been passed and be prepared for gusts especially in the vicinity of Fort Napoleon.

Anchorage

Anchor either in front of the town in 7–13m on sand or in Anse du Fond Cure, which is usually less busy, in 4–6m on sand and weed.

Keep clear of the pier which is frequently used by fast ferries with a lot of wash.

Formalities

There may be a customs post in Bourg but if not, temporary entry can be obtained at the Gendarmerie – if you can find him in.

Facilities

A few small supermarkets. Good fishing gear. Restaurants.

Communications

Airstrip.

Pain de Sucre

15°51'·9N 61°36'·2W

Pain de Sucre is a conspicuous cone of basalt, 53m high, at the western end of the Rade with a pretty anchorage off a beach to its south, edged with coconut palms. There is no danger in the approach but there can be squalls off the peak.

Anchorage

Anchor in 6–12m on sand either west or WSW of the beach. There are underwater rocks between the beaches and it is necessary to pick a spot with care.

Facilities

Several restaurants and bars in the town where it is possible to find a few supplies.

Anse Craven, east of Pointe de Boisjoli, is one of the few 'free' beaches in the Caribbean.

Baie du Marigot

15°52'·9N 61°34'·4W

This wide bay, open to the north, provides a less-frequented but also a less attractive anchorage than Rade des Saintes.

A boatyard with a slipway with 100 ton capacity is situated on the east coast. On the west coast, hotel buildings can be seen.

Approach

When approaching from the west, keep clear of Marigot Caye (0·8m), which is usually difficult to identify and which lies 0·1M NNW of Pointe à l'Eau.

The anchorage at Bourg de Terre-de-Haut, Les Saintes, looking south.
Anne Hammick

Anchorage

Anchor in 3m on sand and weed, 100m WSW of the boatyard jetty. Further south depths decrease rapidly.

Baie de Pont-Pierre

15°52'·5N 61°33'·9W

This very pretty bay on the windward coast of Terre-de-Haut is well sheltered from the trade winds in a wild setting with a beach fringed with coconut palms in the southwest. The easterly swell sometimes makes the approach to this anchorage dangerous.

Approach

Heading SSW towards the entrance, then keep close to the east coast at the narrowest point.

Anchorage

Anchor in 5–7m on sand and weed, 150m from the beach.

Other anchorages

Terre-de-Bas has no anchorages which are protected from the swell at the time of the trade winds and the surroundings are unattractive in comparison with Terre-de-Haut. Anse Fideling (4–5m in the middle) can give quite good shelter if with shallow draught it is possible to get well in and anchor in 3m or less. On the west coast of the island there are anchorages near the little port of Petites Anses and in Anse à Dos (8–10m, 100m from the shore).

Northwest of Grand Ilet one may anchor in a small inlet with a beach and several coconut palms in the south. There are 5m depths on sand approximately 70m from the beach.

Ilet à Cabrit has an anchorage on its southern side in 5–10m off the pier. The wind is apt to eddy onshore. If ashore and feeding the cats, watch your toes as well as your fingers.

South coast: Pointe des Châteaux to Pointe du Vieux Fort

Charts
Imray-Iolaire *A28, A281*
Admiralty *885, 804, 491*
SHOM *3423, 3419, 4519, 7100*
US *25563, 25566*

Coasts, dangers

- The south coast of Grande-Terre which is almost completely straight stretches for about 22M between Pointe des Châteaux and Petit Cul-de-Sac Marin. The approaches to Pointe-à-Pitre are dangerous and are described on page 137.
- Pointe des Châteaux, the eastern tip of Guadeloupe, has a typical rugged outline with two rocks off it. There is a large cross on the top of it.

- East of Ilet à Gosier there is an intermittent coastal reef never more than 0·4M from the shore which creates several lagoons. The sea almost always breaks over it. There is no danger on the seaward side of this reef but watch out for the many floats marking fish traps anchored all along the coast in depths up to 30–40m.
- The principal landmarks are those of Saint-François, Sainte-Anne and Petit Havre (see pages 132 and 134). There is also a conspicuous group of villas with light grey roofs 1·2M east of Sainte Anne.
- The south east coast of Basse-Terre from Pointe-à-Pitre to Pointe de la Capesterre, which is low-lying, is very unsafe. There is a possible anchorage amid the cays at Grosloupe, opposite Sainte-Rose, but local knowledge is very necessary and it is well to give the place a wide berth because of strong winds and currents. In any case it is as well to stay out to sea in depths greater than 50m to keep clear of the numerous fishing floats; they are difficult to see and can easily foul a propeller or rudder. Between Pointe de la Capesterre and Pointe du Vieux Fort the coast is safer. There is often a large area

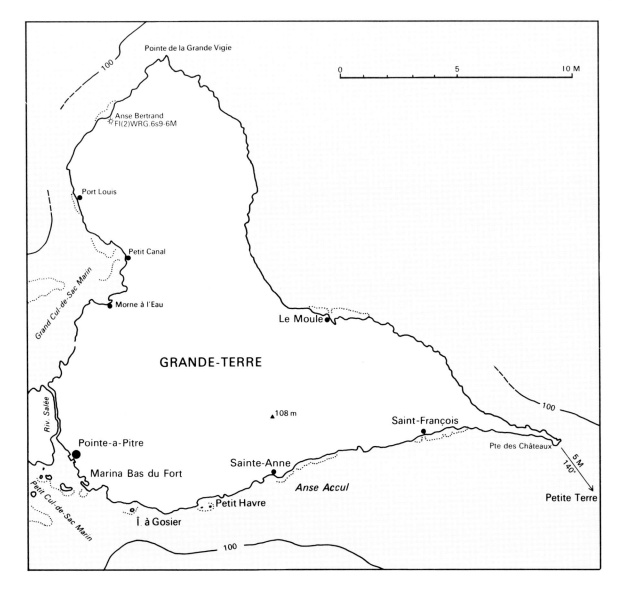

of calm around La Capesterre but, on the other hand, there are often strong gusts around Pointe du Vieux Fort. Capesterre, a village surrounded by radio masts in the north and by a large brick-built factory in the south is the most conspicuous place in this area. There is no possible anchorage there except for those who are completely familiar with the place.

Saint François

16°15′N 61°16′W

Saint François, an old fishing village stretching along the sandy shore of the most beautiful lagoon on the island, is today a lively little seaside resort. Yachts have a choice between anchoring in the lagoon or tying up to the quays of the Marina de la Grande Saline though the latter was badly damaged by hurricanes in 1989. This is one of the most pleasant ports of call on Guadeloupe.

Approach

The landmarks of the old town are the square tower of the church which is not very high and the landing stage on piles. 0·5M further east the modern buildings of the seaside town have conspicuous white roofs. The Grand Hôtel Méridien in the eastern end of the bay is the best landmark but it is not always easy to see when the sun is in the west.

A night approach is possible but only for those familiar with the area.

Entry

Passe Champagne leads to the lagoon and to the marina which is about a mile to the east of the town. This fairly narrow channel between reefs on which the sea breaks is impressive on a first visit but it is not dangerous except in a strong south wind which is very rare. It is essential to identify the green buoy *PC2* which marks the entrance to the channel southeast of the Hôtel Méridien. This buoy is often more difficult to pick out than the red buoy *PC1*. These two buoys in line lead to the entrance of the channel. The swell diminishes very rapidly once the green buoy has been passed. Once past the red buoy alter course towards the red light of the marina and follow the channel marked by small buoys in 2·2–3m depths.

Passe des Pêcheurs, whose entrance is one mile further west in front of the old town, is only of interest to yachts with very small draught.

Anchorage

Anchor in 3–5m on sand, 80–120m east of the red light of the marina. Further east the seabed is uneven with depths below 2m in many areas.

In the marina depths are 2·5–2·7m. The visitors' quay is on the south side in front of the harbour master's office (contact VHF Ch 16).

Facilities

Water, electricity, fuel station, showers in the marina.
3-ton crane.
Market in the town, supermarket next to the marina.
Various restaurants, casino, nightclubs.

Communications

Car hire

Saint François. General view and Passe Champagne

Saint François. Passe Champagne

Saint François. Vieux Bourg and Passe des Pêcheurs looking N

Saint-François. Marina entrance

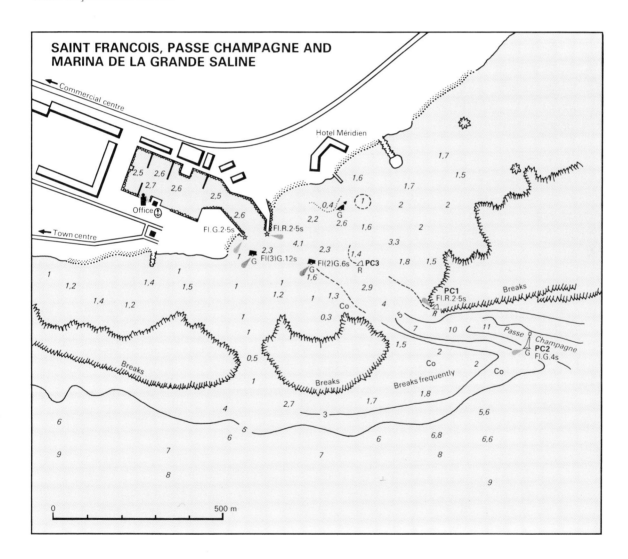

Sainte Anne

16°13'·5N 61°22'·8W

The village of Sainte Anne is situated on the shores of a clear lagoon protected by reefs on which the sea breaks. There is a good anchorage here but the best protected part is only accessible to yachts drawing less than 2m.

Approach

St Anne can be identified by its church steeple and by a small building with arcades on the seafront. A bearing of 350° towards the church will lead to the entrance of La Grande Passe, marked by two small buoys which should be left to starboard. Once past these two buoys bear to starboard and anchor in 2m about 150m from the shore, SSW of the church. It is not advisable to use La Petite Passe which is unmarked. In the approach to the landing stage in the northwest of the bay, there are many shoals with little water over them.

Facilities

Several restaurants, supplies, shops.

Conspicuous houses to E of Sainte Anne

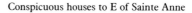

Conspicuous building

Church

Sainte Anne looking N

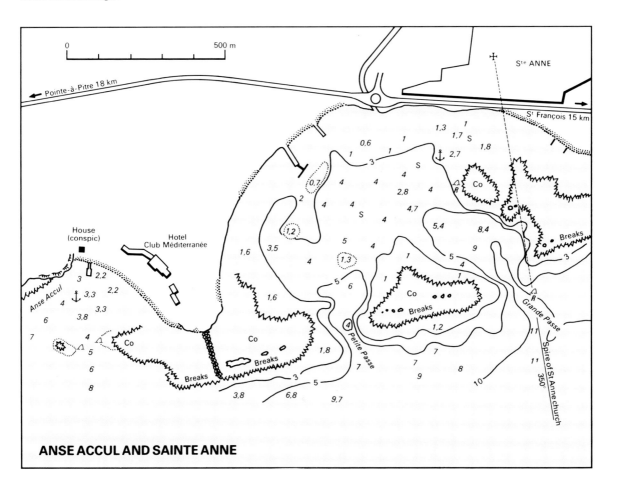

ANSE ACCUL AND SAINTE ANNE

Anse Accul looking N

Anse Accul

16°13′·2N 61°24′·2W

Just west of Sainte Anne this inlet, also called L'Anse de la Caravelle, has a beautiful sandy beach and an area of coconut palms in which the buildings of Club Mediterranée are to be found. The anchorage, partly protected by uncharted reefs, is however open to the southeasterly swell. A large colonial-style house, near the beach, next to the landing stage, makes a good landmark.

Approach

South of the landing stage a channel with 4m depths and about 40m wide is marked by two little buoys. It is also possible to enter by following the west coast of the inlet on a bearing of 052° towards the end of the landing stage.

Anchorage

Anchor in 3·5m on sand near the landing stage.

Le Petit Havre

16°12′·4N 61°25′·5W

Le Petit Havre is protected by a coral reef – partly uncovering – with a rock, Le Diamant, about 5m high, on its western side surrounded by other smaller rocks. This anchorage is uncomfortable and sometimes untenable when the wind and swell are from the southeast. For that reason is has the advantage of being deserted and seldom visited by yachts.

Approach

Keep within 0·5M of the coast to identify Le Diamant. Enter by rounding the reef (which is fairly easy to see) to the east and to the north.

Anchorage

Anchor in shelter in 3–4m on sand and dead coral. The holding is very variable.

In the eastern part of the bay there is a small inlet with a beach and coconut palms which is used by fishing boats. It is not very deep and there are several coral heads not marked on the charts.

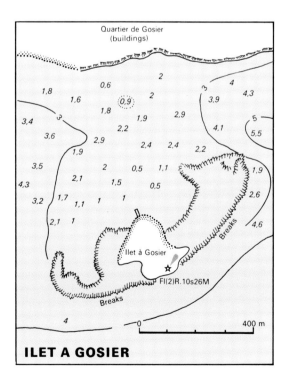

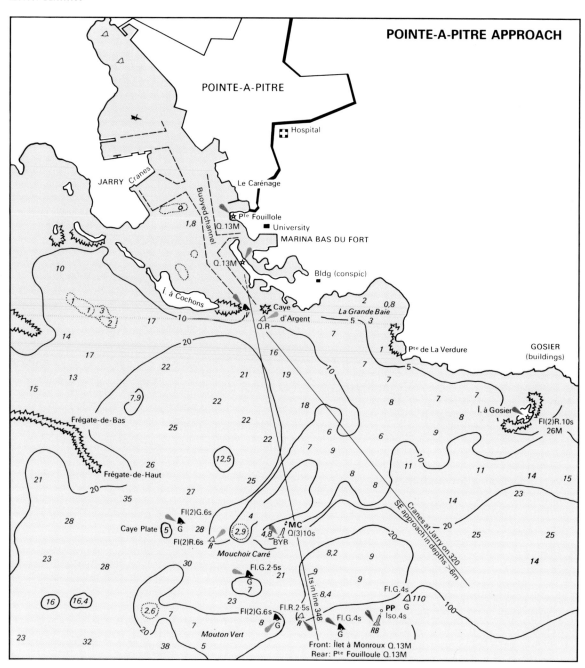

POINTE-A-PITRE APPROACH

POINTE-A-PITRE

Hospital

JARRY Cranes

Le Carénage

Buoyed channel

Pte Fouillole

Q.13M

1,8

University

MARINA BAS DU FORT

Q.13M

Bldg (conspic)

Î. à Cochons

Caye
d'Argent

Q.R

La Grande Baie

Pte de La Verdure

GOSIER
(buildings)

Î. à Gosier

Fl(2)R.10s
26M

Frégate-de-Bas

Frégate-de-Haut

Cranes at Jarry on 320
SE approach in depths >6m

Fl(2)G.6s
G

Caye Plate

Fl(2)R.6s
R

Mouchoir Carré

MC
Q(3)10s
BYR

Fl.G.2·5s
G

Lts in line 348

Fl.G.4s
G

110

PP
Iso.4s

Fl(2)G.6s

Fl.R.2·5s
R

Fl.G.4s
G

RB

Mouton Vert

Front: Îlet à Monroux Q.13M
Rear: Pte Fouilloule Q.13M

Ile à Cochons
Cranes at Jarry

Entrance

Hospital

Building (conspicuous)

Pointe-à-Pitre approach looking NW

Ilet à Gosier lighthouse looking N

Ilet à Gosier

16°12'·1N 61°29'·2W

Gosier is the tourist suburb of Pointe-à-Pitre, where most of the large hotels are situated along the shore. Ilet à Gosier, 400m off shore and 3M from Pointe-à-Pitre, provides an anchorage in clear water protected by the reefs which extend to the northeast and to the southwest of the islet.

Approach
Come in from the west but watch the depths as there are some places where they are less than 2m.

Anchorage
Anchor in 2m on sand, 200m northwest of the islet.

Pointe-à-Pitre

16°14'N 61°32'W

Pointe-à-Pitre and its suburbs has about 100,000 inhabitants. It is a very lively town second only to Fort de France in Martinique. Situated on the shore of a perfectly protected bay, it has a commercial port and the largest yacht harbour in the Lesser Antilles, Marina Bas du Fort (600 places), situated in green and peaceful surroundings 1km from the town centre.

This is a very pleasant port of call with all possible services for yachts.

It is, in addition, the best point of departure for trips to the interior of the island. Although yachts are charged for anchoring in the lagoon there are plenty of places to anchor free; it is a good hurricane hole but crowded.

Approach
Although the approach to Pointe-à-Pitre is well-marked, arrival at night requires great care because the lights, which are quite weak, are difficult to distinguish from the lights of the town. Remember the buoyage system is IALA B.

When approaching from the south, keep well off the coast of Basse-Terre to clear the reefs and shoals which extend from it to a distance of 2·5M. The wreck off Caye à Dupont (16°9'·4N 61°32'·9W) is so conspicuous it can be mistaken for another island.

The best landmarks are two large cranes; the cement works and the power station of the port of Jarry (two identical chimneys); the hospital – a large light-coloured building, standing out clearly against the green background (also easy to identify at night as it has three red lights equidistant from each other on the top of it); a tower block to the west of Grande Baie and, finally, the lighthouse of Ilet à Gosier (white tower with a red top).

At night, the leading lights (which one can do without) are difficult to identify.

Entrance
The entrance to the bay is between the reefs of the Ilet à Cochons and Caye d'Argent. It is well marked as is the approach channel to the marina where there are 3·5m depths.

Berthing
On arrival tie up at the first pontoon or at the harbour master's quay (contact VHF Ch 16, Marina Bas du Fort).

Rade de Pointe-à-Pitre entrance

Pointe-à-Pitre. Marina Bas du Fort entrance looking ESE

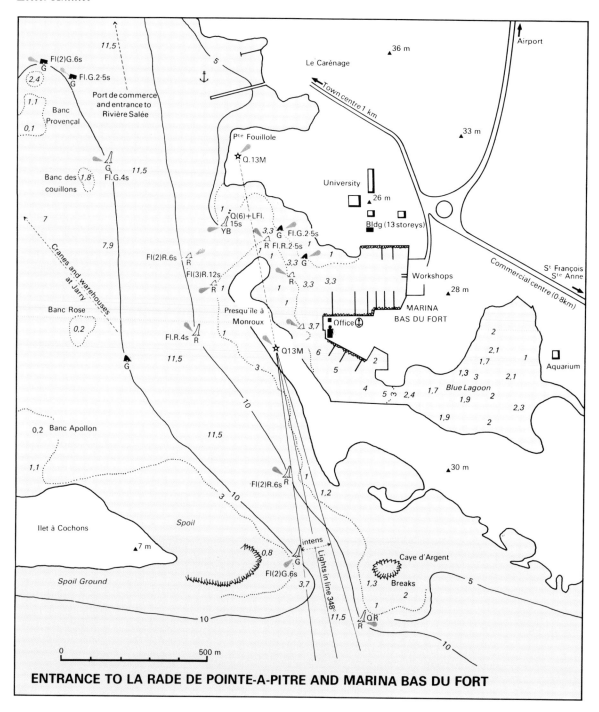

ENTRANCE TO LA RADE DE POINTE-A-PITRE AND MARINA BAS DU FORT

Anchorage

A charge is made for the anchorage in Blue Lagoon where depths are around 2m.

On the south side of the Y shaped dock south of the cathedral, north of the Careenage. The yacht club discourages landing by dinghy but there is a small quay nearby. This is the most convenient anchorage for shopping but the north side is used by cruise ships.

East of Ilet à Cochons or elsewhere outside the buoyed channel.

Jarry is the commercial harbour and it leads to the Rivière Salée.

Facilities

Marina Bas du Fort: water, electricity, fuel at the quay, showers;

25-tonne travel-lift, all maintenance requirements (one of the better facilities in the Antilles). The principal shipyard is Le Merre which has a 500-tonne floating dock but there is a smaller yard with a yacht-sized floating dock in the Careenage.

All the facilities of a large town.

Communications

Car hire

International airport within 4km.

The west coast of Basse-Terre

Charts

Imray-Iolaire *A28*
Admiralty *885, 491*
SHOM *3418, 3127*
US *25563, 25567*

Coasts, dangers

From Pointe du Vieux Fort, the southern tip of the island, to Ilet à Kahouanne the coast is fairly straight and safe. The best landmarks are the lighthouse on Pointe du Vieux Fort, Basse-Terre (page 140), Anse à la Barque (page 141), Bouillante (page 141), Deshaies (page 143). Further inland there are two conspicuous TV masts on Morne a Louis (760m), on a level with Ilet Pigeon (35m). In strong winds there can be very strong gusts for 2M N of Pointe du Vieux Fort and calms most of the rest of the way up the coast.

- Ilet à Kahouanne (74m) and the rock, Tete à l'Anglais (46m), which stand out to the west and northwest of Pointe Allègre are easily identifiable. They are sheer on the western side but very unsafe on the east and southeast. 1·2M SSW of Ilet à Kahouanne lies a shoal, La Perle, (1·8m) 0·2M off the land, on which the sea often breaks. Pointe Allègre itself, the northern tip of Basse-Terre, is low and fairly inconspicuous.

Basse-Terre. Fort Saint Charles looking NE

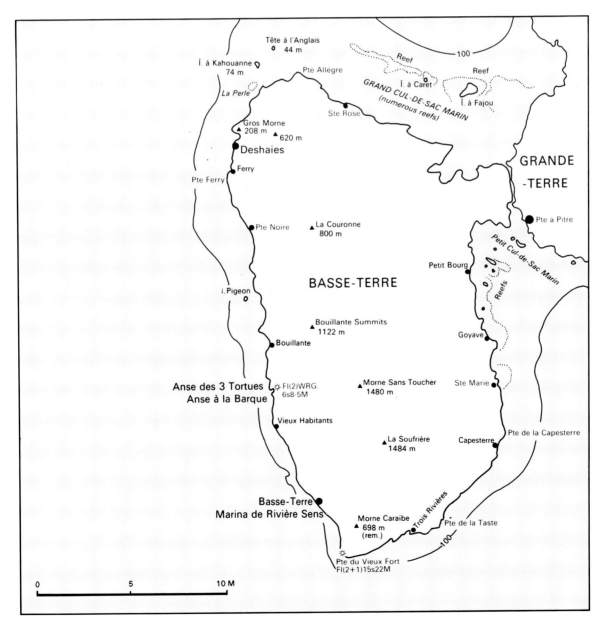

Pointe du Vieux-Fort lighthouse looking ENE

Basse-Terre

15°59'·7N 61°44'·4W

Basse-Terre, prefecture of Guadeloupe and the old capital, is situated on a coast with no protection against the swell though it has a commercial quay totally devoted to loading bananas. Work is in progress (1989) to create a protected area of water to the north of this quay. This would be available to carriers and pleasure boats. Because of the discomfort and the precariousness of the anchorage (where there are frequent strong gusts), yachts normally only call to carry out formalities and it is far better to go on up to Deshaies.

0·5M south of the town the small marina of Rivière Sens is very well protected but always so full of local boats that one cannot be sure of finding a place.

Approach

The landmarks of Basse-Terre are the cemetery to the north of the town, a pointed red tower and the port installations in the centre, and St Charles Fort to the south.

Anchorage

Anchor in 8–10m, 150m off the shore and southeast of the commercial port. Depths increase rapidly further out.

The marina has 3m in the entrance and 2m inside and little else to recommend it. It is crowded with very little room to manoeuvre. There is a starboard buoy in front of the head of the western jetty. If there is not too much swell, it may be possible to anchor outside which might be better than trying to anchor off Basse-Terre itself.

Rivière Sens Marina looking E

Basse-Terre town and port looking NE

N point lighthouse

Leading lights
Landing

La Barque harbour looking ENE

Facilities

Water, electricity and fuel at the marina. Supplies, restaurants and services in the town.

Anse à la Barque

16°05′·3N 61°46′·5W

Anse à la Barque is a useful stopping place with good shelter but very small as it is a narrow cut – several yachts make a crowd and are usual. The light house on the point and a sectored leading light make it accessible at night.

Approach

The yellow and black turret of the light on the northern arm of the entrance and the red and white column of the leading light at the head of the bay are good landmarks. Coming from the north, Bouillante, a village 2·5M north, can be identified by a large square, yellow-ochre building with a tower in the southern part.

Entrance

The entrance is safe with 12m depths.

Anchorage

The choice is between anchoring inconveniently deep on sand or finding space further in off the pier where the bottom shoals rapidly.

L'Anse des Trois Tortues, 0·4M to the north, is an open bay with several villas around it. When entering keep well off the northern arm off which rocks and reefs extend towards the southwest. Anchor in 5–6m, 100m from the beach.

Facilities

Some stores in the village round the north side.

Pigeon Island

16°10′·1N 61°47′·8W

This double islet (35m), is surrounded by an underwater nature reserve where diving for observation is permitted. Cousteau thought it the best diving in the world. Anchoring around the island is forbidden in depths of less than 30m (but see below). Moorings are provided for passing yachts. Vessels are not allowed to circulate in certain areas which are reserved for divers. Glass-bottom boats visit the nature reserve and diving clubs organize guided visits.

One may anchor temporarily in 10–12m about 60m east of the separation between the two islets, or in 4–6m about 130m from the neighbouring beach of Malendure (where diving equipment can be hired).

Deshaies. Landing and church looking NE

The attractive bay at Deshaies, Guadeloupe, seen from near the customs office to the south of the town. *Anne Hammick*

The village of Deshaies, Guadeloupe.
Anne Hammick

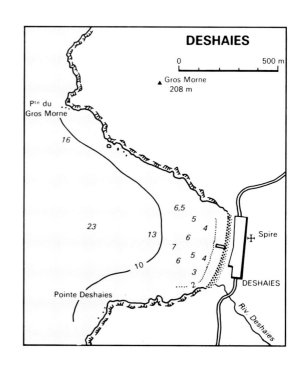

Deshaies

16°18′·5N 61°48′·3W

Surrounded by hills covered in vegetation, the bay of Deshaies is the best anchorage on the leeward coast. The village of Deshaies, with some of the most picturesque vernacular architecture in Guadeloupe complete with basking pigs, lies along its eastern shore near a beach edged with coconut palms. The church, of a light colour, with a red roof and a tall square tower, is easy to identify from the distance. The approach is safe but keep well off both headlands when entering the bay as fishermen spread their nets and pots there.

Anchorage

Anchor in 4–7m on sand and weed, 100–200m from the beach.

Facilities

The usual shore services, including 'typical' restaurants, a doctor and a library but very few shops.
Customs on the S side, 0·5M from the village, on the main road.

Looking S at the NW Point of Basse-Terre between Tête à l'Anglais and Pointe Ferry

La Pointe des Châteaux (Grande Terre) looking N

North coast of Guadeloupe

Charts

Imray-Iolaire *A28, A281*
Admiralty *885, 491*
SHOM *3422, 3367, 3287*
US *25563, 25567*

Coasts, dangers

- From Pointe Allègre to Pointe Gris-Gris is a very large bay, Grand Cul-de-Sac Marin, enclosed by a long barrier of coral with several channels through it (see below). Ilet à Fajou, flat and covered with vegetation, and Ilet à Caret, very small and with a group of trees on it, lie along this barrier and provide the best landmarks from the outside.
- Landmarks ashore are few and difficult to identify for those who do not know the area. The white buildings of La Gabarre (on the Rivière Salée just north of Pointe-à-Pitre) and the hospital there (see page 147) are the only ones worth mentioning.
- There is a marked channel leading to Rivière Salée but sailing in Grand Cul-de-Sac outside it is made extremely difficult by numerous reefs and isolated coral heads and by the absence of landmarks.

There is no reliable chart and in particular the courses and alignments given on SHOM charts 3367 and 3287 are for the most part impossible to identify. Navigation in these areas is only possible when the sun is high and the reefs can be seen. Even then it is strongly recommended that the help of someone familiar with the area be obtained.

- The posts and small markers placed on some of the reefs can only be identified by those who are familiar with the area. The route followed by a dredger which loads up 1·4M west of Ilet à Caret and discharges in Baie Mahault is the only one that is marked – provisionally and as it is needed – by small lateral buoys (a long way from one another and not charted). The direction of the markers is northwest – southeast.
- Part of the Cul-de-Sac (Ilet à Fajou, Ilet du Carenage, La Biche, La Pointe à Lanbis, La Pointe de la Grande Rivière) is a nature reserve where fishing is prohibited.
- From Pointe Gris-Gris on the northwest of Grande Terre to Pointe de la Grande Vigié the coast is comparatively safe. There are two villages: Anse Bertrand and Port-Louis in front of which one can only anchor during the summer months, approaching with caution in order to see and avoid the reefs which lie off the coast.

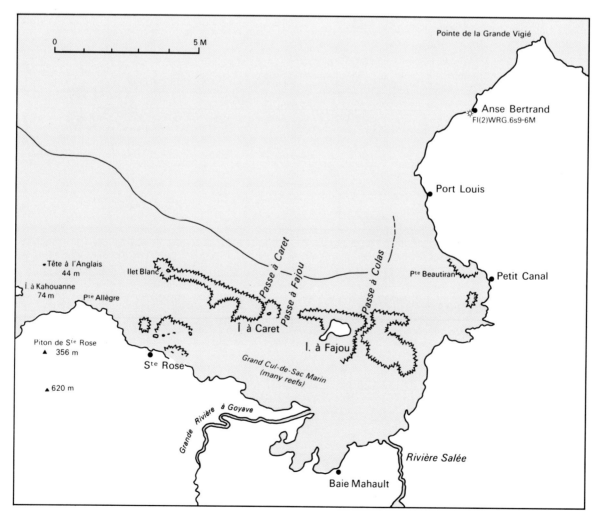

• Pointe de la Grande Vigie (North Point), the northern tip of the island, has grey rocky cliffs and a flat top (84m). The northeast coast from there on to Pointe des Châteaux is completely exposed to the swell and is very inhospitable. There are cliffs reaching heights of 40–80m almost everywhere except around Le Moule where they are lower and where there is a coastal reef. Le Moule, which is the only village on this coast, makes a good landmark (see page 148).

Ilet à Caret and Ilet à Fajou

There are anchorages in these two islets which can be reached either through the Cul-de-Sac or through Passe à Fajou and Passe à Caret but these channels should only be used when there is no northeasterly swell.

Caret 16°21′·4N 61°37′·9W

Passe à Caret is narrow but deep (10–16m) between steep reefs. Approach on a heading of 168° towards the middle of Ilet à Caret, then follow the channel and steer according to the colour of the water (deep blue in the centre, light green on the edges). The difference is very clearly defined. Anchor northwest or southwest of the islet, approaching with caution as the depths decrease very rapidly to below 2m.

Fajou 16°21′·0N 61°35′·4W

Passe à Fajou is wide but the southern part is shallow (2·5–4m). Approach heading on 140° towards the southwestern point of Ilet à Fajou. Turn south to pass 250m west of Gros Mouton de Fajou (on which the sea always breaks) and continue until the middle of Ilet à Fajou is due east. Approach the islet on this bearing, watching the depths. The very white seabed rises gradually towards the east. There are 2m depths 450m from the northwest coast of the islet which is edged by small white beaches. Closer in, the seabed is very uneven and obstructed by a number of uncharted reefs.

Passe à Colas

16°21′·6N 61°34′·5W

Passe à Colas, which is narrow and winding but well-marked and deep, leads safely into Grand Cul-de-Sac. The markers continue to the south of the channel as far as the entrance to Rivière Salée through which vessels drawing less than 2m can reach Pointe-à-Pitre (except in a time of very low tide). There is a project to dredge Rivière Salée to 3m and to mark the whole of it.

The Rivière Salée is a well known hurricane hole. Shelter is good but the bottom is soft mud and the holding poor. There are a lot of side creeks into the mangroves. Storm water building up on the N side of the island can, it is said, produce a 10kt current in the river.

Approach

The best landmarks are Ilet à Fajou – flat and very green, and a group of white buildings near a pylon in the middle of Pointe-à-Pitre on a bearing of 165 degrees from the entrance to the channel. Ilet à Colas, which is minute, has a corrugated iron hut on it.

Considerable caution is called for in the channel because along the sides, which are steep, there are shallows with very little water over them. The entrance is marked by two large and clearly visible buoys in depths of 15–20m. Follow the markers without going too close to the buoys as far as buoy C6. South of this steer 155° for 0·5M as far as buoy C7 (red) then continue on 190° from C7 to C8 (green), 155° from C8 to C9 (red), then due south towards RS1 (small red buoy) which marks the northern entrance to Rivière Salée. There are depths of less than 2m in this last section and it is important to stay exactly on the alignment of the two buoys.

Rivière Salée

After *RS1* go gradually closer, to within 15–20m of the northeastern bank in the first section of the river which winds towards the southeast, watching the depths which are between 2·1 and 2·6m and keep close to the northeastern and eastern shore at the level of the first bend towards the south. After this point, the river is deeper (2·5–5m in the middle) as far as Gabarre Bridge. The bridge opens at 0530, except on Sundays, but only if boats are waiting (1988). Anchor in the waiting area northeast of the bridge in 2·5–3m on mud. South of the bridge the Rivière Salée is still buoyed in the north south direction by two buoys (*RS16* – black and *RS15* – red), but beyond these the markers obey the south north direction of Pointe-à-Pitre harbour.

Proceed with caution in the northern part of the harbour where there are wide shallows off the coast. A shelf with 2·1–2·6m of water over it stretches eastward from Pointe Morne à Savon. See page 147.

Baie Mahoult

16°16′·5N 61°35′·5W

Baie Mahoult, in the south of which lies the quiet little town of the same name, provides a very well-sheltered anchorage but the water is always cloudy.

Approach

The approaches are obstructed by a number of reefs which are almost all marked by poles or small buoys.

From buoy C8 (green) of the approach channel to Rivière Salée head WSW for 1M, then south towards the centre of the village from which two conspicuous palm trees stand out.

Anchorage

Anchor in 3–4m on muddy sand, 150m north of the fishermen's landing stage.

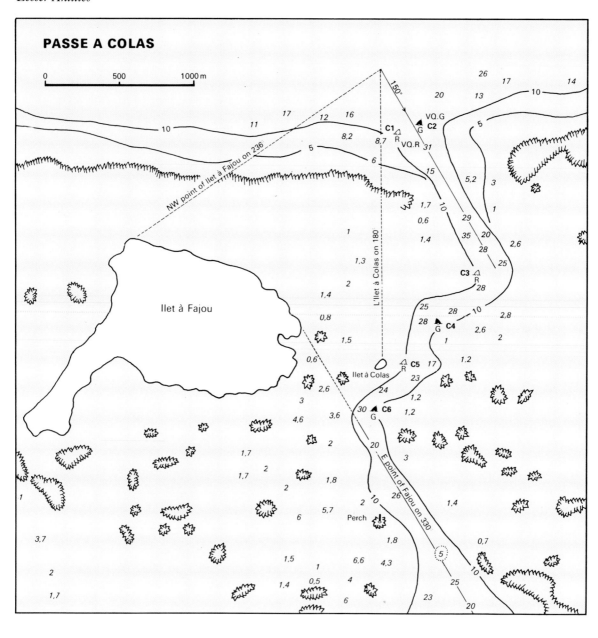

PASSE A COLAS

0   500   1000 m

26   17   14
20   13   10
17   12   16
11
10
8,2   8,7   C1   VQ.G   C2
R   VQ.R   31   5
6   15
5,2   3
1,7   5
0,6   29   20
1   1,4   35   28   2,6
1,3   25
2   C3   28
1,4   R   28
0,8   25   28   10   2,8
1,5   28   C4   2,6
0,6   G   1   2
Ilet à Fajou   2,6   C5   17   1,2
3   23
4,6   3,6   24   R   1,2
2   30   C6   1,2
1,7   20   G   3
1,7   2   1,8
2   10   26   1,4
6   5,7   Perch   2
3,7   1,8   0,7
1,5   6,6   4,3   5   10
2   1,4   0,5   4   25
1,7   6   23   20

Ilet à Colas

La Passe à Colas entrance looking SE
Inset: Detail of background: buildings at Pointe-à-Pitre

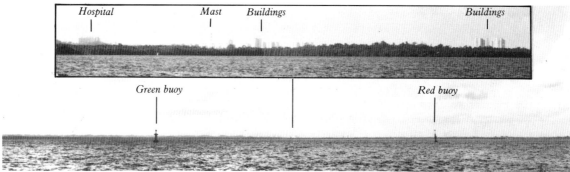

Hospital   Mast   Buildings   Buildings

Green buoy   Red buoy

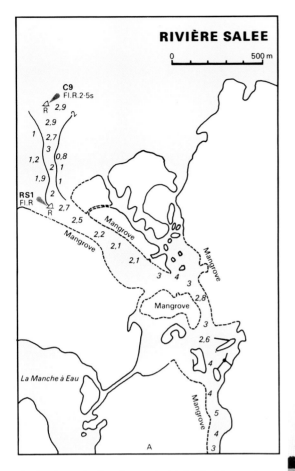

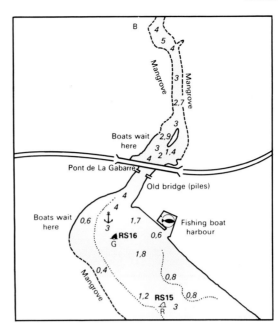

Continued opposite. There is approximately 0·75M of river running N–S from A to B which is not shown. Pointe-à-Pitre airport is conspicuous on the E bank.

Rivière Salée N entrance

Baie Mahault looking S

Petit Canal

16°22'·7N 61°30'·0W

This is the only protected anchorage on the north coast which can be reached without crossing the coral barrier of Grand Cul-de-Sac. It is very well protected and rarely visited but the water is usually cloudy.

Approach

From a point 3M south of Port-Louis steer 073° towards the church of Petit Canal (yellow with a square bell tower). When the 'Maison du Débarcadère' (grey and in ruins) which can be clearly seen on

Pointe Beautiron bears 017° turn on to it and finally on to 100° towards Petit Canal, watching the depths.

Anchorage

Anchor in 2·5–3m on sand, 500m from the shore.

Petit Canal looking E

Port Louis

16°25'·2N 61°32'·2W

An open anchorage though it is possible to get behind the jetty in a dinghy.

Approach

Go for the clock tower or the light on a heading of 090° watching for coral as the shore is closed.

Anchorage

Anchor in 2–3m

Le Moule

16°20'N 61°21'W

A delightful and picturesque little town which provides the only anchorage on the windward side of Grande-Terre. However, only the inner harbour, which has less than 2m, gives any protection and the approach channel is dangerous in a northeasterly or easterly swell. It is best avoided except in very good weather.

Approach

Le Moule is easy to identify from the sea as it is the only village along this coast.

Approach heading south towards the belfry in the middle of the village as far as buoy *M2* (green), then head for the entrance channel marked by a pair of buoys. Once through the channel turn slightly to starboard towards the middle of the bay, watching the depth.

Anchorage

Anchor to draught. The small harbour which has been built in the south of the inlet can only be entered by vessels with a shallow draught (1·2m).

Facilities

Restaurants and supplies in the town.

La Désirade

Charts

Imray-Iolaire *A28*
Admiralty *885, 491*
SHOM *3125, 4519*
US *25563*

General remarks

La Désirade was named by Christopher Columbus at the end of his second visit to the West Indies in 1493 when he found himself short of food and water. Very arid and difficult to approach, it has remained for a long time very isolated from Guadeloupe. Its 1600 inhabitants live mainly from fishing and some raising of livestock.

The island, which is dominated by a high plateau (200–278m) and bordered by cliffs, can be identified from a long distance. The south coast is fringed by a coastal reef which protects the port of Grande Anse, the only place at which it is possible to disembark.

The anchorage at Galet shown on the charts at the western tip of the island is almost always inaccessible because of the swell and the poor holding.

Grande Anse

16°18'·1N 61°04'·8W

Grande Anse, the only port on La Désirade, is a pretty village, full of flowers which stretches along a sandy shore fringed with coconut palms. A small, very well-protected harbour has been built along the front of the village with 1·5–2m. It is only accessible to vessels drawing less than 1·7m and provided there is no southeasterly swell.

La Désirade looking NNE

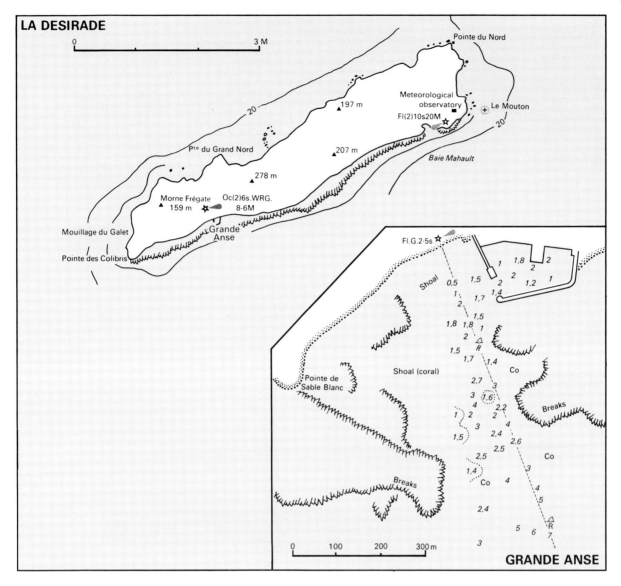

LA DESIRADE

0   3 M

Pointe du Nord

Meteorological observatory
Fl(2)10s20M

Le Mouton

197 m

P^te du Grand Nord

207 m

Baie Mahault

278 m

Morne Frégate   Oc(2)6s.WRG.
159 m   8·6M

Mouillage du Galet

Grande Anse

Pointe des Colibris

Fl.G.2·5s

Shoal   0,5   1,5
1   1,7
2
1,8   1,8   1
2
1,5
1,7   1,4

1   1,8   2   2
2   1,2   1
1,4

Pointe de
Sable Blanc

Shoal (coral)   Co
2,7   3
3   1,6   2,2   Breaks
4
1   2   2
3   2,4   4
1,5   2,5   2,6
Co
2,5   Co
1,4   4   4
Breaks   5
2,4

5   6
3

0   100   200   300 m

GRANDE ANSE

Approach

The approach channel leads in a NNW direction and is marked by two small buoys which should be left to starboard. There are depths of 6m at the level of the first buoy but these diminish rapidly in the channel. Continue towards the lighthouse (clearly visible on the shore in the line of the channel) until 100m beyond the second buoy. Turn to the northeast to enter the port, passing close to the end of the landing stage.

Do not enter by night without local knowledge.

Facilities

One or two restaurants.

Communications

Bicycle and car hire.

Iles de la Petite Terre

16°10'·5N 6°1 07'·5W

5M southeast of Pointe des Châteaux, Petite Terre consists of two deserted islets of coral formation covered in vegetation and surrounded by perfect beaches. The one lying further south possesses one of the oldest lighthouses in the Antilles. Between the two islets a channel, closed at the east by a barrier of reefs, provides one of the most beautiful anchorages in the Antilles in remarkably clear water. Ashore various birds and iguanas are to be seen. Camping is possible provided one does not mind the mosquitoes at night.

Approach

The anchorage is inaccessible with swell from the east or the northeast, when the waves break in the whole of the entrance channel. The breakers form near the west point of Terre de Haut, build up towards the WSW and increase towards the south.

Approach on a bearing of 130° towards the lighthouse and pause in depths of 6–7m in order to ob-

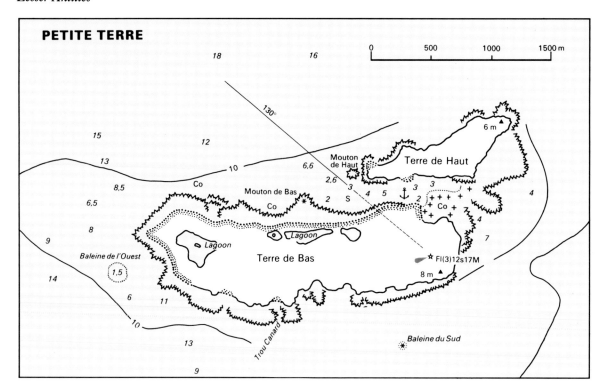

Petite Terre approach from NW. Enlargement of general view of
Petite Terre looking ESE.

serve the waves. Only enter if they are not breaking.
Continue on the same bearing passing over a shelf
with 2·6m depths, then alter course to east to pass
midway between the two islands, but beware of a
coral patch in the middle of the channel opposite the
W end of Terre de Haut.

Anchorage
Anchor in 3–5m on clear sand and do not pass further east than the conspicuous sandy point of the
coast of Terre de Bas.

Marie-Galante

Charts
Imray-Iolaire *A28, A281*
Admiralty *885, 491*
SHOM *3423, 3128, 6948*
US *25563, 25565*

General remarks
Marie-Galante, 15M south of Grande-Terre, is a fertile and gently undulating island covered with dense
vegetation and fields of sugar cane. There are cliffs in
the northwest and a coastal reef on which the sea always breaks in the west, southwest and south. On
the southeast coast Capesterre is only accessible to
those with local knowledge. Grand Bourg, the main
village of the island, is situated on the south coast.

The west coast is safe and provides the best anchorages. In the middle of this coast, the long landing stage at Pointe de Folle Anse, with a crane and
warehouses nearby, is a good landmark.

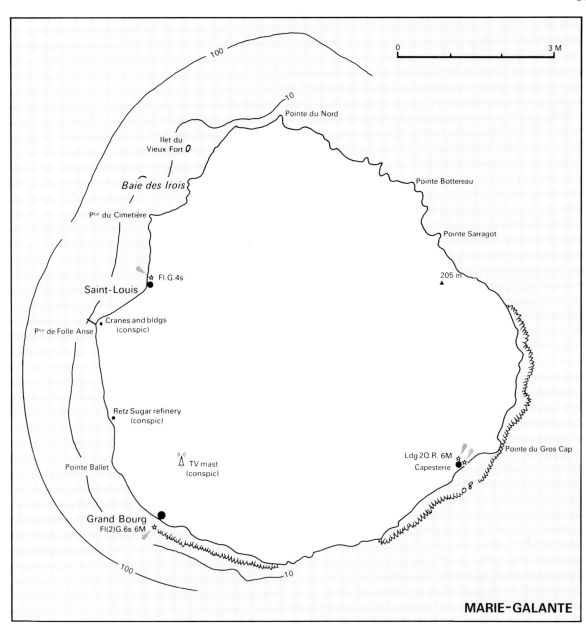

MARIE-GALANTE

Grand Bourg

15°52'·9N 61°19'·3W

The capital of Marie Galante, Grand Bourg is a village of small traditional-style wooden houses and has a warm atmosphere. The port consists only of a landing stage on piles in front of the middle of the village. It is protected by a coral barrier which does not completely shelter it from the fairly frequent southeasterly swell.

Approach

A very conspicuous TV mast, back from the shore 1M NNW of the village, is a good landmark. The approach channel, 300m west of the landing stage, is marked by two buoys which are easy to identify.

Marie-Galante. Conspicuous buildings at Pointe de Folle-Anse

Anchorage

Anchor in 3m on sand, 100m southeast of the landing stage.

Boats with a shallow draught can with caution go further east.

Facilities

Supplies and several restaurants in the village.

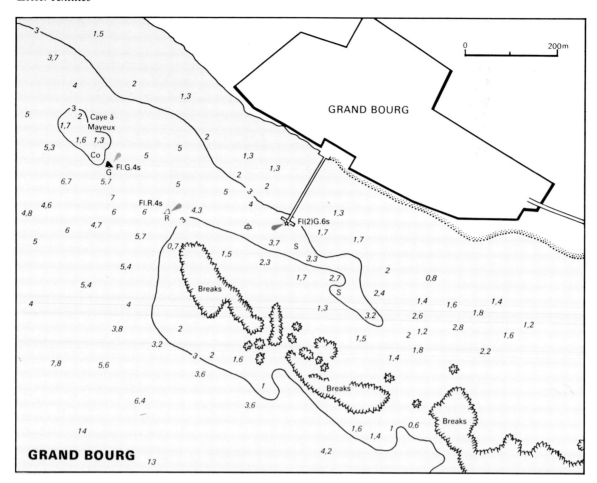

Grand-Bourg looking NNE

Saint-Louis

15°57′·4N 61°19′·4W)

Baie de Saint-Louis provides the best anchorage on the island in front of a quiet village which is easy to identify because of four aluminium-coloured oil tanks situated to the south.

Approach

The approach is open and the sea bed in the bay is very regular.

Anchorage

Anchor in 3m on sand and weed approximately 250m off the landing stage.

Facilities

Several restaurants (simple), food shops.

Communications

Car hire

Baie des Irois

15°59′N 61°19′W

This bay on the northwest coast of the island, better known locally as Anse Canot, has two beautiful deserted beaches shaded by coconut palms. There is a small restaurant hidden in the greenery near the southern beach which is the longer of the two. The swell which rounds Pointe du Nord sometimes makes this anchorage uncomfortable.

There is no danger in the approach. Anchor in 3–4m 150m from one or other of the beaches.

Saint Louis looking E

IX. Antigua and Barbuda

Charts
Imray-Iolaire *A27, A271, A26*
Admiralty *2064, 2065, 254*
US *25570, 25575, 25608*

General remarks

Antigua and Barbuda, linked politically, have another factor in common in that unlike their more volatile neighbours, neither are volcanic. Antigua is flattish, based on limestone which though lacking the abrupt nature of the hills of other islands has been heaved up to 405m. Its indented coastline has several anchorages in water of great clarity and its towns are full of interest for many disciplines but it is, in terms of landscape, dull.

If Antigua is flattish, Barbuda is a pancake. It is a very flat, low-lying island rising only to 60m and surrounded by reefs and shoals. The island is famous for the beauty of its lagoon and the enormous unspoilt beaches along the southern and western coasts. Its anchorages are made the more attractive by the difficulty of getting to them. It has a few hundred inhabitants, almost all of whom live in extreme penury in Codrington.

The two islands together with Redonda are governed from St Johns by a bicameral system of a 17 member appointed Senate and a 17 member elected House of Representatives. It became independent on 1 November 1981 and is a member of the British Commonwealth.

Antigua grows sugar cane and fruits; rum is the main manufacture. An small oil refinery was opened in 1982 but was showing no sign of life in 1989. A major source of revenue is the tourist trade; though hospitable, it is the island which has been longest in this trade and most affected by it. The rate of unemployment is very high. Barbuda fishes.

History
Antigua is one of the earliest islands in the Antilles to be settled by the British. The colony dates from 1632. It remained largely free of the Anglo-French quarrels of the south. Sugar plantations were dominant economically though cotton was also important. After the second world war, a conscious decision was taken to lessen the island's dependence on agriculture and develop tourism as a source of foreign income and this still holds good.

Barbuda is exceptionally dry and was never developed for sugar. It was used as a farm by the Codrington family and stocked with deer and boar for hunting.

Tourism
The tourist attractions of Antigua are the hotels, restaurants and a beach for every day of the year. Antigua race week, organized by the Antigua Yacht Club in Falmouth Harbour (see page 164), takes place at the end of April and is a major international event, attracting yachts from Europe and the USA as well as from all over the Caribbean, including the famous Maxis. It is also a major social event. Barbuda has marvellous reefs and beaches with very few visitors.

Formalities
Ports of entry are: Antigua: St John's; Crabbs Marina, North Sound; Mamora Bay; English Harbour. Barbuda: Codrington. There is a charge for a one month cruising permit, renewable, and also a charge for extending the one month entry permit which can only be arranged inconveniently at the police headquarters outside St Johns.
Flag
Red, with a triangle based on the top edge, divided horizontally black, blue, white, with a rising sun in gold on the black portion.

Maintenance
English Harbour, Crabbs Marina.

Communications
V. C. Bird International airport on Antigua with European, American and Caribbean connections. Airstrips on Barbuda with connections to Antigua.
Buses, hire cars, taxis.
Telecommunications from marinas and hotels.

Hurricane holes
Indian Creek, English Harbour, Falmouth, Parham and Nonsuch Bay.

Antigua

Coasts, dangers

Antigua can be one of the more dangerous islands in the Lesser Antilles to approach. The north and east coasts are low and from Diamond Bank in the northwest, marked by a lattice tower, there is an almost continuous reef extending up to 3M offshore through northeast round to the east of the island. With the exception of Cade reef at the southwest corner, which extends 1½M offshore, the reefs along the southeast and south shores do not extend out beyond the headlands more than 0·2M but in poor visibility – it is often hazy or showery – it is possible to close the coast without seeing the headlands, for instance at Willoughby Bay. North of Cade reef along the east coast the water is shoal with hazardous patches up to the rocks of Five Islands. The approach to St Johns from offshore has the dangers of low lying Sandy Island, marked by a 16m light tower with an unreliable light and a prominent wreck, and to the north, Warrington Bank with a tanker terminal and Great Sister further north.

In good visibility the highest peaks on the island, grouped together in the southwestern part may be seen. The highest, Boggy Peak (406m) has a tall radio mast with several conspicuous parabolic aerials. East of Willoughby Bay there is a long cliff with a flat top and approximately in the middle of it, a conspicuous radio pylon. Further northeast on Friars Point there is a house with a white roof and a cupola which looks like a lighthouse and is visible from a distance.

Approach the coast from all directions with great caution but especially if coming from Guadeloupe and making for English Harbour. On that passage a yacht will often be close hauled, unable to lay the course and set down by the current on to Cade reef. If radar is available, use it.

Inshore passages

It is possible to make an inshore passage from the English Harbour area to St Johns passing Winter Hill Point, through Goat Head Channel (2·5–4m), past Pelican Islet off Johnson Point, Five Islands (15m) (beware the 1m patch 0·75M southwest of Ffryes Point), the Barrel of Beef (2·5m) off Fullerton Point which has another rock southwest of it, Hawksbill Rock (7·5m) and Guard and Shipstern Points. Goat Head Channel is wide enough to beat through but the western entrance has shallows of 2·5–4m and there are shoals on the landward side. The passage between Cade and Middle Reefs is full of coral heads and should not be attempted except in the most favourable conditions.

Boon Channel, on the north coast of the island, is entered between Great Sister and Bannister Bank, south of Diamond Bank and leads to Parham Sound and North Sound. See page 164.

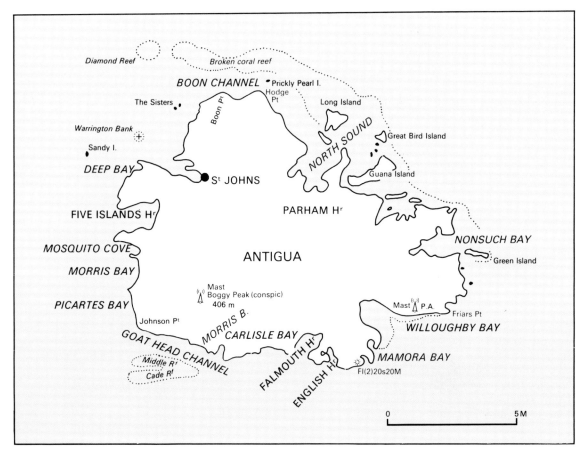

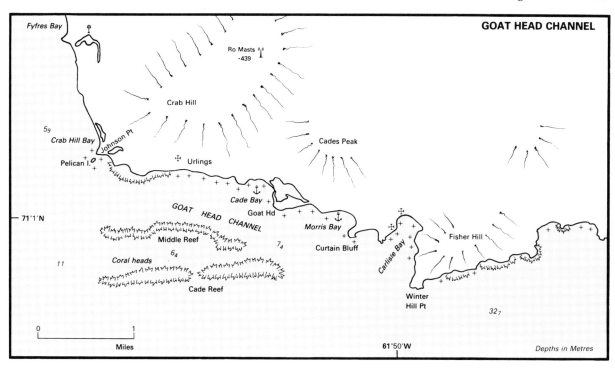

GOAT HEAD CHANNEL

Antigua: harbours and anchorages

Mamora Bay

17°00'·7N 61°44'·0W

This pretty bay, which is sandy and well-sheltered has on its eastern shore the buildings of St James Yacht Club whose light grey, pagoda-shaped roofs are conspicuous from the distance. Mamora Bay is a port of entry.

Approach

Through a buoyed dredged channel, 325°, 3m.

Anchorage

Anchor in the middle of the bay, 3·5–4m on very light sand or moor at the club pontoon, 2–3m, where there are about 20 berths.

Facilities

Water and fuel at the quay. Laundry, chandlery, grocery, restaurant. Casino.

Mamora Bay looking NW, view of the approach channel

157

Indian Creek

17°00′·4N 61°44′·2W

It is said to be named after an event in which the wife of the governor, then residing at Shirley Heights, was kidnapped by Caribs and who, preferring their company to that of British army officers, was not unwilling. The harbour is on a dog leg, surrounded by mangroves, which recommends it as a hurricane hole. It is uninhabited.There is more than a two mile walk through bare country to the shops of English Harbour as there is no direct road.

Approach

The rock just outside the entrance can be avoided by steering 037° towards the cliffs on the west side of the entrance and then keeping 50m off the west side to avoid the reefs.

Anchorage

Anchor in mud, 3–4m, shoaling at the western corner.

English Harbour

17°00′N 61°46′W

English Harbour, the main port of call for yachts on Antigua and a port of entry, is also one of the most important Caribbean centres for yachting and in the maritime history of the area. It is in this perfectly protected bay that the British Admiralty maintained the headquarters of its Caribbean fleet in the 18th and 19th centuries. Barracks, quays, slipways and boatyards were built and after being abandoned at

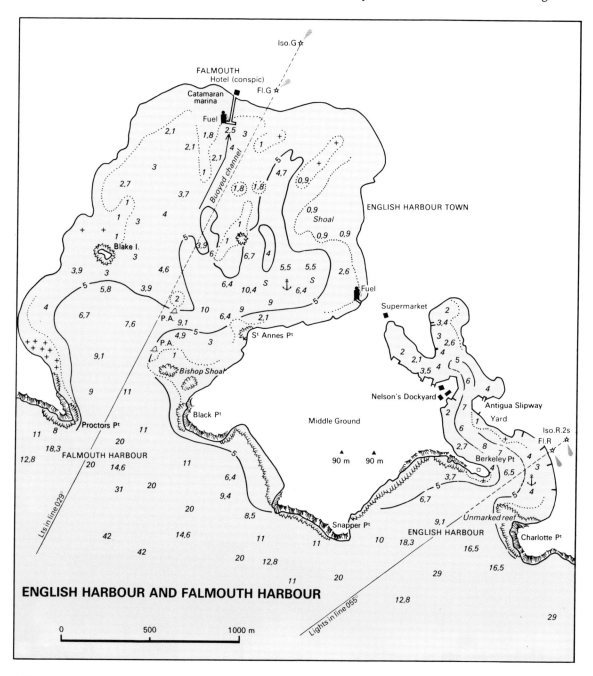

ENGLISH HARBOUR AND FALMOUTH HARBOUR

Berkeley Point (fort)   *Charlotte Point*

Entrance to English Harbour looking NE

the beginning of this century, they were restored in the 1950s. The buildings of the old 'Royal Dockyard' today house several hotels, restaurants, shops, a museum and a library amongst well-kept gardens. In its natural state it was a particularly attractive port of call. Now, though the unmistakable style of a Royal Navy dockyard remains, with complete services on offer to yachts and their inhabitants, it has become more crowded and noisy, with water unconducive to swimming. The name Nelson's Dockyard, which relates to a particular commercial operation within the harbour, is sometime loosely applied to English Harbour as a whole.

In the hurricane season the mangroves are likely to be cluttered with laid-up yachts. Elsewhere large motor yachts may overlay the cables of lesser mortals for hundreds of metres.

Approach

In good visibility the south coast will be spotted long before it is possible to identify Cape Shirley which has a light on a pole and a small fort. In poor visibility or haze it is possible to come up to the reefs before seeing the headlands; see page 156.

Entrance

The entrance is difficult to identify from a distance, particularly approaching from Guadeloupe when the angle of approach is tangential. Though a night approach is not recommended, it is one of the few places it is possible to arrive at night, once the entrance has been identified. There are two red leading lights.

The entrance passes between the crenellated fort of Berkeley Point and the deeply indented cliffs of Charlotte Point off which there is an unmarked reef.

Anchorage

Freemans Bay, a sandy inlet at the entrance. Yachts are supposed to anchor here whilst completing formalities but in practice they shove in and fetch up wherever possible, especially as this bay can be affected by swell. Anchoring in the fairway on the starboard hand is not appreciated.

Within the harbour, yachts can moor stern-to the dock yard, anchor out ahead (call VHF Ch 16). If anchoring within the harbour, do so well away from the quays; large yachts drop their anchors right across

the harbour. Ancient hurricane chains cross the harbour in several places and a tripline may be advisable.

Facilities

Water, electricity, fuel at Antigua Slipway. Gas, see Falmouth's facilities. There are free showers in the Dockyard, and a row of somewhat dilapidated sinks for washing clothes.

Boatyard: Antigua Slipway can handle vessels up to 120 tonnes, 30m and has a trailer hoist for up to 13·7m. All types of work including one of the few facilities in the area for electronics. Chandleries.

Nicholsons Yacht Services, on the peninsula at the head of the harbour, will hold mail, has a fax, a travel agency and a yacht charter agency.

Customs, immigration and harbour authorities; these are grouped together in the Dockyard itself.

Supplies: two supermarkets (one open on Sundays), numerous restaurants, post office, telephones, bank.

Communications

Taxis. Buses to St Johns.

Yachts anchored in Freeman's Bay at the entrance to English Harbour. The jetty gives onto steps leading up to Berkeley Point. *Anne Hammick*

The 'Pillars of Hercules' below Charlotte Point mark the entrance
to English Harbour, Antigua.
Anne Hammick

Nelson's Dockyard, on the western side of English Harbour.
Anne Hammick

Looking down over English Harbour, Antigua, from Shirley
Heights.
Anne Hammick

Anchored off the beach at Green Island, Antigua.
Anne Hammick

Proctors Point   Catamaran Marina   Black Point

Entrance to Falmouth Harbour looking NNE

Falmouth Harbour

17°01'·1N 61°46'·5W

Falmouth Harbour is the home of the Antigua Yacht Club, one of the most important in the Caribbean, and is also base for Antigua Race Week which attracts international competition. It is a well protected anchorage under the same jurisdiction as English Harbour, with the same dues. It is however much less crowded – it is even possible to find a solitary anchorage – more open, breezier, cooler, with fewer bugs and, in a couple of words, less noisome. Though it does not lack facilities, it does not have the range available next door.

As it has more space and fewer yachts than English Harbour, it is easier to lay out multiple anchors in time of hurricanes. The NE corner has mangroves but it is shallow.

Entrance

The entrance itself between Gauldin and Chateau Points (also known as Proctors and Blacks Points) is open but beware Bishops Shoal, a reef on the northern side of Chateau Point, which covers but is easily seen though its buoys may not be in position. The green leading lights are on 029° and are based just east of the Catamaran Pier.

Anchorage

The chief anchorage is in the southeastern part of the bay, off the Antigua Yacht Club. The port authority, which owns the pier, is close by. It can be reached from the entrance by passing between Bishops Shoal and a 2m shoal approximately 300m further north – the channel is marked by two small buoys.

The yacht club has marina facilities for 30 large yachts.

Catamaran Marina, in front of a hotel with light-coloured roofs, is approached by a buoyed channel. Depths at the quay are 1·5–2·5m but contact by VHF Ch 68 to secure a place.

There are other more isolated anchorages north and south of Blake Island.

Facilities

Water and fuel at the Port Authority Pier and Catamaran Marina.

Showers in the yacht club and Catamaran Marina.

Gas bottles can be filled at Pumps and Power, on the shore about 200m north of the port authority building.

It is a short walk over the isthmus to English Harbour (though not to Antigua Slipway).

Communications

Buses to St Johns from the Port Authority Pier and Catamaran Marina

Anchorages between Falmouth and Johnson Point

Carlisle Bay

The eastern arm of this bay is Old Road Bluff, a steep headland in the shape of a rounded hillock which rises to Fisher Hill (142m). Old Fort Point, with its ruin, forms the western arm. On the north coast a large hotel complex is under construction; inshore there is a small village.

Approach

The approach is safe with depths of 10m in the entrance decreasing gradually towards the beach. Within the bay there are rocks off both shores.

Anchorage

Anchor in the middle, 200m from the beach in 3m, sand. Closer in the sea bed is very uneven. The swell can be uncomfortable.

Morris Bay

Morris Bay, 2·7M East of Johnson Point, has a beach and coconut palms. A hotel consisting of a group of low houses with light grey roofs is conspicuous on Curtain Bluff, the eastern arm of this bay.

Approach

The approach is open.

Anchorage

Anchor in 3·5–4m about 150m from the beach, WSW of the hotel landing stage. This bay is uncomfortable in a southeasterly swell.

Cade Reef

In fine weather and with great caution, it is possible to anchor between Middle Reef and Cade Reef in 4–7m on sand. Navigation has to be by eye to dodge the coral heads.

Morris Bay   *Curtain Bluff*

Curtain Bluff looking NW from Goats Head channel

Anchorages between Johnson Point and Five Islands

Half Hide and Ffyres Bay
Anchoring is possible along this stretch of coast 150–200m off-shore in 3–4m. It is wide open to a southeast swell.

Morris Bay
Morris Bay has several hotels near the beach (one the largest on the island) and can also be identified by a radio mast sticking out of the coconut palms a little further back.

The approach is open but with many sandbanks.

The bay has depths of less than 1·8m throughout. Anchor according to draught.

Mosquito Cove
In the season of the year, the name is apt. Sound up the middle towards the shore and anchor according to draught. The bottom is soft powdery sand. It is affected by swell.

A marina to take 500 yachts is being developed alongside the Jolly Beach Hotel; entrance is from Mosquito Cove.

Five Islands Harbour
17°06'N 61°53'W

Five Islands Harbour is a large, quiet harbour with a choice of anchorages, surrounded by green hills. It is subject to swell.

Approach

Coming from the south it is possible to pass through the Five Islands; the safest channel is between them and the mainland, keeping well in the middle. From the north, clear the rocks off Fullerton Point. The isolated, unmarked Cook Shoal (2·6m) is about 0·8M south of west from Maiden Island (30m) which is rounded, covered in vegetation and clearly visible in the middle of the bay.

Anchorages

The best anchorage is Hermitage Bay on the south side which has 4m over most of it. Sand.

Deeper draught yachts anchor west of Maiden Island in 5–6m. Vessels with less draught can sound north and south of the island towards the mangroves where the swell may be less. A reef extends from Maiden Island ENE as far as the shore.

There is some shelter from the swell in the bay on the north side but it is foul with shoals extending 200m off shore, especially at the west end.

Deep Bay
17°07'·7N 61°53'W

A well sheltered anchorage in a sandy inlet useful for access to St Johns.

Approach

The approach is open but there is a wreck below water in the middle of the bay; pass either side.

Anchorage

Anchor off the beach, 3–5m.

Facilities

The Royal Renaissance Antigua Hotel has a restaurant and bar.

Barracks and other ruins line the road up to Shirley Heights, Antigua.
Anne Hammick

St Johns

17°06′N 61°51′W

The capital of Antigua is situated at the head of a very well-sheltered bay, the inner part of which is almost completely silted up (0·5–2m depths). However, the harbour has been dredged and the customs area enlarged. The port is unattractive and is only worth visiting to shop economically at the main supermarkets or deal with arrival formalities, a job better done away from a commercial port. (See page 155)

Approach

A red and white marker buoy is anchored in the WNW of the entrance. Approach the port through the dredged channel which is marked by buoys, none of them standard. Depths diminish rapidly ESE of the commercial port.

Anchorage

The anchorage near the town has 1·6m or less; approach very carefully (1988). There is 4–5m near the south coast SSW of the commercial quays. This is quite a long way out but is cleaner and more secure. Some yachts and the trading schooners make their way further in, even up to the quays. It is also possible to get round behind the steamer dock on the north side where there is a small jetty for dinghy landing.

Facilities

Supermarkets. Heritage Quay complex at the head of the harbour has duty free facilities.

Other anchorages

Fort Bay, north of Fort James. Anchor in 4m, sand.
Dickinson Bay, 2M north of Fort James. Go round outside the Sisters. It is a shallow bay, 3m, used by big charter yachts and by Maxis in Antigua week, with hotels, restaurants and a night life.

North Sound and Parham Harbour

17°08′N 61°46′W

North Sound and Parham Harbour is a large area with many islands, mostly uninhabited, and anchorages which are sheltered from the swell by the reefs but not from the wind. It is a fine sailing ground, very much less crowded than the area around English Harbour possibly because skill is needed. There are isolated coral patches all over the place but they are visible and can be avoided. Imray-Iolaire chart A271 is essential.

The huge parabolic aerials of the satellite tracking station 1M SE of the E end of the airport runway and the masts of the BBC relay station between the airport and Parham are conspicuous.

Approach

The easiest approach is Boon Channel, which is wide enough to beat through from the west (to get into Boon Channel, see page 156). The reef shows in good light but watch out for a few shoals on the shore side. Prickly Pear Island can be passed either side but the south channel, Prickly Pear Channel, has reefs extending northwards half way from the shore; the wider and deeper channel is on the north side and is safer when sailing. Maid Island Channel leading to Crabbs Peninsula was dredged for coasters and is marked by unorthodox buoys (though red to starboard). It passes very close to a shoal on its west side marked by a stake and to reefs off the southwest corner of Maid Island marked by a buoy. A yacht can go safely outside the channel elsewhere and must do so if it is occupied by a coaster.

A more difficult approach is by leaving Horseshoe Reef, which is generally awash, to starboard with Prickly Pear Island on a bearing of 192°. Prickly Pear Island blends in with the land behind and, though it shows on radar, is hard to identify by eye until close

Saint Johns, entrance to the approach channel

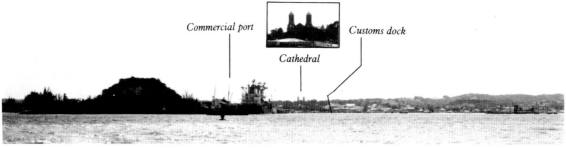

Saint Johns. Detail

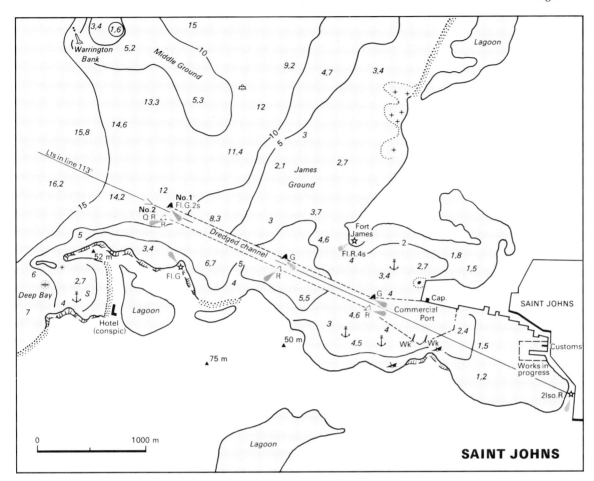

SAINT JOHNS

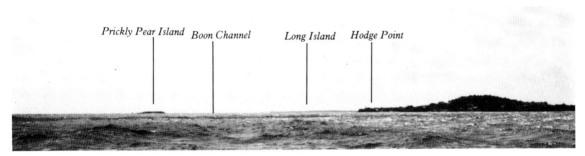

Entrance to North Sound. Boon Channel looking E

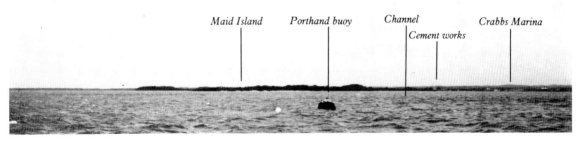

Entrance to approach channel from North Sound

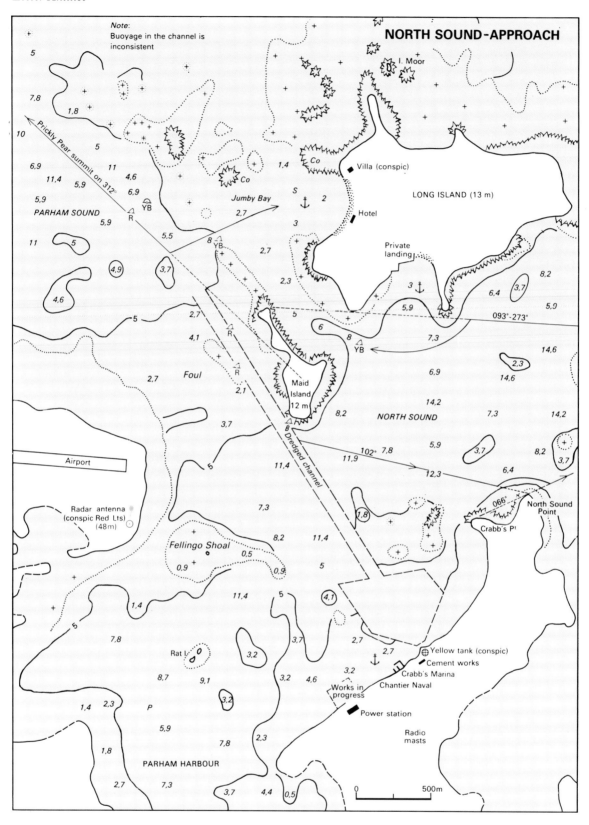

NORTH SOUND-APPROACH

Note:
Buoyage in the channel is
inconsistent

I. Moor

Villa (conspic)

LONG ISLAND (13 m)

Hotel

Co

Private
landing

Jumby Bay

PARHAM SOUND

Prickly Pear summit on 312°

093°-273°

YB

Foul

Maid
Island
12 m

NORTH SOUND

Airport

102°

Dredged channel

North Sound
Point

Crabb's Pt

066°

Radar antenna
(conspic Red Lts)
(48m)

Fellingo Shoal

Rat I.

Yellow tank (conspic)
Cement works
Crabb's Marina
Chantier Naval

Works in
progress

Power station

Radio
masts

PARHAM HARBOUR

0   500m

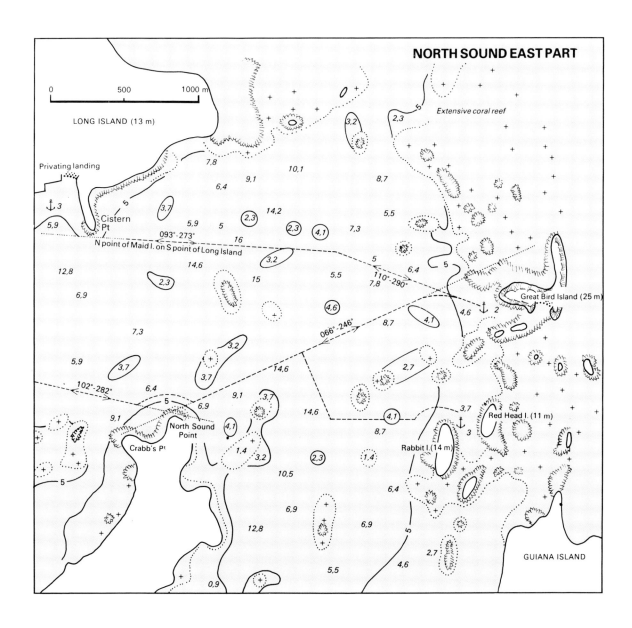

NORTH SOUND EAST PART

LONG ISLAND (13 m)

Privating landing

Cistern Pt

093°-273°
N point of Maid I. on S point of Long Island

110°-290°

066°-246°

102°-282°

North Sound Point

Crabb's Pt

Extensive coral reef

Great Bird Island (25 m)

Red Head I. (11 m)

Rabbit I. (14 m)

GUIANA ISLAND

North Sound. Cement works and conspicuous tank

North Sound. Crabbs Marina

but on that bearing is somewhere below Boggy Peak. The reef to port at the entrance is hard to see unless the sea is breaking on it. Radar is also useful here to give a safe range off Prickly Pear island; if Horseshoe Reef has not been identified at a safe range, abort and go round Diamond Bank to enter the channel.

There are various other approaches. Coming from the east the most attractive may appear to be Bird Islet Channel but it is very dangerous, not to say frightening, with a 20m passage leading in from the windward swell and surf.

Neither Horseshoe Reef nor Bird Islet channels should not be attempted without very good local knowledge. They are best used for the first time when leaving and only from seaward when they are familiar.

North Sound anchorages

Parham Parham was the first capital of Antigua, possibly because this side of the island was the most suitable for sugar cane. The town, which is fairly squalid, has an interesting church with its roof built like a boat. The harbour is well sheltered, serves moderately well as a hurricane hole and has a pier. There are shallows in the west part which extend round to a spit to the north of the pier. Anchor in 3–4m off the pier or in the bay under Old Fort Point whence Crabbs Marina is within dinghy range.

Crabbs Peninsula Between Parham and Crabbs are the masts of the Voice of America relay station. The area is not very attractive with its desalination plant, power station, cement works and a commercial dock handling sand. It can be choppy in a northeasterly wind but has no swell. But it has places at the quay with 3m depths, there is plenty of room to anchor and the main attraction is Crabbs Marina (see Facilities below).

Red Head, Rabbit and Lobster Islands – North Sound, Southeast side If care is taken, there are deserted anchorages to be found among the reefs on the southeast side of North Sound such as those in the lee of Red Head, Rabbit and Lobster Islands. The Guana shore also has anchorage but the island is a nature reserve and walking inland further than the beach is discouraged.

Great Bird Island An islet covered with scrub and cacti, Great Bird provides a well sheltered anchorage on its WSW side. It is a popular barbecue site for day charter yachts when it is best avoided. Follow the headings shown on the plan to avoid the dangers in North Sound but it is possible to nudge in further than indicated on the plan (on page 167). There is a landing on a small beach (not visible from the anchorage) on the southern coast of the islet.

Long Island Davis Bay, on the south side of Long Island, is quite well protected and quiet though not outstandingly pretty; the quay is private. Anchor in the middle, 3–5m.

Jumby Bay On the west coast of Long Island, has a very white beach and low-lying hotel buildings among the coconut palms. Long Island is private and owned by a hotel; visitors ashore are not encouraged unless using the hotel's facilities. It is 1½M to windward of the airport runway. It should be avoided if the wind comes round to the northeast. Anchor in 2–3m on white sand 200m from the beach.

Maid Island There are anchorages on either side of the start of the isthmus leading NNW from Maid Island. The channel between Maid and Long Islands has 2·3m. The bottom is sand but watch for coral near both islands.

Facilities

Crabbs Marina: water, electricity, fuel at the quay, showers, laundry, restaurant. Boatyard with 50-ton travel-lift and a large fenced hard standing part of which is inside a locked security fence for long-term storage. Chandlery. The marina is one of the better places in the Caribbean to haul out and one of the safer ashore in the hurricane season. Owners can do their own work but hauling rates are cheaper if yard labour is used. Contact Sun Yacht Charters on VHF Ch 68.

Communications

Car Hire at Crabbs Marina. Bus to St Johns from Parham and from the main road 1M from Crabbs Marina.

Nonsuch Bay

17°04'·5N 61°41'·3W

This huge lagoon which is well sheltered by a coral barrier provides fairly deserted anchorages in clear waters. There are several villas scattered over the hills both to the north and to the south of the bay. The approach is through a channel to the west of the deserted Green Island. Conk Point, on the western side of the channel is steep and has several conspicuous villas on top of it.

Approach

Approach on a bearing of 322° towards the middle of the channel. This route passes over the shoals (6–8m depths) which extend from the reef SSW of Green Island and leaves to port a conspicuous rock separate

Buoy

House (conspicuous)

Access to Jumby Bay (Long Island)

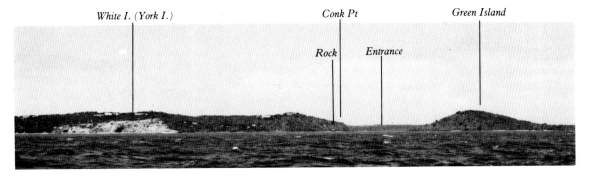

White I. (York I.)   Conk Pt   Green Island

Rock   Entrance

Entrance to Nonsuch Bay on 322°

from the coast of Antigua and surrounded by reefs. The channel is safe in the middle (18–20m depths) but in the bay one must avoid a large reef, awash situated approximately 250m NNE of Conk Point.

The approach to Nonsuch Bay through Spithead Channel north of the coral reef should only be attempted with local knowledge.

Anchorages

The most pleasant anchorages are to be found in the eastern part of the bay, either in a small inlet with a white beach, northwest of Green Island, or on light sand north of this island where the depths decrease gradually toward the coral barrier. Green Island is a favourite day trip from English Harbour; it, and the nearby mainland, is owned by the Mill Reef Club and access to some beaches is restricted.

In the western part of the bay, which requires careful navigation because of the shoals, the anchorages are less attractive and the water not so clear; Ayres Creek, however, is almost Devonian with trees coming down to the water's edge.

Willoughby Bay, between Nonsuch and Mamora Bays, is of little interest. The entrance between inadequately charted reefs and shoals is difficult to identify.

Barbuda

Charts

Imray-Iolaire *A26*
Admiralty *254*
US *25608*

Coasts, dangers

Barbuda is very difficult to see at a distance of more than 5 or 6 miles. It lies on the same shelf as Antigua and approaching from the south it is possible to see the bottom all the way. The sea breaks on Codrington shoal, south of the island, in bad swell. Near the coast there are numerous coral reefs and it must be assumed that they are either incorrectly charted or not charted at all; there are two hundred known wrecks. Always sail by eye as well as using the usual coastal techniques.

It is most important to take back bearings on Antigua and calculate the set carefully. The first marks to come into view are usually the white buildings of the hotel on Cocoa Point, a headland covered in vegetation, and a pile of very white sand with a loading chute at a sand pit 2·2M east of Palmetto Point. Palmetto Point, which has exceptionally white sand, extends 0·5M further south than is shown on the charts and there is a Martello Tower, difficult to spot, between the point and the sand chute. Keep west of Codrington Shoals by sailing on 012° at the sand chute or, better, the Martello Tower if identified, until Cocoa Point bears 060°. There are also reefs 1M southwest of Cocoa Point but they have wide and clearly visible passes and are sheltered by Pallister Reef.

Bungalows   Main building

Barbuda. Conspicuous hotel at Cocoa Point looking ESE

Martello Tower

Sand hill (conspicuous)

Landmarks on the S coast of Barbuda

Pallister Reef stretches from the vicinity of Cocoa Point to Spanish Point, at the southeast of the island. This reef extends two miles off shore and it is essential not to approach the shore between those two points.

There is no particular landmark on the west coast, which is edged by a very white beach with off-lying reefs, and a dangerous bank, Nine Feet Bank, which means what it says, just north of Palmetto Point. The whole length of the east coast is made inaccessible by a reef on which the sea breaks constantly.

Barbuda anchorages

Cocoa Point

16°32'·5N 61°46'·1W

The best protected anchorage on the island is to be found to the west of Cocoa Point, between the hotel beach and a line of reefs parallel to the shore about 400m out.

Approach

Pass west of the reefs lying off Cocoa Point and when well north of them, turn onto 125° towards the main building of the hotel, work your way inshore and as far south as possible between the reefs and the land.

Anchorage

To draught, sand. Watch for coral.

Facilities

None. The Hotel at Cocoa Point is a 'free' hotel at which guests do not pay for drinks and it is unable to offer service to casual visitors.

Spanish Point

16°32'·6N 61°44'·0W

The anchorage at Spanish Point is less well protected than that at Cocoa Point but has the advantage of being less used.

Approach

The easiest approach is from Cocoa Point inside Pallister Reef dodging the coral heads on the way – many of which are deep anyway.

A shoal draught boat with a more experienced crew can make the same passage but inside Gravenor Reef.

The third approach is by going north towards Spanish Point, keeping Pigeon Cliffs open, and turning in towards the Hotel at Cocoa Point on 286°; this leads between Pallister Reef and the reefs S and SW of Spanish Point. The sea breaks on both. It is necessary to get that bearing precisely and navigate by eye.

Anchorage

Pick an anchorage between widely spaced coral patches according to draught, 2–3m 200m off shore, fine powdery sand. The further you can get in, the better the protection from the reef off Spanish Point

Facilities

Absolutely none. A real desert island.

Tourism

Excellent snorkeling on Pallister reef. The area is a National Park and no fishing (especially spearfishing) is allowed.

If walking ashore, look out for cactus spines which penetrate flip-flops and sandals.

X. Montserrat, Nevis, St Kitts, St Eustatius and Saba

Charts
Imray-Iolaire *A25*
Admiralty *254, 489, 487*
US *25601, 25608, 25607*

General remarks

Geography

This group is a chain of high volcanic islands and a steep isolated islet, Redonda, between Montserrat and Nevis. They are comparatively undeveloped and are less often visited by yachts for the good reason that landing is awkward and shelter poor.

Redonda (305m) belongs to Antigua and Barbuda. It has no anchorage and landing is very difficult. It is like an overgrown Rockall.

Montserrat, with 13000 inhabitants, is high and massive, dominated in the south by Soufrière (913m). It is a British crown colony and has strong Irish connections and even a resemblance to the peninsulas of Kerry. It was devastated by the hurricane of 1989.

Nevis is separated from St Kitts by a narrow strait, The Narrows, 1·5M wide (see page 174). It is dominated in the centre by the crater of Nevis Peak (1096m) which slopes gently towards the southwest and the northwest. It has a population of 12000, a third of whom live in Charlestown in the middle of the leeward coast which is very green and fertile.

St Christopher (St Kitts) is the largest island in this group. It is dominated by two volcanic mountain ranges of unequal height joined together by a long, low isthmus which makes it look like two islands when seen from the northeast or southwest. The southwest and biggest range reaches 1115m at Mount Misery and is often covered in cloud. The southeastern range is 319m high. St Christopher has about 35000 inhabitants, half of whom live at Basseterre, the capital of the island, situated on the southwest coast. It has the best anchorages in this group of islands. St Christopher and Nevis form an independent state within the British Commonwealth.

St Eustatius, known also as Eustache and commonly referred to as Statia, has 1400 inhabitants and is part of the Netherlands Antilles. Together with Saba and the southern part of St Martin, it is administered from Curaçao where the Government is responsible for certain internal affairs. It is dominated by two ranges of hills, separated by a low, cultivated plain. The highest, in the south east, reaches 600m. Oranjestadt, the only village on the island was one of the richest freeports on the Caribbean where pirates, traffickers and established traders carried on a lucrative trade. When in the course of their quarrel with England the Dutch allied themselves to the new, rebel, American government the British Navy found its excuse to take out St Eustatia which it had long detested as the headquarters of the privateers. It never recovered.

Saba (860m) is a steep sided volcano partly covered in vegetation. It has about 1000 inhabitants who almost all live at The Bottom, a pretty village which extends along the edge of the ancient crater – the only inhabitable part of the island. It is almost inaccessible and has the quiet charm of a forgotten island outside the normal tourist and trade routes.

Formalities

Ports of entry and flags are as follows:

Montserrat Plymouth
Flag The British blue ensign with the shield of Montserrat in the fly.

St Kitts and Nevis Basseterre
Flag Diagonally green, black, red, with the black fimbriated in yellow and charged with two white stars.

St Eustatius Oranjestadt
Flag Whiteground with horizontal blue stripe and vertical red stripe, six white stars on centre of blue stripe.

Saba Fort Baai
Flag Whiteground with horizontal blue stripe and vertical red stripe, six white stars on centre of blue stripe.

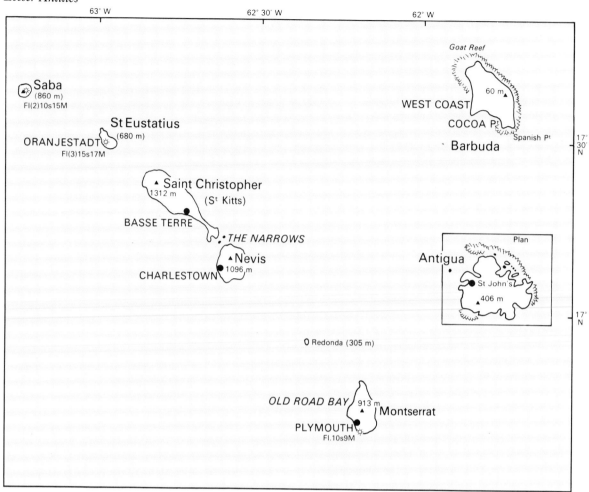

Maintenance
Nil.

Communications
Montserrat, an airstrip at Blackburne.
Nevis, an airstrip.
St Christopher, airfield at Golden Rock.
St Eustatius, an airstrip.
Saba, VHF shore station Ch 27.

Hurricane holes
None.

Montserrat

Coasts, dangers
The whole coastline of Montserrat is fairly steep with the exception of a small area on the west coast where the control tower of Blackburne airstrip provides a good landmark. There is no anchorage on the island with complete shelter from the swell.

Approach
There are no underwater dangers more than 0·1M from the shore.

Montserrat looking NNW (6M). Soufrière Hill hidden by clouds

Montserrat looking SSE (17M)

Plymouth

16°42'·2N 62°13'·3W

Plymouth, the capital of Montserrat, is a quiet little town on the southwest coast. Few yachts call in here as the anchorage is uncomfortable most of the time but a temporary visit to carry out the formalities and take on board a few stores is possible.

Anchorage

Anchor about 300m southeast of the conspicuous commercial jetty in 6–10m on sand and weed.

Old Road Bay

16°44'·4N 62°13'·6W)

This bay, 2·2M WNW of Plymouth, provides better shelter from the swell which rounds both the northern and southern extremities of the island. The northern arm is Old Road Bluff with steep cliffs and numerous villas on the slopes. In the northern corner of the bay is a little harbour for small boats.

Anchorage

Anchor in 6–7m depths, 150m from the grey, sandy beach fringed with coconut palms.

Carrs Bay

16°47'·9N 62°12'·5W

This sandy inlet with a steep promontory forming its northern arm is fairly open to the swell. There are a number of villas on the surrounding hills.

Anchorage

Anchor in 5–7m in the centre of the inlet.

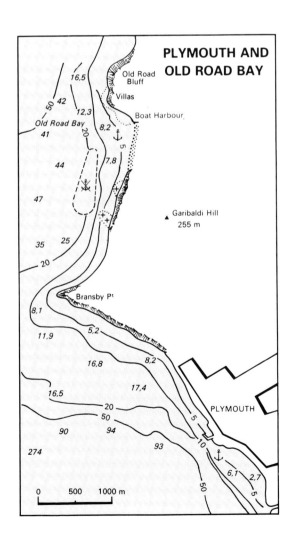

Town and port of Plymouth looking NE

Redonda looking NNE

Nevis

Coasts, dangers

There are coastal reefs along almost every part of the coast of this island, except to the west, for about 4M north of Fort St Charles.

There are very few landmarks on this island apart from those of Charlestown (see below). Hurricane Hill (363m) with a red and white radio mast on it, in the north, is the most conspicuous.

The Narrows

The Narrows is the name given to the 1·6m wide strait separating St Christopher from Nevis. In the northeastern entrance there are unmarked reefs and shoals. In the central part of the channel, Booby Islet (38m), a steep rock with a top covered in vegetation, is easily identifiable. On the other hand Cow Rocks

(2m) have little to characterize them. By following bearings shown on the plan (page 175) the dangers in the northeast entrance will be avoided. The south channel should only be taken in good weather, and bearing in mind that the currents here are stronger than elsewhere.

Charlestown

17°08'·2N 62°37'·9W

Charlestown, the main village of Nevis, has ancient, traditional-style houses. A warm welcome is always to be found. A short jetty in front of the village provides a landing stage for local coastal craft.

Approach

From the south the low headland of Fort Charles, on which there is a villa (the ruins of the fort have disappeared) must be rounded at a distance of 0·2M.

Charleston looking ENE and Nevis Peak in the background

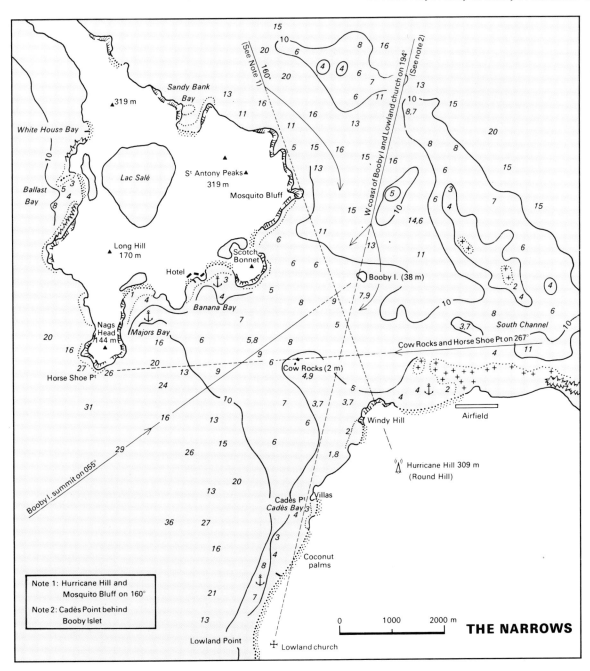

Note 1: Hurricane Hill and
      Mosquito Bluff on 160°

Note 2: Cadès Point behind
      Booby Islet

THE NARROWS

The Narrows on 195° approximately

The Narrows. Hurricane Hill and Windy Hill looking S

Anchorage

Anchor in 4–5m on sand and weed, NNW of the jetty.

Facilities

There is a public water point on the north side of the jetty and there are two or three restaurants. Supplies are limited.

Anchorages

0·9M SSW of Cadès there is an anchorage off a small landing stage with a bar easily visible in the middle of a long beach, fringed with coconut palms. There is 3m 150m from the shore. This anchorage is used by local craft.

At the entrance of Cadès Bay, to the north of which is a small bluff with several villas, there is an anchorage in 2–3m.

Nevis looking NW

Saint Christopher looking NW

Saint Christopher looking SE

St Christopher (St Kitts)

Coasts, dangers

The southwest coast has no inshore dangers except between the Nags Head and Guana Point. The coast is high and arid southeast of Basseterre and covered in vegetation to the northwest.town. The landmarks on this coast are those of Basseterre itself (see below) and the conspicuous fortress of Brimstone Hill, on a steep hill (236m) 2·5M southeast of the west point of the island.

The northeast coast of the island which is almost completely straight has a few reefs extending just over 0·5M from land. The best landmark is a conspicuous radio mast standing on a height of 409m at the northwestern tip of Canada Hills.

South coast anchorages

On the coast of St Christopher, Majors Bay (deserted) and Banana Bay (where there is a hotel) are accessible in fine weather. There are shallows in most of the western halves of both these bays. In the first, anchor in 4m on sand and weed, 100m from a small rocky point on the east coast. In the second, anchor in 3–3·5m depths, 100m from the east coast and 200m from the beach.

Anchorages on the Southeast coast to Basseterre

To the southeast of Basseterre there are several easily accessible sandy inlets offering pleasant and almost deserted anchorages. The best shelter is to be found in Ballast Bay and Whitehouse Bay situated respectively 1·6M and 2·3M north of Horseshoe Point, the southern extremity of the island. The first is in arid surroundings. The northern arm of the inlet is extended 250m towards the southwest by a series of

reefs and shoals. Anchor in 3–4m on sand, 100m from the east coast, where there is a beach. The second is bordered by a small beach with a landing stage, also in arid surroundings. Anchor in 3–4m on sand, 120m west of the landing stage.

Basseterre

17°17'·8N 62°42'·5W

The capital of St Christopher is a picturesque, small town whose streets, bordered by old colonial-style buildings, converge upon a small square, The Circus, in the middle of which stands a strange Victorian clock fountain. The town is situated along the shores of a wide bay which is quite well sheltered from the prevailing winds but often uncomfortable because of the southeasterly swell. There is a small commercial port on the east coast of the bay with 5–9m depths.

Approach

The landmarks of Basseterre are a grey spire in the western part of the town, the customs building with a red roof and white dome in the centre, petrol tanks in the east and two large hangars in the commercial port. There is no danger in the approach.

Anchorage

The best anchorage is in the east of the bay in 5–6m, sand, to the north of the commercial quays. As long as there is no swell, one can anchor in front of the town where there are three landing stages, two of which are in ruins.

Facilities

Supplies in the town (market and fairly well-stocked supermarkets), restaurants, taxis. Yacht yard.

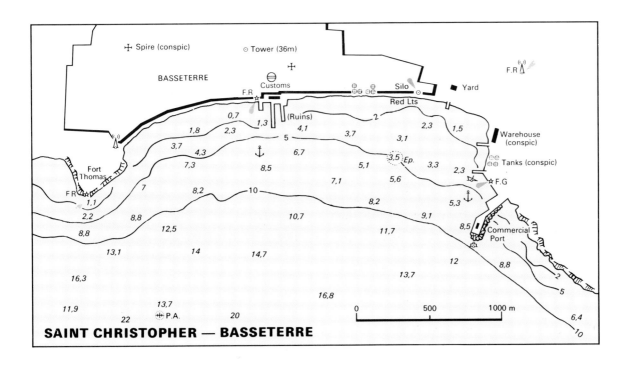

SAINT CHRISTOPHER — BASSETERRE

Basseterre looking N

Tourism

The imposing 18th-century fortress at Brimstone Hill is well worth a visit. It was built on the top of a steep bluff (256m) on the west coast of the island. This fortress, nicknamed the Gibraltar of the Caribbean, is one of the largest and best preserved of the Antilles.

St Eustatius

Coasts, dangers

St Eustatius (Statia) has a safe coastline. The only isolated danger is a rock, awash, 0·15M off the land, 1M southeast of the jetty at Oranjestadt. 1·2M Northwest of this village large green oil tanks and a landing stage 900m long make good landmarks.

Oranjestadt, St Eustatius

17°28'·8N 62°59'·3W

The capital of St Eustatius is a pretty, flowery village on the shore of a sandy bay near the ruins of an 18th-century town which extends along the shore.

This bay, which offers the only mooring on the island is fairly well sheltered from the prevailing winds but often uncomfortable because of the swell. In the southern part, a dilapidated jetty on piles provides berths for coastal vessels.

Approach

There is no danger in the approach.

Saint Eustatius looking SE

Oranjestadt looking NE

Anchorage

Anchor north of the jetty, in 4–5m on an even sandy seabed, 150m from the shore. The best place to go ashore is the small beach just to the north of the jetty near the customs office.

Facilities

Ashore there are a few restaurants and limited supplies.

Saba

Coasts, dangers

Saba has a sheer coastline except in the northwest near Torrens Point, 0·2M off which lies Diamantrots, a whitish rocky spur 24m high. The channel between this rock and the land is dangerous.

Fort Baai, Saba

17°13'·2N 63°14'·6W

There is no properly sheltered anchorage and a visit should only be contemplated in very calm weather. The sole port on the island, Fort Baai on the south coast, is minute. It is protected by a 70m breakwater with a quay on its inner side 3m above sea level which is high for a yacht. It is possible to come alongside if there is room (4–7m) but there is frequent surge. A road leads into the village. It is often better to anchor on the west coast of the island near Ladder Landing, a small landing stage connected to the village by steps up the side of a mountain where there are 8–10m depths, sand and rock, about 120m from the shore. A few mooring buoys in 12–15m are in place to the south of Ladder Landing.

Fort Baai, Saba looking N

Saba looking S (3M)

XI. St Barthélémy, St Martin, and Anguilla

Charts

Imray-Iolaire *A24*
Admiralty *2038, 2047, 2079*
SHOM *1488, 6090*
US *25613, 25608*

General remarks

Geography

This small group extends approximately 30M from northwest to southeast. The islands were discovered by Christopher Columbus who named them – Anguilla possibly because of its shape. It is a microcosm of the political hotchpotch that is the Caribbean.

St Barthélémy, commonly called St Barts, is administered by France through Guadeloupe; the name of its capital betrays a former connection – France bought the island from Sweden in 1877. It is a small rugged island reaching a height of 302m with an indented coastline. It is characterised by a 90% white population (2500 inhabitants) of Breton and Norman origin which remains opposed to miscegenation and has retained a number of 'old French' customs. Tourism is fairly well developed but still fairly unobtrusive on this island which is not without charm and is worth visiting with Gustavia (see page 183) as a starting point.

The southern half of St Martin is part of the Netherlands Antilles. Together with Saba and St Eustatius it is administered from Curaçao where the Government is responsible for certain internal affairs. The northern half is French and administered through Guadeloupe. Though mountainous with a peak of 415m it is fringed with lagoons and was a great exporter of salt. Many battles were fought before it was divided between the two nations in 1648. The population of approximately 21,000, 14,000 Dutch and 7,000 French, is permanently increased by a large transient tourist influx. The whole island is, in effect, a free port and it is difficult to see in the circumstances how it might otherwise be administered. This concession to circumstance has encouraged the development of hotel complexes and casinos which is out of character and makes St Martin the least Caribbean of all the islands. It is however a good place to have spares sent for collection and to stock up with all kinds of normally dutiable goods.

Anguilla is a long, low-lying, scrub-covered island (66m) with coasts which are for the most part deserted. It is a member of the British Commonwealth; it was formerly grouped with St Kitts and Nevis with whom the Anguillans disagreed. The friendly population is mainly black and consists of about 7000 inhabitants. Although there are a few hotels of international standing tourism is undeveloped and the majority of visitors come on day trips from St Martin. It has about the highest charge in the Caribbean for a cruising permit.

Formalities

St Barthélémy and St Martin are free ports.
St Barthélémy: immigration at Gustavia.
St Martin (south side): immigration at Philipsburg.
St Martin (north side): immigration at Marigot.
St Barthélémy and St Martin (north side) wear the tricolour, blue, white red vertical stripes and St Martin (south side) wears the Netherlands Antilles flag, white ground with horizontal blue stripe and vertical red stripe, six white stars on centre of blue stripe.
Anguilla: immigration at Road Bay and Blowing Point. *Flag*: White ground with narrow blue/green stripe at the bottom. On the white, three interlocking orange dolphins.

Maintenance

St Martin: Bobby's Marina, Phillipsburg.

Communications

St Martin has an international airport in the south, with US and European connections as well as with the Lesser Antilles, and an airstrip at Grande Case in the north. Anguilla has an airstrip and a regular ferry service to St Martin.
VHF: Saba Radio on Ch 27

Hurricane holes

Simpson Baai Lagoon and Oyster Pond, St Martin.

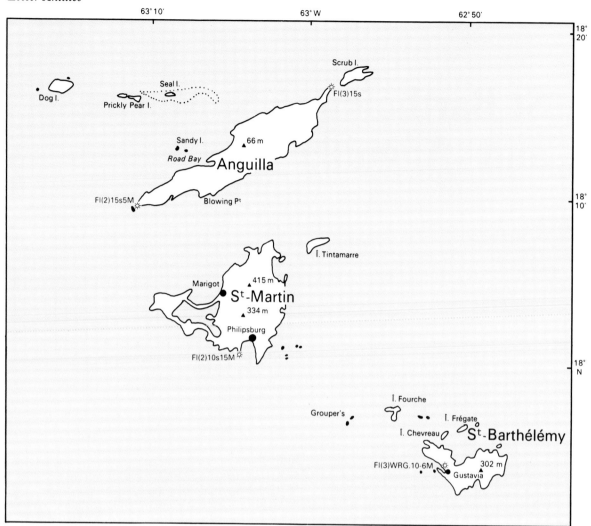

St Barthélémy

Coasts, dangers

Morne Lurin (192m) 0·8M to the north of Pointe Negre, the southern tip of the island has two radio masts, one with a parabolic aerial, which are clearly visible from all directions except east.

The southeastern coast of the island, which is mainly deserted, has four rocky promontories separating sandy bays which offer little protection. Off the coast there are several small rocks from 6–12m high and Ile Coco (38m). There is a dangerous shoal approximately 200m north of Ile Coco.

Off the southwest coast in the approaches to Gustavia there are several islets and rocks of which Pain de Sucre (54m) is the most conspicuous. 2M northwest of Gustavia dangerous reefs extend 300m out to sea from the islets and rocks off the southern point of the Anse du Colombier (see page 184). On the north coast, where the main headlands are without dangers there are several bays full of reefs (see page 186). On the eastern side the islet La Tortue is joined to the land by a continuous reef and 300m off its northern shore is a reef on which the sea breaks.

Saint Barthélémy looking NW

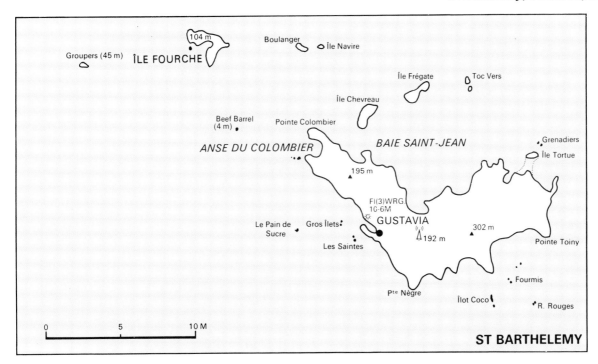

Saint Barthélémy to ESE

A further ten or so islets and rocks, all clearly visible and comparatively safe, extend to the north and to the northwest of St Barthélémy. There is an anchorage on the southwest of Ile Fourche (104m) which is the largest of this group of islets (see page 186).

Ile Fourche looking N

Gustavia

17°54'·2N 62°51'·3W

The capital of St Barthélémy is a smart little town, full of flowers on the edge of a natural harbour which is well protected from the prevailing winds. On the northeastern side of the port there are quays reserved for pleasure boats, 250m long and with 2·5–4m depths. The quays on the southwest side are privately owned.

Gustavia, which largely lives off tourism, is a pleasant port of call.

Approach

The lighthouse of Fort Gustave, a white tower with a red top (64m) is the principal landmark. It is easiest to enter by coming north of Gros Ilets (32m) or by passing between Gros Ilets and Les Saintes. If approaching from the south between Les Saintes and the Fort Oscar headland keep very close to the eastern side of the channel.

If passing to the west of Gros Ilets look out for La Baleine, a small low rock (1m) which is sometimes difficult to see and should be marked by a south cardinal.

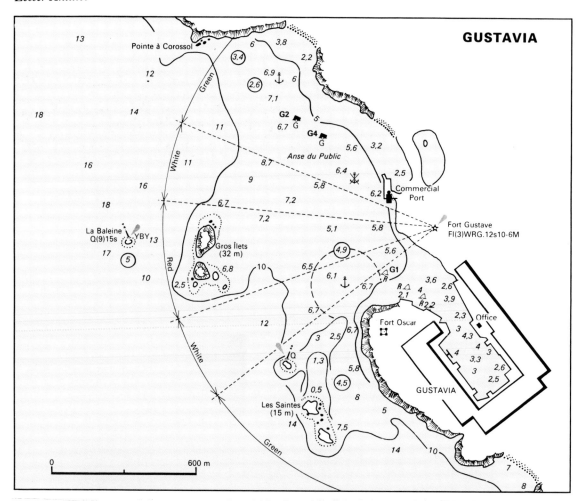

Gustavia looking SE

Anchorage

Anchor in the middle of the harbour in 3–4m depths and go stern to the northeastern quay. The southern part of the harbour, dredged to 2·5–3m is full of local yachts on moorings. There is an anchoring area (for which a charge is made) to the NNW of Fort Oscar in 5–7m depths on sand and weed. Anchoring is forbidden in the approaches to the commercial port in Anse du Public.

Facilities

Water points on the quay, showers, fuel station on the southern side of the commercial quay (3·5–5m depths at the foot of the quay).

Supermarket, a few shops, various bars and restaurants.

Communications

Scooter and car hire.

Anse du Colombier

17°55'·2N 62°52'·2W

This beautiful semi-circular bay near the northwestern tip of the island has a deserted white beach at the foot of low rocky cliffs.

Approach

Off the southern arm of the bay there is an island, some rocks and reefs which should be rounded at a distance of 300m.

Gustavia Harbour, St Barts, looking northwards to St Martin.
Anne Hammick

The clear waters of Marigot Bay, St Martin, looking south-west over the Grand Etang.
Anne Hammick

Anchorage

Anchor according to draught about 200m from the beach in 4–6m on sand and weed. The seabed is even.

Baie St Jean

17°54'·2N 62°50'·2W

Baie St Jean has two white sandy beaches separated by a small rocky headland. In the eastern part there is a pretty anchorage in a lagoon which should be entered only if there is no swell and with a good light. It is advisable to get help from someone with local knowledge.

Approach

The channel leads in a southeasterly direction. The seabed is clear sand and there are minimum depths of 2·5m over a shelf. To the west there is a wide reef on which the sea breaks and to the east some less clearly defined shoals.

Anchorage

Anchor in 3m depths on sand, 120m northeast of the headland between the two beaches. On this headland there is a conspicuous small hotel with a red roof.

Ile Fourche

17°57'·4N 62°54'·5W

Ile Fourche (100m) is deserted, steep and extremely rocky. It is possible to anchor on the southwestern coast.

Approach

From the south keep well clear of a rock which is barely visible, 100m west of the southern tip of the island.

Anchorage

In the entrance to the bay depths are 12–14m and decrease steadily towards the beach along the eastern shore. Anchor in 5m depths about 150m from this beach.

St Martin

In Dutch the island is called Sint Maarten.

Coasts, dangers

Off the south coast there is a single isolated danger, Proselyte Reef, 1½M south of Pointe Ouest, Philipsburg (see page 193). The clearest landmarks on this coast are Philipsburg and Simson Baai (see page 194). Away from the shore a white radome on St Peter Hill (317m) is clearly visible from the southwest and the northwest. Pic de Paradis has a radio

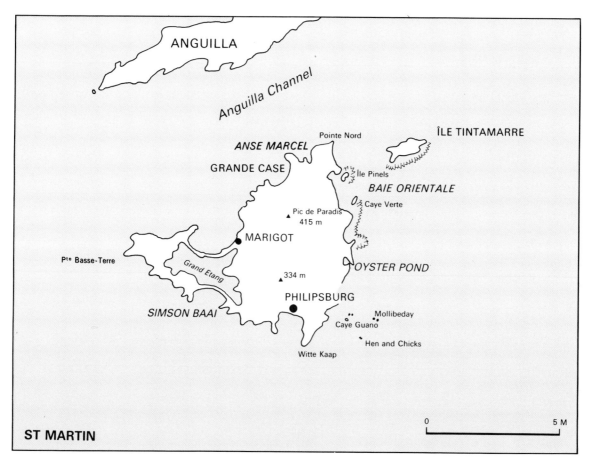

Saint Martin looking NE (7M)

Saint Martin looking SSW (8M)

mast which is less easy to distinguish but which can best be seen from the east and there are several other masts on its southeastern slopes.

Pointe Basse Terre, the western tip of the island has shoals off it for a distance of 0·75M and should be given a wide berth.

The north coast of the island into which the large Marigot Bay (see opposite) cuts deeply is comparatively safe. The only isolated danger is a shoal (1·2m) 400m north of the western arm of Grande Case Bay (see page 190). The landmarks on this coast are those of Marigot and Grande Case Bays.

Pointe Nord which is high and steep has a dangerous shoal, Basse Espagnole (Spanish Rock), lying 1·2M ENE of it. It consists of two rocks with less than 1·7m of water over them and is not easy to identify though it breaks in heavy weather. The east coast of the island has a reef with an irregular edge extending in places 0·3M from the coast. Tintamarre Island (see page 191) lies to the northeast and off the southeast of the island there are several islets and groups of rocks. They can be clearly seen and have safe channels between them but Pelican Cay (Guana Cay) has shallows for 250m to the NNE. With the exception of a large group of green roofed villas north of Oyster Pond (see page 191) there are few landmarks along this coast.

Marigot

18°.04′N 63°06′W

Marigot, sub-prefecture of Guadeloupe, has undergone considerable development in the last ten years. The modern area which has been built around Port La Royale Marina is today larger than the old town with its traditional colonial-style houses. This is the most 'civilized' port of call in this area with several restaurants, bars, nightclubs and shops selling luxury articles. The wide bay of Marigot provides a well sheltered anchorage, sometimes affected by a slight swell, in crystal clear waters.

Approach

There are no dangers in the approaches. 'La Belle Creole', a phoney Provençal village, to the west of the bay with yellowish pink houses and a tall square tower is a conspicuous landmark from a distance from the northeast and from the northwest. In the town the clearest landmark is the red and white radio mast.

Anchorage

Anchor in the eastern part of the bay in 2·2–3m depths on sand. It is possible to go ashore either at the town quay or at the landing stage of a restaurant 300m further west.

Facilities

Supplies in the town (market and well supplied supermarket), restaurants.

Communications

Car hire.

See also Grand Etang page 194

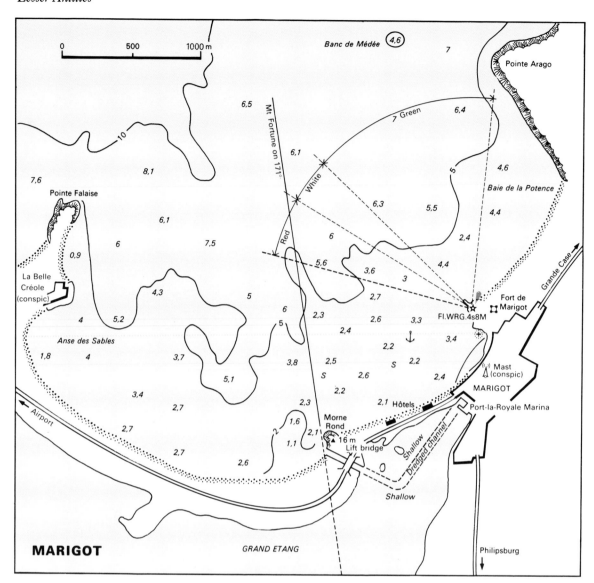

MARIGOT

Marigot looking SE

Marigot. Approach line of access channel to the Grand Etang

Marigot. Post office mast

Marigot. Commercial port and lighthouse

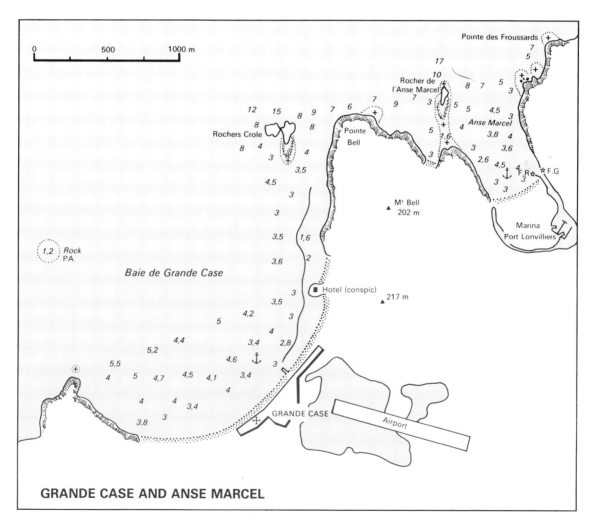

GRANDE CASE AND ANSE MARCEL

Landing and Grande Case village looking SSE

Grande Case

18°06′·2N 63°04′·5W

Grande Case, the prettiest village in St Martin, stretches along the south east coast of a wide bay edged with a sandy beach. The anchorage is well sheltered from prevailing winds but sometimes affected by a slight swell. A dangerous shoal (1·2m) which is unmarked and always difficult to identify lies 400m north of the western arm of the bay.

Anchorage

Anchor in the area of the landing stage in 3–4m depths on an uneven, sandy seabed.

Facilities

Several restaurants and the possibility of limited supplies.

Communications

Airstrip

Anse Marcel

18°07′·0N 63°03′·0W

This beautiful inlet surrounded by green hills is fairly well protected from the prevailing winds. On the southern shore there is a white beach behind which a colonial-style hotel and a marina situated in an old lagoon have been established. The marina provides perfect shelter in all conditions.

Approach

The hotel buildings with yellowish orange roofs are easily visible from the distance.

Enter leaving Rocher de l'Anse Marcel to starboard and anchor in 3–4m depths on sand 150m from the beach. The access channel to the marina is very narrow and it is not possible for two boats to pass each other. It gets sanded up and has to be dredged periodically (for information call the port office on VHF Ch 1 or 16).

Facilities

Water, electricity and fuel at the quay. Showers. Restaurants.

Communications

Car hire.

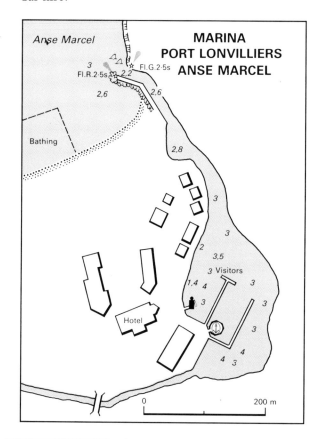

Marina Port Lonvilliers entrance

Tintamarre Island

18°07′N 62°59′W

The west coast of this deserted island, partly covered in scrub, is edged by a beautiful sandy beach between two rocky headlands. Anchor close to the beach on sand, weed and coral. The three metre contour passes approximately 50m from the shore. There is exciting diving through caves.

Baie Orientale

18°06′·0N 63°01′·5W

Pinels Islet (30m), in the northern part of the bay, provides a pretty anchorage edged by a beach and coconut palms and sheltered from the northeast.

Approach
Pinels Islet has reefs extending for 200m towards the east and the south. Round it at a safe distance and then head northwest towards Petite Clef Islet. Enter the bay leaving to starboard a mass of coral which is marked by an oil can.

There is a passage between the reefs and the isolated masses of coral to the north of Pinals Islet but it is more difficult to identify.

Anchorage
Anchor on sand and weed between Pinels and Petite Clef in 2–4m.

In the south of the bay, bordered by a long white beach, there is an anchorage sheltered from the south east by Caye Verte (20m) and by the reef which joins it to the coast in the south. Keep well off the reefs which extend from Caye Verte towards the NNE and anchor in 2·5–4m depths on clear sand 200m from the beach.

Oyster Pond

18°03′·2N 63°01′·5W

Oyster Pond, a small bay providing complete shelter surrounded by hills, is the base for a charter fleet with which it fills up in storm conditions. Captain Olivers Marina on the north coast of the bay has about 40 places at the quay in 1·5–3m depths.

In storm conditions the marina is cleared and its contents anchored in the lagoon, leaving little room for others.

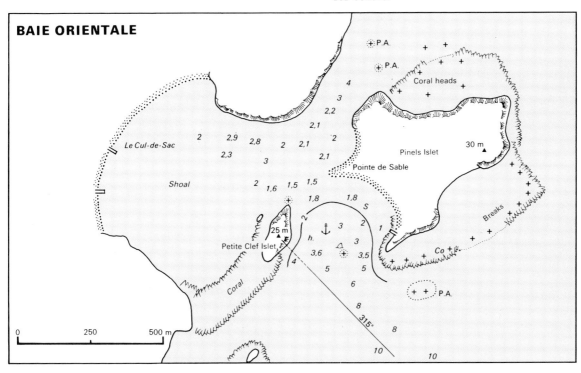

Pinels Islands anchorage looking NW

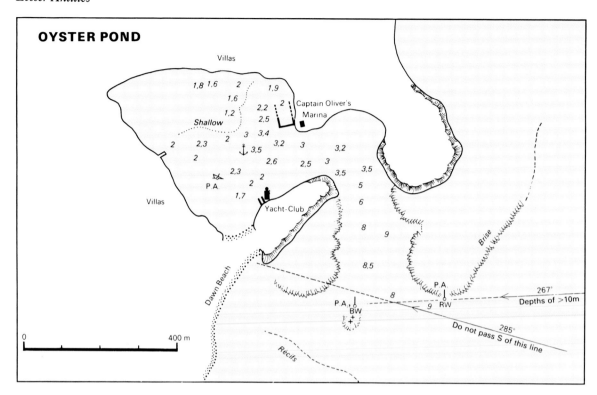

Oyster Pond approach

Oyster Pond. Details of entrance to passage

Entrance

The entrance is difficult to identify from a distance and there are reefs and shallows in it. The channel through them is marked by two poles (red and white to starboard, black and white port). A bearing of 285° towards the northern tip of Dawn Beach passes over a wide shoal (6m depths) and then leaves the red pole to starboard. Continue on the same bearing for 100m before turning to starboard towards the entrance. Access is difficult in a swell and dangerous in very strong trades, but you can call La Vida Charters

on Ch 16 and they will send a small boat to guide you. The posts wobble and may be laid flat by the waves.

Anchorage

Anchor on mud in the southeastern half of the bay. Be careful of a shoal in the middle of the bay, west of the marina, which is difficult to see.

Alongside at the marina.

Facilities

Water, electricity, showers, bar and restaurant at the marina. A fuel station is contemplated.

Philipsburg

18°01'·0N 63°03'·2W

The capital of the Dutch area of St Martin is situated on the shores of Grootbaai which is large but often uncomfortable for small boats because of the swell which enters it. The town consists mainly of one long road where there are numerous tax-free shops (jewellery, electronics, fashion) and restaurants, several hotels and two casinos. Philipsburg is a port of call for shopping and nightlife and has two marinas.

Approach

From the sea Philipsburg can often be identified by the large ferry boats anchored in the entrance to the bay or berthed at the landing stage of Witte Kaap. Ashore the best landmarks are the conical point of Fort Willem (216m) on which there is a pylon, and Witte Kaap, a steep whitish headland with a landing stage for large vessels on its western side and a white oil tank (only visible from the southwest). In Klein Bay a large white hotel with arcades is also a good landmark.

When entering the bay be careful of the shoal (1·9m) near the east coast.

Anchorage

Anchor in the northeastern part of the bay which is less subject to swell on an even, sandy seabed.

Bobbys Marina and Great Bay (Grootbaai) Marina) have berths in 1·5–2·3m. Call on VHF Ch 16.

Facilities

Water, electricity, fuel on the quay at both marinas. Showers, WC, laundry at both marinas. Restaurants, chandleries at the marinas and in town.

Well stocked supermarkets in town (1·5km)

Boat yard with 70-ton travel-lift (Bobbys Marina).

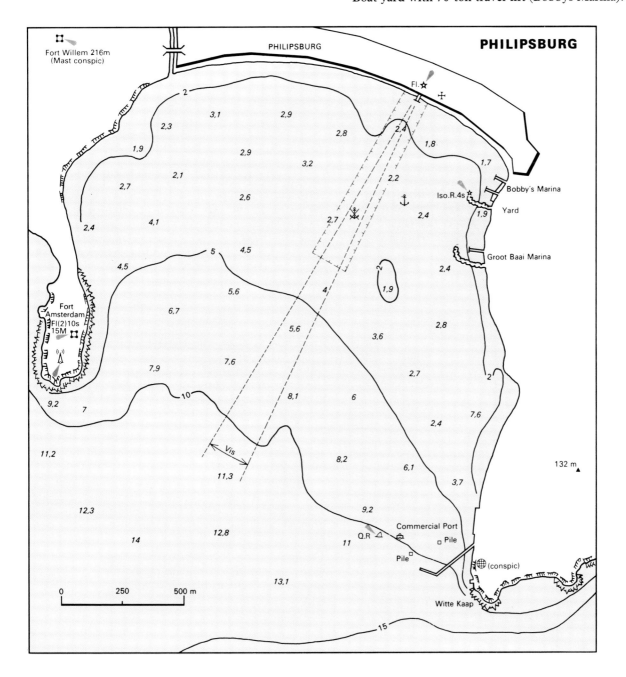

Fort Amsterdam   Mont Willem (mast)   Berth for merchant ships   Witte Kaap

Philipsburg looking NNW

Simson Baai. Entrance to approach channel leading to Grand Etang and lifting bridge

Simson Baai

18°02'·0N 63°06'·5W

Simson Baai is the best protected anchorage on the south coast in winter when the trade winds blow. The eastern arm is Pelican Point which has obstructions extending northwestward 400m. The whole bay viewed from seaward presents a 'mediterranean wall' of development.

Approach

There is no danger in the approach as long as one does not go too close to the coast of Pelican Point.

Anchorage

Anchor in the middle of the bay on sand according to draught.

Grand Etang

18°03'N 63°06'W

Grand Etang is a good hurricane hole but it gets crowded as yachts and coasters from far away seek shelter and it can get quite rough with waves of 1·5–2m. The holding is not good and there is much damage in storm conditions from other boats – but it is better than being outside.

Entrance

From Marigot: the swing bridge which crosses the approach channel opens between 0900 and 1700 hours just long enough to allow waiting boats to pass through. By lining up the sugar loaf shaped summit of Mont Fortune and the right hand side of a house with arcades on the western side of the channel on a bearing of 171° one may approach in depths which never decrease below 2m. Leave this alignment to go

around Mon Ronde at a distance of 50m. The width between the piles of the swing bridge is 7m and there are 4–5m depths. The current is often very strong. Once through the bridge, keep slightly to port along some reefs which are easy to see as far as the entrance channel to the marina dredged to a depth of 2·5–3m and buoyed. There are very irregular depths along the edges of this channel (1–3m). The swing bridge is in poor repair and the channel is silting; it is possible that this approach to Grand Etang will be closed whilst improvements are made. Inquire locally.

From Simson Baai The channel which has a lifting bridge marked by a conspicuous blue crane. The width between the piles is 8m. Opening times: 0600 and 1700. A red and green light, similar to a traffic light, controls movements.

Anchorage

At the Marigot end: there is a small marina but it is always very full. Otherwise anchor outside the channel, but go carefully.

At the Simson Baai end Anchor either in the inlet just east of the bridge or further north where there are 2–3m depths. Vessels drawing more than 2m must proceed with caution as the muddy bottom is very uneven.

Facilities

Water and electricity in the marina. There or elsewhere boatyards, chandlery, mechanics, sailmaker. Bars, restaurants and hotels.

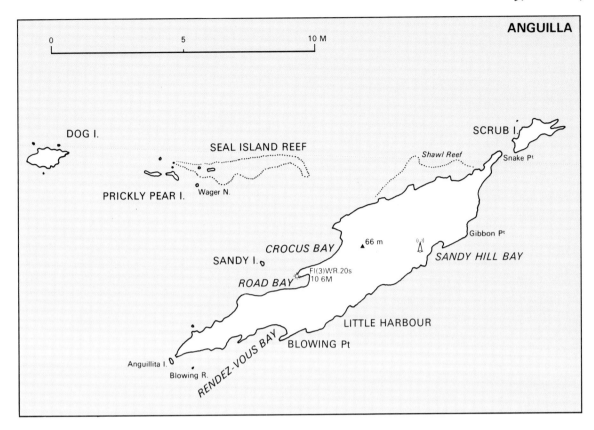

Anguilla and neighbouring islets

Coasts, dangers

The southern coast of Anguilla which is almost straight is bordered in several places by a coastal reef and it is advisable to keep more than 400m off the southern side of this. The clearest landmarks are those of Blowing Point (see page 197) and a radio mast WSW of Sandy Hill bay. Off the southwestern point of the island there is a low lying islet Anguillita on which there is a light and 0·3M ESE there is a small rock, Blowing Rock (1·8m). The channel between Anguilla and Anguillita is dangerous.

The western half of the northwest coast of the island is quite safe but the eastern half is not so. There are dangerous reefs extending almost 1M out to sea.

The northeastern tip of Anguilla is separated from Scrub Island (see page 196) by a wide channel which has 12m and no obstructions in the channel.

The islands and reefs to the northwest of the island are described on pages 198 and 199.

Road Bay

18°12'·0N 63°06'·5W

The commercial port of Anguilla lies in Road Bay and consists of a single landing stage for cargo boats but trade is so small that the peace of the anchorage is not disturbed. On the east coast lies the hamlet of Sandy Ground near a long sandy beach.

Entrance

The entrance is open except for a conspicuous wreck in the middle; pass either side but there is more room to the south.

Anchorage

Anchor in 3m on sand, WSW of the hamlet and 150m from the beach.

Facilities

A snack bar and two restaurants.

Road Bay looking E

195

Sandy Island

18°12'·6N 63°07'·2W

In fine weather and with no swell this is a splendid little anchorage by a sandy islet covered in coconut palms. It is 1·6M WNW of Road Bay.

Approach

Approach the centre of the islet from the southwest. There is a patch with less than 2m to the south of the islet and rocks awash to the northwest.

Anchorage

Anchor SW or W of the reef which surrounds the island in 4–6m on sand.

Crocus Bay

18°13'·3N 63°04'·5W

Northeast of Road Bay, Crocus Bay is not as well protected from the northeasterly swell. Two oil tanks at the northern end of the beach provide a good landmark.

Anchorage

Anchor in 5m on sand about 150m from the shore.

Shoal Bay and Island Harbour

18°15'·5N 63°01'W

Island Harbour houses the local fishing fleet. Both it and Shoal Bay have extremely tricky entrances which should only be attempted with local knowledge, in calm conditions without swell and have to be done by eye. Do not forget that coral grows.

Approach

Shawl Rock, which is north of Shoal Point about 450m out from the reef, and Seven Stars reef break heavily. A course of 135° on to the northwest point of Island Harbour passes about 0·6M NE of Shawl rock, 375m NE of the first showing reef and the same distance SW of Seven Stars reef. This leads to the inner passage.

The inner passage can also be entered from the east and the west; it is narrow – the eastern passage narrows to less than 100m.

Entrances

Both bays are protected by their own reefs. The entrance to Island Harbour is north of Scilly Cay. The entrance to Shoal Bay is right under Shoal Point. Both entrances are very narrow indeed.

Anchorages

The two bays have many coral heads. Shoal Bay has about 1·8m, Harbour Bay 1·5m. Anchor towards the head of either bay – if you can get there.

Scrub Island

18°16'·9N 62°57'·5W

Scrub Island is edged on its western side by a large, very white beach in front of which there is a large reef. A narrow channel from this reef permits yachts drawing less than 2m to reach the beach over a clear, sandy seabed. This anchorage should only be used in calm seas for a temporary stop.

Sandy Hill Bay

18°13'·0N 63°06'·0W)

Sandy Hill Bay, 5·8M ENE of Blowing Point, can be identified from a radio mast to the west and a tourist complex with white houses on the eastern arm of the bay.

Entrance

Several coral reefs with very little water over them lie in the entrance and centre of this bay. Enter with caution keeping fairly close to the reef (which uncovers) off the eastern arm, then keep close to the eastern shore on a bearing of 320° towards a conspicuous villa with arcades.

Anchorage

Anchor in 4–6m in a sandy area, 100m from the northwest beach.

Villa with colonades

Tourist complex

Sandy Hill looking NW

Little Harbour

18°10'·7N 63°02'·7W

Little Harbour is an anchorage used by fishermen. It is a wide bay enclosed by a reef. It is only suitable for a visit in calm weather without swell.

Entrance

A narrow channel with 5m about 200m from the western arm of the bay provides the entrance to the lagoon.

Anchorage

Anchor a little to the east of a deserted beach near which an isolated coconut palm is conspicuous (2–3m

depths). Be on the lookout for isolated outcrops of coral. The central and eastern parts of Little Harbour are only accessible for small craft.

Blowing Point

18°10'·0N 63°06'·0W

Blowing Point is a port of entry on an extremely small scale: two small landing stages, a customs post and a few little houses on the shore of a sandy lagoon almost enclosed by reefs. It is the landing point for the small passenger craft which provide a continuous service between Anguilla and St Martin.

S side of Blowing Point

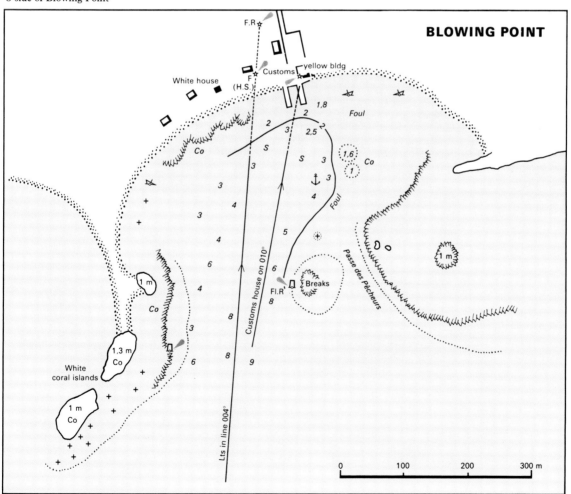

Approach

The square yellow customs house is a good landmark and the coral headland which forms the western arm of the entrance is easy to identify. Approach on a heading of 010° towards the customs house to find the entrance channel which is marked by two easily distinguishable beacons.

Anchorage

Anchor south of the landing stage in 2·5–3m. The eastern part of the bay is unsafe.

Rendezvous Bay and Cove Bay

18°10'·0N 63°07'·5W

This wide bay bordered by a long white beach is sheltered from the east by Shaddick Point on which some villas can be seen.

Round this point at a distance of 200m and anchor in 3–4m depths approximately 150m from the east coast where there are two ruined landing stages. Avoid the western half of the bay which is full of wrecks.

Cove Bay, 1·5M further west, is a sandy inlet where local fishing boats anchor. A hotel with arcades is being built on the north coast. Keep well off the shore when rounding the eastern arm of the bay to avoid the reefs which project some 140m towards the WSW. Anchor in 2·7m depths, 120m from the eastern shore.

Prickly Pear Island

18°16'·0N 63°11'·3W

Prickly Pear consists of two islets, very close together off the western tip of Seal Island Reef, Northwest of Anguilla. This is a magnificent anchorage in a clear lagoon between the eastern islet and the coral reef. The anchorage can be dangerous in swell which may get up at short notice. It is inadvisable to stay overnight.

Approach

Two approaches are possible: either pass to the west then to the north of the western islet or take the channel, narrow but quite safe, between the two islets, 3·5m minimum depths. The current can be strong in this channel.

Anchorage

Anchor in 3–5m on sand, north or south of the rock called Prickly Pear North. There are coral heads scattered throughout the cays but beware particularly of isolated outcrops of coral to the east of this rock. Yachts drawing less than 2m can, with care, reach the small lagoon in front of the beach through a narrow channel near the shore of Prickly Pear East.

In fine weather it is possible to anchor south of Seal Island Reef, a long coral reef from which several sandbanks and islets emerge of which the largest islet is Seal Island (4m) itself. It should be approached with extreme caution as none of the charts are exact for this area.

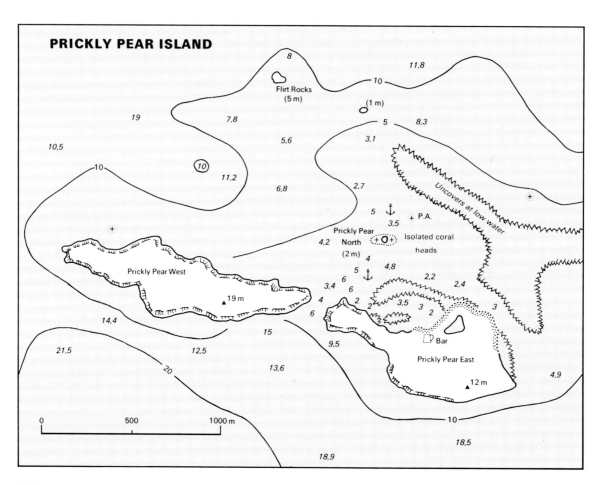

Dog Island

18°14′·6N 63°15′·3W

Dog Island, 3M west of Prickly Pear can only be approached when the sea is absolutely calm.

Anchor in 4–6m depths near the south coast where it is easy to go ashore. Watch out for a small rock (Bay Rock) about 200m off the shore.

XII. The Virgin Islands

Charts
Imray-Iolaire *A23, A231, A232*
Admiralty *2008, 2019, 2452, 485, 130*
US *25609, 25611, 25641, 25647, 25649, 25644, 25645*

General remarks

Geography

The Virgin Islands consist of a large group of islets and rocks all close together and situated on a bank extending about 90M ENE of Puerto Rico, to which St Croix, standing about 30M south on the far side of a very deep ocean trench, is attached politically. For the sailor, the Virgin Islands owe their reputation to the great beauty of their coastline with its numerous bays and creeks with beaches of very fine sand. They are almost all in sheltered waters and are particularly well suited to a seaward approach. With the exception of Anegada the islands are volcanic though dormant. The terrain is hilly (the highest peak, in St Thomas, is 472m) and the coastline is generally very indented. Anegada is coral, very low lying (9m) and surrounded by reefs. With lower rainfall than the other islands of the Lesser Antilles, the Virgins have in some areas a typically tropical vegetation and in others scrubland and cactus plants which are almost Mediterranean in appearance.

The eastern islands, the Tobagos, Jost Van Dyke, Tortola, Virgin Gorda, Anegada and the neighbouring small islands are a British crown colony with a governor appointed by the British crown responsible for external affairs, defence and internal security, supported by a legislative assembly, partly elected, for other matters.

The western islands, St Thomas, St John and St Croix, are under the jurisdiction of the United States, administered by the Department of the Interior and technically are 'unincorporated territory'. There is an elected Governor and an elected single chamber legislature with limited powers. Though their inhabitants are US citizens they may not vote in Presidential elections and their representative in Congress has no vote.

Agriculture (livestock, fish, fruit, vegetables and animal feedstuffs) and Industry (rum, watch assembly, pharmaceuticals), such as they are, tend to be on the British Virgins and St Croix. St Thomas is given over to Government and tourism which also provides three quarters of the income of the British Virgins.

History

The Virgin Islands were named by Christopher Columbus who discovered them in 1494 during his second voyage. Like all the Lesser Antilles they were fought over for a long time and often changed hands between the Spanish, Dutch, English and the Danes. Pirates and buccaneers such as Captain Kidd, Francis Drake, George Bond 'Black Beard' also used the islands as safe havens on the return route of the Spanish galleons. The British and the Danes lasted longest. Whilst there is still a British presence in the eastern islands, after two and a half centuries of uninterrupted occupation the Danes sold St Croix, St Thomas and St John to the United States in 1917 for twenty-five million dollars. Their presence for so long explains the typically Nordic style of architecture in the US islands' capitals.

Arrival

Most yachts arriving in the Virgin Islands come either from the Leeward Islands, that is to say from ESE, or from Puerto Rico.

Approaching from ESE it is wise to plan to arrive in daylight as lighthouses on the islands and the numerous small islands which surround them are few and far between and not very powerful. The first landmark, sometimes seen from more than 20 miles away, is the summit of Virgin Gorda (416m) shaped like a wide cone. Subsequently the whole island gradually comes into view with the south western part (148m) appearing to be separate, then the hills of Tortola and the small islands on the southern side of the Sir Francis Drake Channel. Round Rock Channel, between Round Rock and Ginger Island, is the safest entry. There is a lighthouse on Ginger island and an aerobeacon on Beef Island though this only operates when a plane is expected. A vessel approaching east of Virgin Gorda may be set north towards Anegada, which is very flat and never visible.

Road Harbour on Tortola is the main port of entry for the British Islands.

Coming from Puerto Rico should present no difficulty as land can be kept in sight.

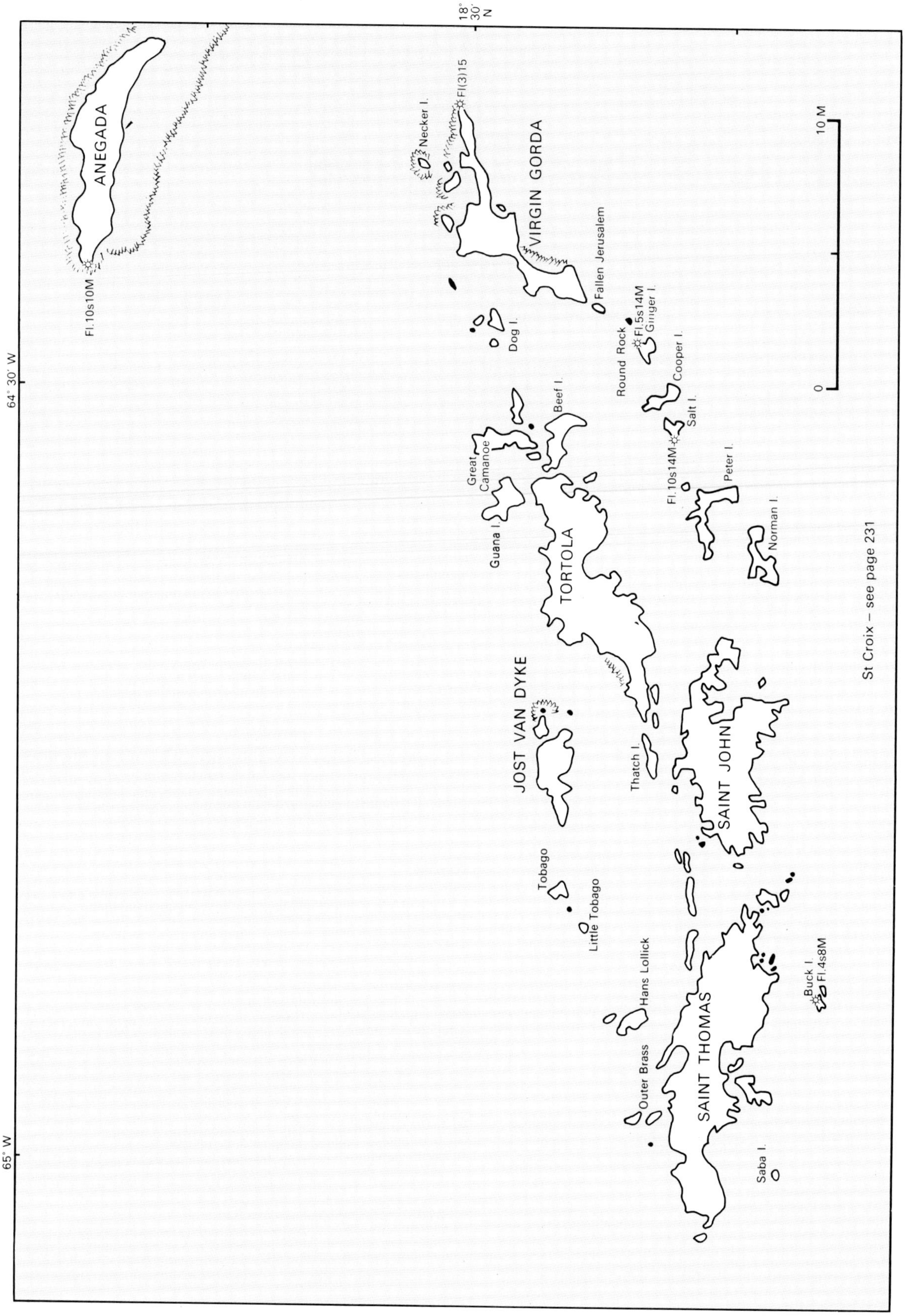

ANEGADA

Fl.10s10M

64° 30′ W

65′ W

18°
30′
N

Necker I.

☆ Fl(3)15

VIRGIN GORDA

Dog I.

Fallen Jerusalem

Round Rock

☆ Fl.5s14M
Ginger I.

Cooper I.

Salt I.

Fl.10s14M ☆

Peter I.

Norman I.

Beef I.

Great
Camanoe

Guana I.

TORTOLA

JOST VAN DYKE

Thatch I.

SAINT JOHN

Tobago

Little Tobago

Hans Lollick

Outer Brass

SAINT THOMAS

Saba I.

Buck I.
☆ Fl.4s8M

10 M

0

St Croix – see page 231

Formalities

Entry ports are as follows:

The British islands: Jost Van Dyke, Tortola (Road Harbour and Westend) and Virgin Gorda Yacht Harbour

The US islands: St Thomas (Charlotte Amalie, Redhook Bay), St John (Cruz Bay), St Croix (Christiansted).

The US Virgin Islands are a separate customs area; they are not part of the US and Puerto Rico area. Movement between the three, the US Virgins, the UK Virgins and the USA, requires customs clearance on arrival in each area.

Flags

The British Islands: the British blue ensign with the arms of the territory in the fly.

The US islands: white ground, centre a large gold eagle with outstretched wings with a blue topped white shield with 13 red stripes. The letters V and I on either side in blue.

Maintenance

Yacht yards at Road Harbour, Tortola; Nanny Cay, Tortola; Sopers Hole, Tortola; Yacht Harbour, Virgin Gorda; Charlotte Amalie, St Thomas; Christiansted, St Croix;

Communications

Airfields on St Croix and St Thomas have scheduled flights to Europe, the USA and St Martin. Beef Island airfield, 16km from Road Town, Tortola, has scheduled flights to Puerto Rico and St Kitts. There are air and ferry services between the islands.

Buses, car hire etc

VHF shore stations on St Thomas (Ch 25 and 28) and Tortola (Ch 27).

Hurricane holes

None can be suggested. Overcrowding is considerable and the standard of seamanship, particularly of anchoring, generally very low. In an otherwise safe haven, the chances of escaping a dragging vessel are slim.

Virgin Gorda and Anegada

Coasts, dangers

The central part of Virgin Gorda is dominated by Virgin Peak (416m) with a conspicuous white pylon on its northern side. The only lighthouse on the island (Fl(3)15s16M) is situated on the eastern extremity (Pajaros Point) which is rocky and indented. A line of islets and rocks is to be found off the southwestern tip of the island and the southern-most of these, Round Rock (57m) is sheer on the seaward side. The channels between Round Rock and Virgin Gorda are dangerous. Several other islands and reefs off the northeast of the island almost surround Gorda Sound and Eustatia Sound where the shores are unsafe (see page 205).

Elsewhere there are no dangers outside a line joining the main headlands of the coast. The islets and steep rocks which extend off the northwestern coast are easily identifiable and comparatively safe.

Anegada is very low-lying (7m) and surrounded by unmarked reefs which extend for more than 9M SSE. These reefs are particularly irregular and difficult to pick out to the south of the island. The only point at which it is safe to approach is near the eastern tip (see page 208).

Virgin Gorda Yacht Harbour

18°27′·1N 64°26′·2W

This yacht harbour built in an ancient lagoon near Spanish Town, the main village of the island provides perfect shelter in a modern, attractively developed setting. It is often extremely full.

Approach

A red and white radio mast (conspicuous in Spanish Town) lined up with the landing stage for local boats, on a bearing of 105°, leads to the entrance of the marked channel. This leads to the port entrance behind a reef covered with very little water. Depths are more than 3m in the channel and in most of the port. To reserve a place, call on Ch 16 or tie up to the south quay. It is also possible to anchor in 7–10m, sand and weed, in the northwest of the port in St Thomas Bay where Colison Point gives some shelter. There are shoal patches off the beach and the bay is dangerous in a strong northerly which occurs occasionally in winter.

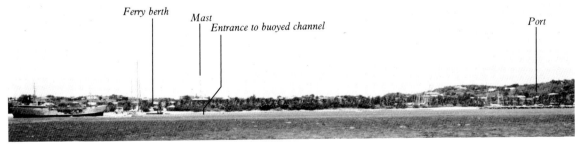

Ferry berth Mast Entrance to buoyed channel Port

Virgin Gorda Yacht Harbour

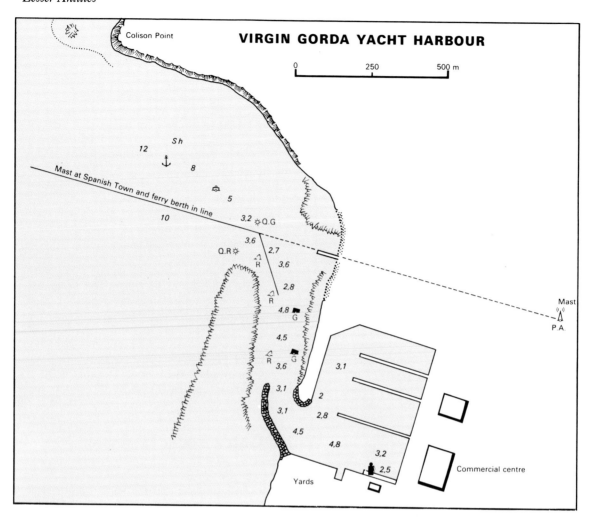

Colison Point

VIRGIN GORDA YACHT HARBOUR

0   250   500 m

Sh

12

8

Mast at Spanish Town and ferry berth in line

5

10

3,2 ☼ Q.G

3,6

Q.R ☼   2,7

R

3,6

2,8

R

4,8

G

4,5

R   G

3,6

3,1

2

3,1

2,8

4,5

4,8

3,1

3,2

2,5

Yards

Commercial centre

Mast
P.A.

Approach to Virgin Gorda Yacht Harbour

Facilities

Water, electricity, fuel at the quay. Showers. Supplies from the port shopping centre and in Spanish Town, bar and restaurant.
Boatyard with 60-ton travel-lift, repairs of all kinds.

The Baths

18°25'·8N 64°26'·8W

The Baths is the name given to a series of small sandy beaches near the southwestern end of Virgin Gorda. The beaches are extremely white and there are coconut palms amongst piles of enormous granite blocks polished by erosion. The beauty of this setting – the most famous in the Virgin Islands – is enhanced by the exceptional clarity of the water. The anchorage in the Baths is easily accessible but often uncomfortable because of the swell but it is worth even a short stay just to see this extraordinary geological curiosity.

Anchorage

Anchor 100m from the shore in 8–12m depths on sand and weed. There is room for one or two boats in the middle of the most southerly bay in 5–6m depths on sand, lying to two anchors to avoid swinging.

The spectacular rock formations at The Baths, Virgin Gorda.
Anne Hammick

Savana Bay

18°28'·3N 64°25'·4W

This beautiful bay on the northwest coast of the island is almost entirely enclosed by a reef covered by
very little water and has four deserted beaches (one
small one to the south, two larger ones to the south
east, one small one to the northeast). It is a little frequented anchorage only practicable if there is no
northerly swell. The light must be right when approaching it so that the reefs can be identified. A
white villa standing alone on the east coast is a good
landmark for the bay. Enter through a channel with
5·5m depths keeping 100m off the west point of the
bay and heading ESE. On the inside of the reef there
are depths of 11–14m decreasing towards the
beaches.

Anchorage
Anchor in front of the westernmost of the two large
beaches in 4–6m, 100m from the shore. To reach this
anchorage yachts must pass across a coral shelf with
3–4m depths which runs parallel to the coast and
150–200m off it. The beaches further to the north
east are also accessible but must be approached with

care, in particular look out for a reef covered with
very little water 150–200m from the shore between
the two big beaches.

Gorda Sound

18°30'N 64°22'W

Gorda Sound is a vast bay enclosed to the north by a
chain of green islands and reefs amongst which there
are several anchorages. Groups of villas and hotels
have been built here to the east and to the south but
the greater part of the coast remains undeveloped.
On the eastern side Gorda Sound joins the well-
sheltered lagoon, Eustatia Sound.

Approach channels
Approaching from the east take care to avoid the
dangerous shoal, the Invisibles, east of Necker Island
and the reefs in the southern half of Virgin Sound
which are difficult to see.

The main approach to Gorda Sound is through the
northern channel between Colquhoun Reef, which is
easily identifiable (largely uncovering) and the partly
hidden reefs off the northwest point of Prickly Pear
Island. This channel, 150m wide and 6m deep is
marked by two buoys. The western approach to the
south of Mosquito Island has minimum depths of

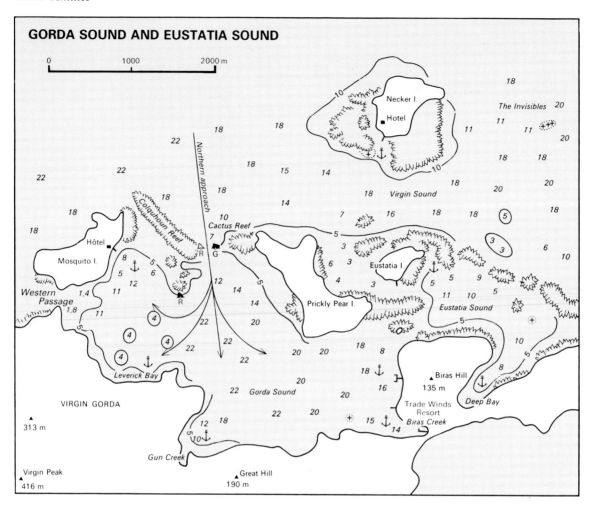

GORDA SOUND AND EUSTATIA SOUND

Gorda Sound looking S

Gorda Sound. Biras Hill looking E.

1·8m. Enter the channel, steering due east as far as the narrowest point, then on a heading of 115° to avoid the shoals south east of Mosquito Island.

The channel between Prickly Pear Island and Eustatia Island leads to Eustatia Sound. Enter the channel keeping 150m from the northeastern coast of Prickly Pear Island until the landing stage on the southern point of Eustatia Island comes into view. Head east to pass 80m to the south of this landing stage and continue on the same bearing for 350m before turning south.

To pass from Eustatia Sound to Gorda Sound take the channel between Saba Rock and Biras Hill, keeping 50m off the latter. Minimum depths are 2·3m.

Anchorages

Mosquito Island Anchor in 5–9m depths on sand, ESE of the landing stage of a solitary hotel which stands on the southeast coast of the island near a beach bordered with coconut palms. In the approach keep well clear of the shoals south of Colquhoun Reef which are marked by a discoloured buoy.

Leverick Bay On the coast of Virgin Gorda is a tourist centre with a hotel and villas. A small marina (3–5m depths) provides all services at the quay (water, electricity and fuel) and buoyed moorings for passing yachts. This anchorage is open to scend from the northeast.

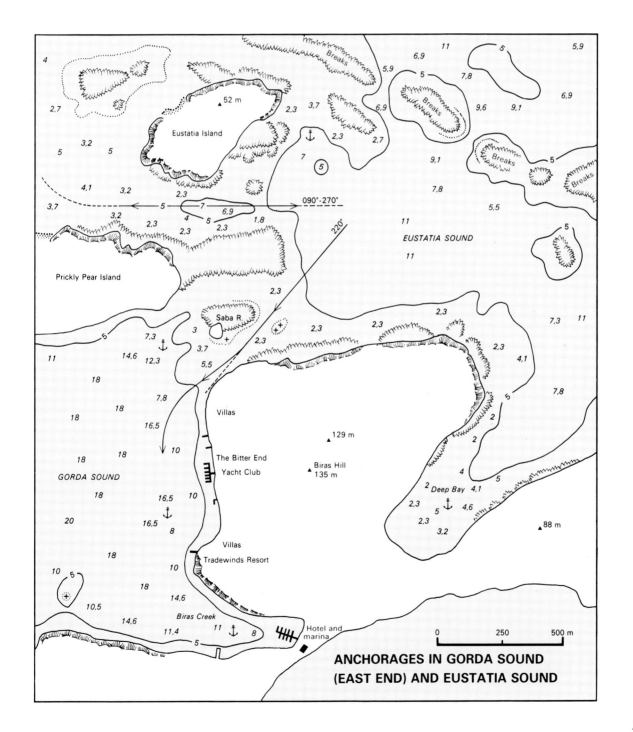

ANCHORAGES IN GORDA SOUND (EAST END) AND EUSTATIA SOUND

Gun Creek Where there is a landing stage for Creek Village is also open to scend from the east and northeast. Anchor in 6–10m depths towards the opening at the head of the bay.

The Bitter End Yacht Club On the west coast of Biras Hill is a tourist complex consisting of a hotel, restaurant, villas and complete services for yachts (water, electricity, fuel, showers). There are fifteen or so places at the quay and a large number of mooring buoys in 6–14m depths. There is not much room to anchor.

The Tradewinds Resort Owned by and just south of the Bitter End Yacht Club, can be identified by a group of villas with brown roofs on the hillside. There is a landing stage with water and fuel (4–5m depths) and mooring buoys.

Biras Creek There is a marina with about twenty places at the quay in 2·5–4·5m depths. There is also a good anchorage in 8–11m depths on sand and weed in the middle of this creek but the setting is unattractive.

Eustatia Sound Has some very quiet anchorages in Deep Bay (3·5–4·5m depths, sand, 200m from the beach) and between the reefs approximately 100m ESE of the east point of Eustatia Island (3–4m depths, sand).

Necker Island

18°31'·5N 64°21'·6W

This steep-cliffed island, surrounded by reefs, has a conspicuous hotel, royally patronised, with two brown pointed roofs standing on the southwestern headland. There is a landing stage on the south coast.

From the middle of Virgin Sound head north towards this hotel and pass between the reefs to the southwest of the island. Anchor 80m southwest of the landing stage in 3–3·5m, fine sand.

Rounding the southwest point of the island at a distance of 25m leads to an anchorage in 3m depths on sand, between the attractive beach of the west coast and a line of barely covered reefs 80–100m to seaward.

South Sound

18°29' N 64°23'W

South Sound, the only anchorage on the southeastern coast of Virgin Gorda is a lagoon well sheltered by a barrier of coral, 2m high at its centre. This lagoon is rarely visited by yachts. The approach, which must be undertaken with care, should not be contemplated at all unless the east to southeast swell is moderate and the light is favourable (sun in the east).

Approach
The entrance channel, near the north coast of the bay has an isolated shoal with less than 1·5m over it.

Approach on a northerly bearing towards Great Hill and be sure to identify the reef: a pile of coral emerging at the centre and the northern tip awash with the

water breaking over it. Head northwest towards this, leaving to starboard the shoal in the entrance (the channel between the two is about 60m wide and 15m deep). Round the steep, north side of the reef at a distance of 30m and continue in a westerly direction towards a beach bordered by coconut palms.

Anchorage
Anchor in 3m depths on sand in front of this beach. The hurricane hole surrounded by mangroves in the south of the lagoon can only be approached by keeping about 40m off the west coast. It has 2–3m decreasing to 1·5m over half its area and can only hold a few boats.

Anegada

18°43'·4N 64°23'·2W

Anegada is rarely visited by yachts because the only sheltered anchorage near Setting Point has to be approached with great care and then only by yachts drawing less than 2m.

Its shores, which are almost deserted are bordered by vast white sandy beaches in front of a shallow coral lagoon which can be explored by dinghy.

Approach
The approach to the Setting Point anchorage should only be attempted in fine weather and with the sun high so that the reefs and isolated coral heads in the approaches can be seen through the clear water. Extreme vigilance and caution is necessary as the marks (scanty at best) have disappeared in places.

A good approach is on 351° to West End. Remember the current, which bears towards the east. The following landmarks will come into view: two clusters of tall trees east and north of the anchorage, then West End and the very white beach of Pomato Point on which there are two houses (one conspicuous with a white roof) and lastly a greyish brown square building near the landing stage. Enter with caution on a bearing of 050° from this building leaving a single (1988) red buoy to starboard.

Anchorage
The best anchorage is in the shelter of Setting Point Reef in 1·8–2·3m depths on sand. Anegada Reef Hotel has 10 moorings; contact on Ch 16. There are two restaurants on the waters edge.

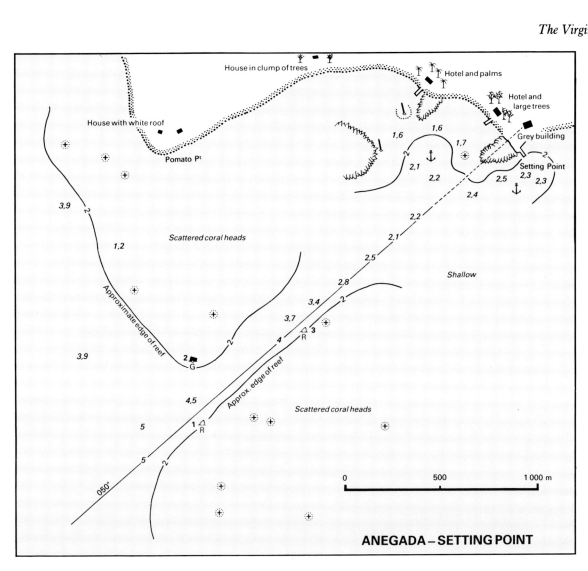

House in clump of trees
House with white roof
Pomato Pt
Hotel and palms
Hotel and large trees
Grey building
Setting Point

3,9
1,2
Scattered coral heads
Approximate edge of reef
3,9
2 G
4,5
1 R
5
5
2
050°
2 G
4
3 R
3,4
3,7
2,8
2,5
2,1
2,2
2,4
2,2
2,1
1,7
1,6
1,6
2,5
2,3
2,3
Shallow
Scattered coral heads

0   500   1 000 m

ANEGADA – SETTING POINT

House and clump of trees
Hotel and coconut palms
Hotel and clump of trees
Grey building
Red buoy

Anegada. SW side of anchorage at Setting Point

Hotel and clump of trees
Grey building
Landing

Anegada. Conspicuous marks at Setting Point

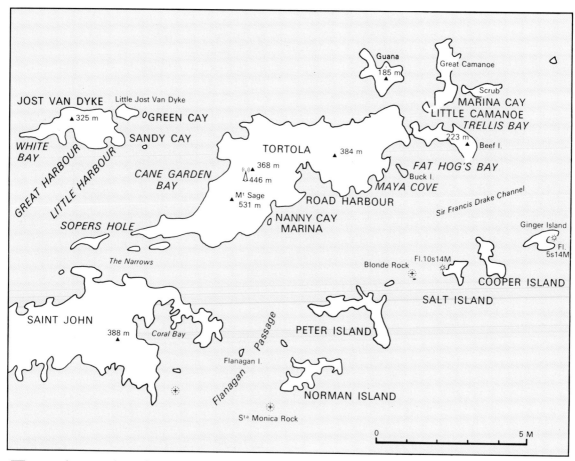

Tortola and neighbouring islands

Coasts, dangers

Tortola is the most important of the Virgin Islands. It is mountainous and the coasts are steep-to but quite safe except within the bays. Off the west end are two steep islands Great and Little Thatch Cays. Off the east end there are seven small islands which are quite safe on the seaward side and with usable channels on the landward side (see page 215).

The clearest landmarks on the island are two large radio masts one of which has parabolic aerials visible from all directions except the southwest. These are on a height (531m) 2M WNW of Stanley Point. There are three yacht harbours on Tortola and numerous anchorages.

Jost van Dyke (352m) less than 3M NW of Tortola is a steep and safe island with several good anchorages. About 2M to the west the islets of Tobago and Little Tobago have no shelter to offer. 0·5M south of Tobago is an isolated rock awash. The south side of the Sir Francis Drake channel, 2·3–3M south east of Tortola is made up of a series of volcanic rocks. A number of easily accessible anchorages are to be found here. Three separate dangers should be noted: Santa Monica Rock (3m) 0·8M SW of Norman Island, Carrot Shoal (2·7m) in the middle of the channel between that island and the south point of Peter Island and Blond Rock (2·7m) 1M west of Salt Island.

Jost Van Dyke

This steep and sparsely populated island has several pleasant anchorages on the south coast and near the islets off its east coast.

Great Harbour, a port of entry, is a deep bay on the south coast and one of the most beautiful in the islands. It is well protected from the prevailing winds. It is bordered by the houses of a small village scattered amongst the hibiscus and coconut palms near a long white sandy beach. From a distance the customs house (white) and the church (yellow with a red roof) can be seen.

Approach

There is no difficulty in the approach provided one does not go too close to either shore.

Anchorage

Anchor in 6–8m on sand, 300m from the beach off which there are reefs.

Facilities

There are two restaurant bars ashore.

White Bay just to the west of Great Harbour is partly enclosed by a coral reef and bordered by two beautiful beaches. Two black and white markers (a square

Jost Van Dyke. Great Harbour

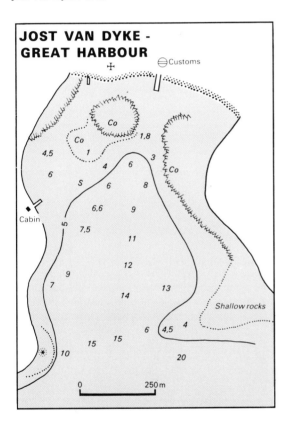

JOST VAN DYKE - GREAT HARBOUR

⊖Customs

Co

Co
Co
1,8

4,5
1
6
4
6
3
Co
S
6
6
8

6,6
9

Cabin
5
7,5

11

12

9
7
13
14

Shallow rocks

6
4,5
4

15
15
6

10
20

0   250m

and a triangle), difficult to see, on a bearing of 360°
lead to the entry of the channel which is marked by
two small red buoys. There are 3m depths in the
channel and from 1·8–2·6m in the lagoon which is
tiny. This anchorage is very prone to swell and easily
becomes uncomfortable and even untenable. There is
a restaurant ashore.

Little Harbour is a small bay near the south east point
of the island. It is bordered by rocky cliffs where
several small houses (three of which are restaurants)
can be seen in fairly arid surroundings. Enter keeping clear of both shores off which there are rocky
shoals. There are depths of 14–16m in the centre
which decrease rapidly over a narrow coastal shelf

(4–6m). It is preferable to anchor in the northwestern
arm in 4–10m on sand. There are moorings (which
can be rented) near the landing stages in the north
east corner.

Green Cay is a rocky island joined to Little Jost Van
Dyke by a reef and projecting southwards in the
form of another reef which uncovers and a sand bank
covered in vegetation (Sandy Spit). A shelf about
150m wide with 2·5m depths, easy to see through the
clear water, extends westwards from Sandy Spit reef.
Anchor on sand with good holding (there are a few
areas of coral). Do not anchor on the edge of the
shelf as depths increase suddenly from 5–6m to
12–16m. This anchorage is not comfortable in a
swell.

Sandy Cay is a low wooded island bordered in the
southwest by a very white beach. In fine weather anchor on the sandbank to the west of the beach (3–6m
depths). The northeast and south coasts of the islet
are not safe.

Road Harbour

18°25′N 64°37′W

Road Harbour is a large bay surrounded by hills in
which the small capital of the British Virgin Islands,
Roadtown (3000 inhabitants) is situated. The commercial port (a quay on the northeastern shore of the
bay) is of far less importance than the installations of
the yacht harbour which make Road Harbour one of
the main yachting centres of the Antilles. It is a port
of entry and a useful port of call on the technical side
but the natural surroundings are of little interest.

Approach

In the entrance to Road Harbour there are several
buoyed sandbanks with 3–4m of water with wide
channels between them. The best landmark is a
group of white oil tanks on the eastern shore of the
entrance. Enter either through the main channel or
keeping 300m off the west coast to pass between it
and Lark Banks and Denmark Banks.

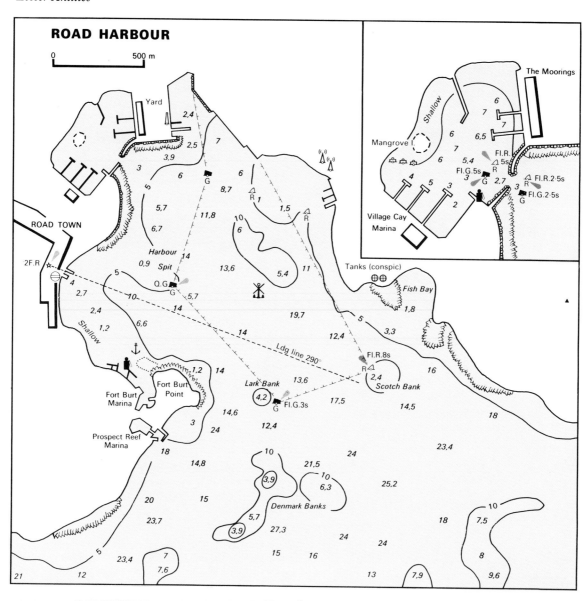

ROAD HARBOUR

0   500 m

Yard

ROAD TOWN

2F.R

The Moorings

Mangrove I.

Shallow

Village Cay
Marina

Fl.R.
5s

Fl.G.5s

Fl.R.2·5s

Fl.G.2·5s

Harbour
Spit

Q.G

Tanks (conspic)

Fish Bay

Ldg line 290°

Fl.R.8s

Fort Burt
Point

Fort Burt
Marina

Lark Bank

Scotch Bank

Fl.G.3s

Prospect Reef
Marina

Denmark Banks

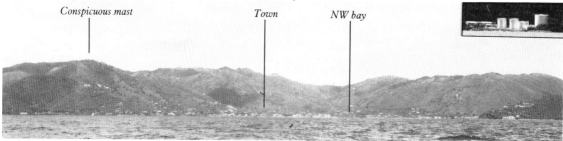

Conspicuous mast   Town   NW bay

Road Harbour looking NW

Road Harbour. Entrance to NW bay

Anchorage

Anchor temporarily 100m off the customs pontoon in 3–4m to carry out the necessary formalities (this anchorage is often uncomfortable and the holding is poor). The harbour in the northwest is well protected with 3m depths in the narrow entrance. It is possible to tie up to the quay of the Moorings (VHF Ch 12) or of Village Cay Marina (VHF Ch 16) if places are available. A small anchorage in the centre of the harbour is always very full.

It is also possible to anchor north of Fort Burt Marina in 2·2–6m depths on sand. Look out for unmarked shallows with very little water over them WNW of Fort Burt Point (extending about 60m North east of Fort Burt Marina Quay) and those near the west coast of the bay.

Prospect Reef Marina, a tiny basin on the west side of the entrance to the bay is only accessible to yachts with a very shallow draught (1·5m through a very narrow channel).

Facilities

Water, electricity, showers, laundry at the moorings, Village Cay Marina and Fort Burt Marina. Two fuel points in Fort Burt Marina harbour.

Supplies: there is a well-stocked supermarket near the harbour, several restaurants and bars.

Boatyard with a lifting capacity up to 100 tons and repair and maintenance work of all kinds. Sailmaker, chandlery.

Communications

Car hire. Airfield at Beef Island (see page 203).

Nanny Cay Marina

18°24'·1N 64°38'·2W

This yacht harbour in a very well-sheltered mangrove lagoon offers complete services but is of no other interest for passing yachts.

Approach

The land marks are: the pink buildings with grey roofs of Nanny Cay Marina centre; a large square yellow house to the east of the entrance and the masts and sails which can be seen from a distance.

Approach

The approach channel between two reefs is marked by buoys. In the port keep very close to the landing

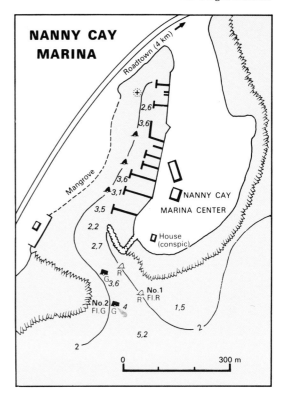

stages in order to avoid the shallows in the west bank which are only scantily marked and keep a constant watch on the depths as the seabed is very irregular.

Contact the harbour master (VHF Ch 16 and 68) for a place.

Facilities

Water, electricity, fuel. Showers, laundry, bar and restaurants.

Boat yard with a lifting capacity of 180 tons, sailmaker, chandlery.

Communications

Taxis.

Sopers Hole (West End)

18°23'·3N 64°42'·3W

Sopers Hole on the extreme west of the island is a well-sheltered bay surrounded by hills and bordered by the village of West End. It is a port of entry and a pleasant port of call with a small yacht marina (Stevens Yachts).

Nanny Cay Marina looking NNW

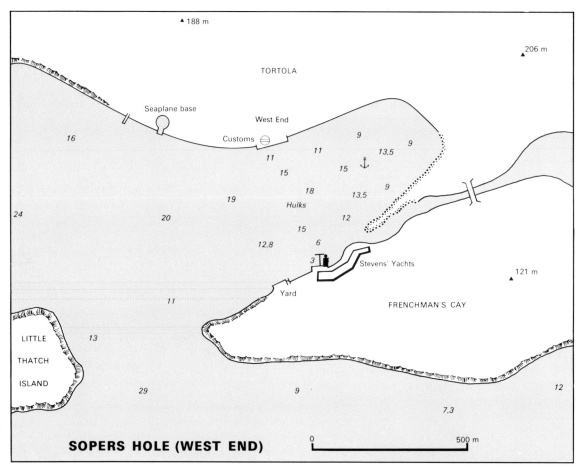

SOPERS HOLE (WEST END)

Approach

There are no dangers in the channels leading to Sopers Hole but there are strong currents which can reach three knots and there may be sudden changes of wind. The centre of the bay is very deep.

Anchorage

It is preferable to anchor in the eastern part in 12–15m on sand or to take one of the many moorings of Stevens Yachts (a charge is made). It is possible to come alongside at the customs quay but it is always very busy with small motor boats ferrying passengers and it is inadvisable to stay longer than necessary to carry out formalities.

Facilities

Water, electricity and fuel at Stevens Yacht Pontoon (3m depths).
Boatyard with slipway for 200 tons.
Supplies (limited) in the little market and the shops near the customs building. Several restaurants.

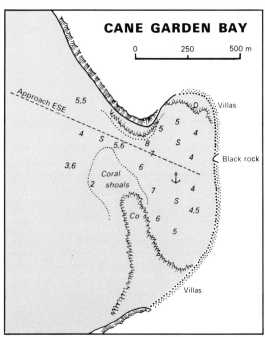

CANE GARDEN BAY

Cane Garden Bay

18°25'·8N 64°39'·6W

This beautiful bay surrounded by green hills is the only anchorage on the northwest coast of Tortola. The water is very clear and there is a long sandy beach with coconut palms. There are several hotels and villas round the shore.

Anchorages

It is inadvisable to anchor here if there is a swell. A reef and shoals cover three quarters of the southern side of the bay and there is another reef off the point on the north side. About 100m SSW of this point there is a channel leading ESE which is 5–6m deep. It is easy to see the light-coloured sand through the clear water.

There are 4–8m depths over sand in the bay except in the extreme north and in the south where there are coral reefs. Take one of the moorings – which are in the hands of Rhymers Beach Bar (in the middle of the beach).

On shore there are several bars and restaurants and a grocery.

Note Anchoring is forbidden in Brewers Bay, 1·2M northeast, where there are cables and extensive reefs.

Islands northeast of Tortola

Close to the northeastern tip of the island is a group of islands and islets consisting of Guana, Little Camanoe, Great Camanoe, Scrub, Marina Cay and Beef Island. Beef Island is linked to Tortola by a bridge.

Channels

The channel between Tortola and Guana is safe. The channel between Beef Island and the two Camanoes has dangerous reefs marked by small buoys. The shallow southwest of Little Camanoe is marked by a green buoy which should be left to the north. Those off the north coast of Beef island extending to the middle of the channel are marked by two red buoys which should be left to the south.

The channel between Great and Little Camanoe is narrow but safe (a minimum of 4–6m in the south part) except for an uncovering reef near the southeastern point of Little Camanoe and a rock awash of its northeastern point.

Finally, the channel between Great Camanoe and Scrub is safe in the centre but there are reefs off both shores, particularly on the west side.

Anchorages

Guana Northwest of monkey Point, sand, 7m.
Great Camanoe Island. Lee Bay Keep in the centre and anchor in 6m, sand. Both these anchorages are affected by northerlies.

Marina Cay

18°27'·7N 64°31'·6W

Marina Cay, a green island with a hotel and several villas, is surrounded by a reef which extends 250m towards the southwest. A red buoy and several posts mark the southwestern tip of this reef.

Marina Cay looking ENE

Anchorage

There is a pleasant anchorage in clear water with 5–10m depths on sand to the west of the islet in the lee of the reef. A number of buoyed moorings for which a charge is made are available in this anchorage.

Facilities

Bar and restaurant in the hotel near the landing stage.

Trellis Bay

18°27'N 64°32'W

Trellis Bay on the north coast of Beef Island is a well-sheltered anchorage surrounded by a low-lying and arid shore but it is often very full. In the middle of the bay on Bellamy Cay there is a conspicuous hotel.

Approach

Leave to the south the red buoy which marks the shoals off the west end of the bay.

Anchorage

The best anchorage is in the eastern part of the bay in 2·5–4·5m depths on sand at a safe distance from both east and south coasts where there are shallows.

Facilities

Restaurants on Bellamy Cay and on the west coast.

Communications

Buses to Road Town and fast ferry to Gorda Sound. The airport is about a ¼M west of the anchorage.

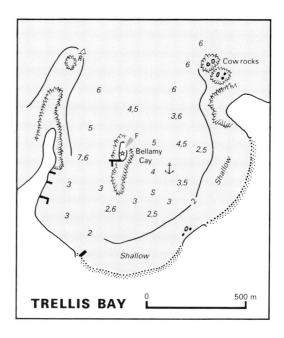

TRELLIS BAY

Fat Hogs Bay and Maya Cove

18°26′·2N 64°33′·7W

Fat Hogs Bay is bordered to the north by East End which has little attraction. It provides a well-sheltered anchorage in clear water for a bare boat fleet of 75 boats. It is only accessible well inshore to yachts drawing less than 1·8m.

Entrance

Enter leaving a group of reddish rocks (about 20m high) to the north and a green buoy to the south. Then head NNW, watching the depths.

Anchorage

1·8–2·5m on sand about 200–300m from the shore.

Maya Cove

Maya Cove, west of Buck Island is a small creek whose shores are covered in vegetation and well protected by an uncovering reef. It is a popular, calm, anchorage for live-aboards, a good alternative in a strong E or SE to Road Town which can be easily reached by ferry.

Approach

The approach is narrow and winds between the reefs which are marked by buoys. The entrance is on a heading of 345° towards a low white-roofed house standing on a height in the northeast of the creek. Follow the channel with caution in order to avoid a shelf where there are only 2m depths.

Anchorage

2·5–4m on sand in the shelter of the reef.

Facilities

There is a restaurant.

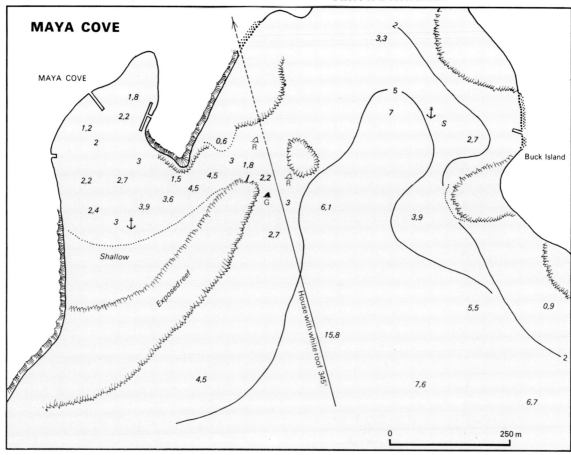

Maya Cove looking NNW

Norman Island

18°19′N 64°36′W

According to local legend, Norman Island is the 'Treasure Island' of Robert Louis Stevenson's famous novel. It is covered in scrub and cactus and has a large, deserted bay on the west coast (The Bite). The coasts are, on the whole, safe.

The Bite is well sheltered from prevailing winds and provides a good anchorage with plenty of room but it is much frequented by yachts. There are no dangers in the approach and the entrance is very deep. The best anchorage is in the eastern corner where the sea bed, sand and weed, is level, 10 and 6m at 100 and 50m from the beach. In the south eastern corner, where an old hulk, now a bar restaurant, is anchored there are 12m depths 100m from the beach.

Other anchorages

The approaches to the following three bays are safe and very deep. Anchor within 100m of the shore in 8–12m depths on sand, bearing in mind the probability of a sudden change in wind towards the west:

A small cove north of the entrance to the Bite, surrounded by rocky escarpments with knotted trees and huge creepers growing out of them.

Privateer Bay, south of the Bite, surrounded by low cliffs and with caves at sea level which are reputed to be the hiding place of Black Beard's treasure.

Brenures Bay on the north coast of the island, surrounded by scrub.

Peter Island

18°21′N 64°35′W

This is a dry and sparsely populated island which has several anchorages and a small yacht harbour.

Little Harbour, a pretty bay on the northeast coast, is not much frequented. It can be identified from a villa with a white roof standing predominantly on the northern arm of the bay. The approach is safe with considerable depths in the entrance. Anchor in 7–12m on sand and weed at the head of the bay where there are two privately-owned landing stages.

Deadman Bay, Peter Island, looking east towards Dead Chest Island.

Elizabeth Hammick

Conspicuous houses   *Entrance*

Peter Island Yacht Harbour. Approach from N

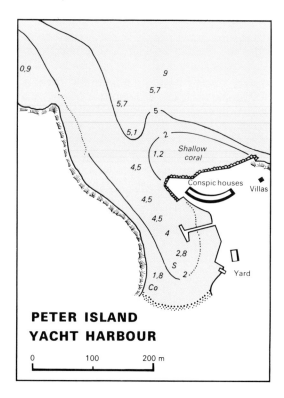

**PETER ISLAND
YACHT HARBOUR**

0   100   200 m

the south keep clear of Carrot Shoal (see page 210). Anchor in 5–6m depths on sand, 100m from the beach in the northeastern corner.

Salt Island and Cooper Island

18°22'·5N 64°31'·0W

Salt Island has only one fair-weather anchorage on its north coast near a beach bordered by coconut palms where the ruins of a village can be seen. Anchor in 7–10m depths on sand, 60m from the landing stage. The mooring buoy on the west coast of the island are for divers exploring the wreck of the steamer *Rhône*, sunk by a cyclone in 1867. They are government owned and free and are there to stop anchoring. They may not be used as overnight moorings.

The northwest coast of Cooper Island is bordered by a beach with coconut palms and the poisonous Manchineal; it has a bar restaurant. Either anchor in 10–12m depths approximately 60m from the beach or take one of the moorings (for which a charge is made) near the restaurant pontoon.

When passing through the channel between Salt and Cooper islands keep close to Cooper Island to avoid a dangerous rock northeast of Salt Island.

Great Harbour is large with sheer cliffs and considerable depths at the centre. The best anchorages are along the northeastern coast which is rocky in 14–17m depths. It is best to avoid the head of the bay where fishermen from the village spread their nets.

Peter Island Yacht Harbour, situated in a well-sheltered bay on the north coast is easy to identify from a group of houses with white roofs on the eastern arm of the entrance. Approach on a bearing of 165° towards the middle of the entrance in order to avoid the shoals in various places off both coasts (especially the east). Either tie up to the port pontoon (2–4m depths) or anchor in the southern part of the bay (2–2·8m depths, sand).

Deadman Bay, fringed by a sandy beach and a row of coconut palms, is prettier than those previously described but open to the swell which frequently comes round the northeastern part of the island. When entering be careful of the reefs off the east and west coasts. The best anchorage is in front of the beach in the southeastern corner in 3–6m depths on sand.

The south coast of the island forms one large bay not much frequented by yachts. When approaching from

St John

St John, the greenest of the Virgin Islands, has in contrast to St Thomas very little urban development as a national park covers two thirds of its area. The administrators of the national park control entry to some of the anchorages. From Cruz Bay (see page 221) it is possible to visit the interior of the island which is very beautiful and affords splendid views over other islands.

The coast, dangers

The North coast

Off the SW of Moravian Point, the western tip of St John is Mongo (Mingo) Rock, barely above sea level and a series of reefs the end of which is marked by a red buoy. 0·4M to the north of this point Cruz Bay (see page 221), in which there is the only port on the island, can easily be identified. 0·4M WNW of this same point Steven Cay (9m) is a rocky islet surrounded by rocks and reefs with a light on its northern point.

The north west coast of St John has several deep bays where it is possible to anchor. They are separated by headlands, of which Hawks Nest Point is the largest. Off this point are three steep islets between which it is possible to pass but where the current is often strong. The northern swell sometimes breaks on a shoal of 4·2m, 350m to the NNW of the eastern islet. Windward Passage between these islets and Lovango Cay is quite safe.

Further off to the ENE, Johnson Reef which is often difficult to see, extends over 0·3M. The north-ern extremity of this reef is marked by a green buoy (easily visible) and the southern extremity by a small red buoy. The channel on the landward side of the reef is safe. Mary Point, the northern tip of the island, is a high steep promontory (176m). 300m west is Whistling Cay (61m), the western part of which is unsafe.

Mary Point marks the southern shore of the entrance to The Narrows, a safe channel bounded to the north by Tortola and Thatch Cay. The current in this channel is capable of reaching 3 knots and the wind strengthens noticeably. The north coast of St John to the east of Mary Point is safe and offers several anchorages. The eastern tip of the island is safe close to as is also Flanagan Island (42m) 0·7M to the SE.

South Coast

Very indented between jutting but safe capes, the most prominent of which is Ram Head, the southern most tip of the island. The south coast is rocky and very steep.

Eagle Shoal (1m), unmarked, situated 0·9M ENE of Ram Head is the only danger on the route from cape to cape.

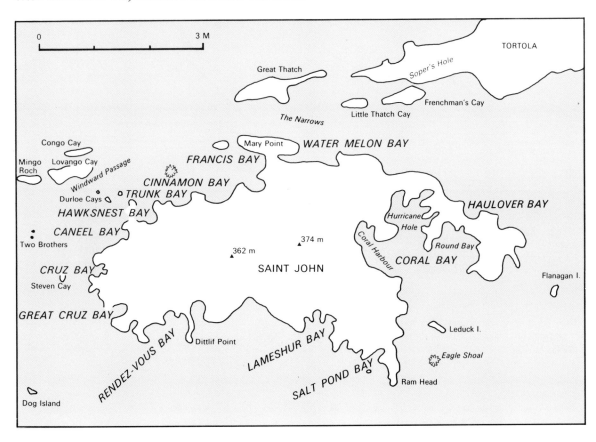

Cruz Bay looking E

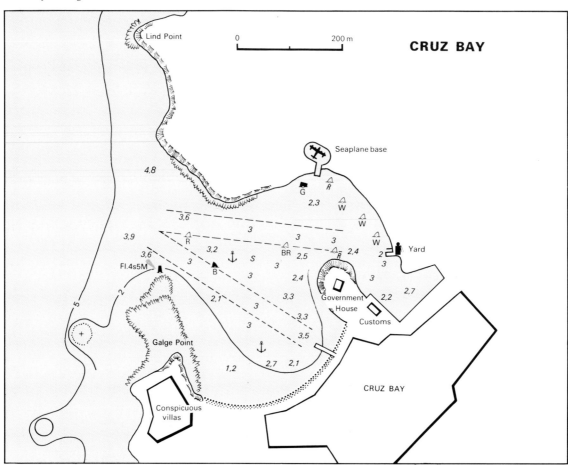

Cruz Bay

Cruz Bay

18°20′N 64°47′W

In Cruz Bay is the only port on St John. It is small and near a pretty village which lies amongst the vegetation and tropical flowers. It is the easiest port at which to carry out the formalities necessary when passing from the US to the British islands or vice versa but the anchorage is always very full.

Approach

From the west Cruz Bay can be identified by a group of light grey villas with light roofs situated conspicuously on Galge Point and by Government House, white with a red roof on Battery Point. Leave to starboard the buoy which marks Galge Point Reef and anchor either in the southern part of the bay, always very full, or WNW of Battery Point between the channels of approach to the port and to the southern landing stage (3–4m depths, sand). One may only tie up to the Customs Quay (2·2m depths) for the time required to carry out the formalities.

Facilities

Fuel at the quay (2·1m) in the northern creek, small boat yard with 10-ton travel-lift, many bars and restaurants. Car and scooter rental, bus tours of the island.

Bays on the northwestern coast of St John

On this coast are to be found some of the most beautiful bays of the islands in enchanting and almost deserted natural settings. The anchorages are in crystal clear water near beaches of white sand backed by hills covered in tropical forests. With the exception of Francis Bay these anchorages are open to a northern swell.

Caneel Bay, 0·8M NW of Cruz Bay, is bordered by two beaches, one to the east, the other to the south. Some buildings can be seen close to the eastern beach where there is a landing stage, the approach to which is marked by buoys. Anchor on sand in 4–5m about 150m from the eastern beach outside the buoyed channel. It is also safe to anchor close to the southern beach where there is a footpath leading to Cruz; this is handy for groceries or clearing when Cruz is packed. Another bay, 0·3M further north, affords a similar anchorage (6–8m depths, 120–150m from the beach).

Hawksnest Bay is less busy but very open to the swell. Anchor in front of any of the three beaches (west, south and south east) in 5–9m depths, sand. Beware of the reef 100m off the southern beach.

The anchorage in Trunk Bay is bounded to the east by the rocky islet Trunk Cay (15m). Anchor southwest of this islet in 7–10m depths in front of a deserted beach. The southwest corner of the bay is unsafe.

Cinnamon Bay is similar with a rocky islet (18m) in the eastern part. There is a wreck in the centre. Anchor in 6–8m depths to the WSW of the islet which is joined to the coast by a reef.

Francis Bay, which is very wide, is the best anchorage on the north coast. This can be approached through Fungi Passage which is safe but subject to sudden shifts of wind. Anchor preferably in the north

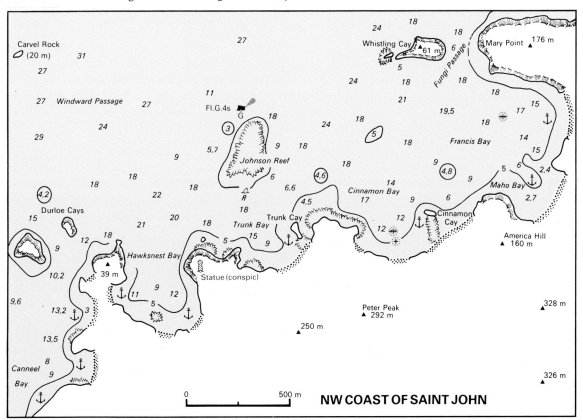

NW COAST OF SAINT JOHN

eastern part of the bay on sand and weed in 12–14m depths. The south eastern creek called Maho (Mahoe) Bay has shoals in the whole of the south-western half.

Bays on the north coast of St John

This well-sheltered area has several pleasant anchorages in surroundings which are deserted but less spectacular than those of the northwest coast of the island.

Watermelon Bay is the eastern creek of a bay situated just to the east of Mary Point headland. The small island of Watermelon Cay and an old mill visible on the south coast make good landmarks. There are no problems in the approach. Anchor in 5–9m depths on sand and weed in the middle of Watermelon Bay or in 10–13m just to the south of Watermelon Cay. There are 3m depths in the middle of the passage to the east of this island.

Haulover Bay is a small deserted bay not popular with yachts some 1·3M WNW of the east point of the island. Anchor in 9–10m depths close to the small southeastern beach taking a line ashore as the depths increase rapidly towards the centre of the bay (20–30m). Beware of the reef off the northern end of the beach.

A very calm anchorage is to be found 0·6M WNW of the east point of the island in a deserted bay almost enclosed by a reef which uncovers. A narrow passage on a bearing of 215°(4m depths) crosses this reef and leads to the centre of the bay where depths are 2·7–3·5m over a light sandy seabed. Approach with caution keeping about 20m from the eastern side of the passage which is safer than the western side.

Coral Bay

18°20'·0N 64°41'·5W

This huge bay on the southeastern coast of St John is divided into three secondary bays which are all very different in appearance and offer several anchorages of which Hurricane Hole and Round Bay are the most beautiful. Coral Harbour, the westernmost bay, is less attractive.

Approach

Eagle Shoal with 1m of water over it situated 0·9M WNW of Ram Head must be well cleared when approaching from the west and the south. The west coast of the entrance is bordered by a coastal reef which uncovers.

At the entrance of Coral Harbour a passage marked by two buoys approximately 60m from the east coast makes it possible to reach an anchorage keeping clear of the shoals to the west. Anchor in 3·5–4·5m sand in the middle of the bay. There are a lot of local craft on moorings.

On land: a snack bar, a limited grocery store and a small boatyard.

Hurricane Hole is divided into several creeks, totally deserted and very well sheltered, bordered by tufted mangroves. Anchor in one or other of the three creeks on the east coast in 4·5–8m of water on mud.

In Round Bay, the most beautiful anchorages are to be found on the east coast bordered by two sandy beaches. Between them on a height stands a conspicuous villa with a red roof. For a distance of 150m or so off the point which separates the two beaches there are rocks and shoals. Anchor in 4–5m on sand, 120m from the southern beach which is bordered with coconut palms. In front of the northern beach which is very white a coral reef with 2·5m of water over it extends for 120m from the shore. Anchor a little further out on sand.

Other bays on the south coast of St John

The south coast of the island which is fairly dry has a number of anchorages which are less attractive than those previously described.

Salt Pond Bay (not named on the charts) is situated 0·5M NW of Ram Head. It is bordered by a white beach surrounded by scrub and aloes.

Booby Rock (12m) can be easily seen in the south of the bay but in the centre of the bay there is a line of dangerous rocks. To enter pass to the east of these rocks and anchor in 3m on sand about 100m from the beach.

Great Lameshur and Little Lameshur Bays 1·5M WNW of Rams Head are separated by a rocky headland off which a small rock and some reefs extend for 50m towards the SW. The approaches are safe. Anchor in either bay in 3–4m on sand about 120m from the north shore in somewhat austere surroundings.

A little further east Reef Bay and Fish Bay are unsafe.

In Rendez-vous Bay sheltered from the east by Dittlif Point, anchor 150m from a small beach on the east coast in 3m of water.

Great Cruz Bay (Calvary Bay) 0·8M south of Cruz Bay is well sheltered from the trade winds but always extremely full. Depths are from 2·5–4·5m over a sandy seabed. A hotel with a grey and mauve roof near the beach is conspicuous from the sea.

St Thomas and neighbouring islands

The coast, dangers

The whole length of St Thomas Island is dominated by a mountain range whose two highest peaks are Crown Mountain (472m) and Signal Hill (457m). There is a pylon with aerial warning lights on top of Crown Mountain. On Signal Hill there is a conspicuous television tower with aerial warning lights. These landmarks are visible from both north and south.

North Coast

This coast is steep-to and covered with vegetation. It is for the most part quite safe close-to. Along the shore are about ten small islands and high rocks which are easily identifiable. Other separate dangers are Ornen Rock, a dangerous, isolated shoal 0·5M to the WNW of Picara Point and Hans Lollick Rock, awash, 0·35M to the SE of the island of the same name.

South Coast

More indented than the north coast, this shore also has many small islands and rocks close-to which present a greater hazard than those on the north coast. The submerged rocks are buoyed with the exception of one shoal of 2·1m in the approaches to Jersey Bay (see page 229). St Thomas Harbour (see opposite page) and Charlotte Amalie are about half way along the coast.

Off the western tip of the island are two islets, West Cay and Salt Cay, which are almost joined; the passage between St Thomas and these two islands is dangerous. Passage between St Thomas and the islands off the eastern tip is possible (see page 230).

St Thomas Harbour

18°20′ N 64°56′ W

St Thomas Harbour, the main port of the US Virgin Islands for passenger and yacht traffic is situated in well-protected roads which are completely safe except in a hurricane.

Charlotte Amalie (25,000 inhabitants) which spreads along the northern shore of these roads still enjoys the status of free port granted to it by the Danes in 1724. It is a bustling small town of great historical interest with narrow streets and shady alleyways along which stand 18th and 19th century houses and shops.

Although it is always crowded this is nevertheless a pleasant port of call and all services for yachts are available.

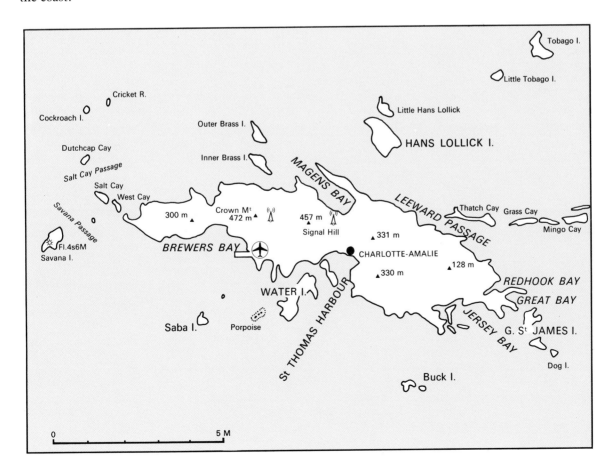

Watermelon Bay, St John (USVI), looking westwards over
Leinster Bay. The hills of St Thomas and its offlying islets can be
seen in the distance.
Anne Hammick

The waterfront at Charlotte Amalie, St Thomas (USVI).
Anne Hammick

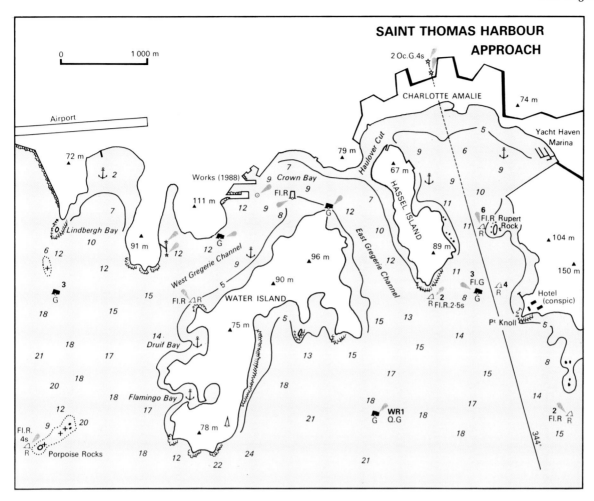

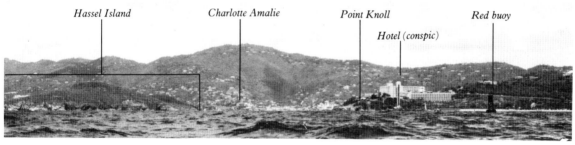

St Thomas Harbour. Eastern approach looking NNW

St Thomas Harbour. Approach – West Gregerie Channel

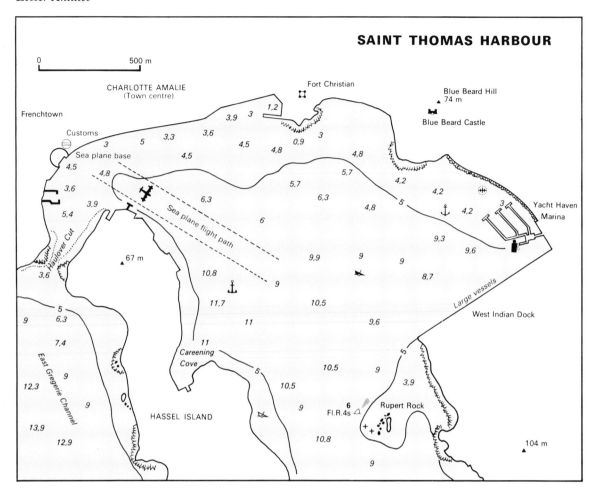

SAINT THOMAS HARBOUR

Approach

The dangers which lie in the approaches to St Thomas and the roads are all well marked. The best landmarks are a large hotel on Point Knoll to the east of the entrance and a conspicuous pylon shaped like a look-out on the east side of the southern tip of Water Island.

The approach is normally made through the channel to the east of Hassel Island where lights can be aligned. It is also possible to come in through West or East Gregerie Channels and through the narrow passage to the NW of Hassel Island (Haulover Cut) which has 4m depths in the centre but the sides are unsafe. This passage and a strip to the NNE of Hassel Island are an area where seaplanes frequently take off and land. Make sure that no seaplane is in sight (to the SW) before entering Haulover Cut.

Anchorages

Yacht Haven Marina Hotel and landing stages are in the eastern corner of the roads with 3–4·5m depths (contact VHF on Ch 16). Places at the quay are often difficult to find; the best anchorage is to the west of the marina with 4·5–9m depths, sand and good holding. There is sometimes a slight swell.

There are other anchorages in the Roads but these are less convenient because of their distance from the town centre. The most usual ones are along the NE coast of Hassel Island (6–10m depths, sand, subject to swell); along the NW coast of Water Island (6–9m depths, poor holding, sheltered from the SE swell); in Druif Bay (Honeymoon Bay) calm and bordered by a beach with coconut palms (3–7m depths, sandy bottom); in Flamingo Bay next to the previous bay but of little attraction (3–5m depths, sand, subject to swell) and finally in Lindbergh Bay to the west of the town, very close to the airport in front of a sandy beach with coconut palms (5–10m depths, sand, except on an isolated shoal of 2m in the middle).

In Crown Bay construction work is in progress to build a basin for small vessels.

Brewers Bay (SW Roads) is 2·5M to the west of the town centre. This small bay is bordered by two quiet, sandy beaches and is well sheltered from the SE by the long embankment (750m) of the aerodrome jutting out to sea. Go round this embankment, which is very easy to identify from the sea, and anchor in 3–4m depths 150m from the NE beach. Note: the sea bed is very uneven in this bay (depths vary from 7–9m to 3–4m over sand banks). There is a taxi and bus service to town.

Facilities

Water, electricity, telephone, TV sockets and fuel can be found at the quay of Yacht Haven Marina.

Nearby are chandleries, mechanics, sail-makers, a supermarket (very well stocked), exchange, car and scooter rental, bars and restaurant.

In town there are many shops selling duty free goods (particularly perfumes and jewellery), other shops of all kinds, restaurants, and bars.

Tourism

The most picturesque parts of Charlotte Amalie are the town centre and the area to the west of the town, known as French Town which comes to life in the evening. It is perfectly possible to do a complete tour of the island by car in a day. Coral World aquarium on the NE coast is well worth a visit.

Communications

Car hire. Frequent seaplane services to the other Virgin Islands. From the international airport there are daily links with the United States, the French Antilles (St Martins) and Europe (see page 203).

Magens Bay

18°22′N 64°56′W

The northern limit of Magens Bay is Picara Point, the rocky tip of a high, steep promontory on which there is a pylon. The SE coast of the bay is bordered by coconut palms and a long beach of white sand close to which there is a pleasant anchorage as long as there is no northern swell.

When approaching watch out for the dangerous isolated shoal, Ornen Rock which is difficult to lo-

cate at 0·5M to the WNW of Picara Point. Keep 200m from the NE coast of the bay to avoid a reef at its southern part barely covered by the water. Depths and the extent of this reef towards the north are uncertain. Anchor in 6–8m sand at about 200m from the northern part of the beach. The other bays on the north coast of the island, west of Magens Bay are easily accessible but often uncomfortable or even untenable because of the swell.

Anchorages in Leeward Passage and Hans Lollick Island

Leeward Passage is the channel between the NE coast of St Thomas and Thatch Cay the westernmost of the chain of islands blocking the northern entrance to Pillsbury Sound. It is possible to anchor here when the northern swell is not too strong.

Coral World aquarium, built at sea level, can be identified as a group of white buildings with cupolas on the coast of St Thomas. One may anchor temporarily in 13–16m of water, 100–120m from the little beach immediately west of these buildings.

Water Bay bounded to the north by Coki Point is edged by a beach and surrounded by a number of buildings. Anchor in the middle in 6m, sand. A shelf with less than 2m extends 150m from the beach.

Hans Lollick Island (220m), steep and covered in greenery, is joined to Little Hans Lollick to the north by a series of reefs and shoals. In fine weather anchor in 4–5m, sand, to leeward of these reefs but

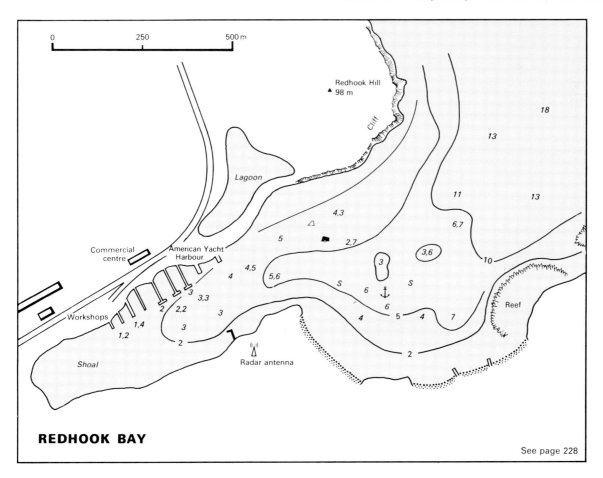

REDHOOK BAY

See page 228

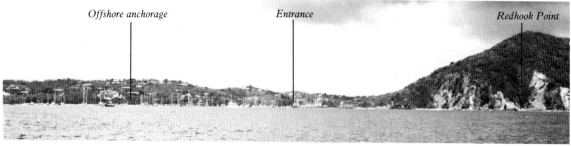

Redhook Bay looking WSW

approach very carefully from the west. It is possible to go ashore on a white sandy beach on the southern point of Little Hans Lollick.

Redhook Bay

18°19′·6N 64°51′·0W

The interior of this bay which opens just to the north of Cabrita Point is an excellent natural harbour part of which has been developed into a yacht harbour which is always extremely full. Passing yachts can tie up to the pontoons of the 'American Yacht Harbour' if there is room (contact by VHF Ch 16).

There is a frequent motor boat service from Redhook Bay to St John. This port of call has good services but the surroundings lack charm.

A new yacht harbour is being built in Redbay 0·5M to the NW of the entrance of Redhook Bay (1989).

Approach

On the north coast of the entrance are the red cliffs of Redhook Point. There is no difficulty in the approach but there is often heavy traffic in the entrance. Depths are from 1·3–3m at the landing stages. Outside the bay one may anchor in 3–9m on sand but the swell is greater. Take care to avoid the reefs up to 150m off the SE coast.

Facilities

Water, electricity and telephone at the landing stages. Two fuel supply points (2·8 and 2m depths). A well-stocked supermarket next to the marina. Restaurants. Bars. Mechanics.

Great Bay and Cowpet Bay

18°19′·4N 64°50′·5W

At the eastern tip of St Thomas, these two bays bordered by white beaches and coconut palms are constantly being developed and built up. A large number of local yachts have permanent moorings here.

Great Bay, the larger of the two, has not yet suffered too much development (1988). Enter, keeping clear of the north and south coasts where there are reefs and anchor in 5–6m, sand, about 180m from the west beach. Look out for a reef between this and the smaller southwest beach.

Cowpet Bay is edged by a complex of residential villas with white roofs which are easily identifiable. The head of the bay is completely blocked by the moorings (all occupied) of the St Thomas Yacht Club. Anchor just short of these moorings in 6–7m on sand.

The passage from one bay to another is through Current Hole.

Islets to the east of St Thomas

Close to the eastern tip of St Thomas there are three arid islets. Great St James, Little St James and Dog between which the currents can be very strong.

Passages

Current Hole is the passage with 8–9m of water between St Thomas and Great St James. In the middle is a low rocky islet (Current Rock) marked by a red and white flashing beacon. The only safe channel 150m wide is to the east of Current Rock. Approach on a bearing of 015°–195° taking care to avoid the reefs off Current Rock 100m to the south. A strong current (4 knots), sudden changes of wind and very heavy traffic must also be taken into account.

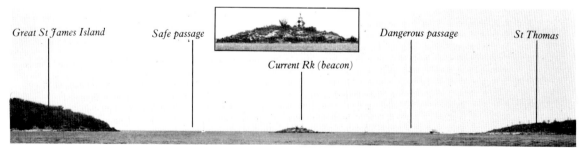

Current Hole looking SSW

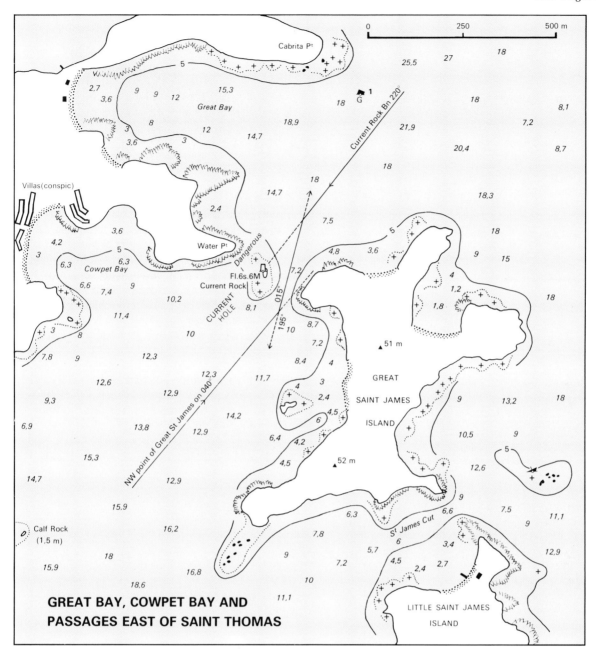

GREAT BAY, COWPET BAY AND PASSAGES EAST OF SAINT THOMAS

St James Cut between Great and Little St James is deep in the centre but in the eastern approach there is a group of low rocks surrounded by reefs.

Dog Island Cut between Little St James and Dog Island has a dangerous shallow in the centre of the northern entrance and should not be attempted.

Anchorages

The west coast of Great St James has a small, deep, well-sheltered bay with an islet in the middle (the north and eastern coasts of which are unsafe). Anchor to the NNE or to the south of this islet on sand in 4–8m depths. The passage between the islet and Great St James has 2·4m depths.

The creek on the NW coast of Little St James, where there is a villa and a landing stage, is much less frequented but offers poor shelter from the SE. Anchor in 3–4m on sand and weed in the centre of the creek.

Jersey Bay

18°19'·0N 64°52'·4W

The northern part of Jersey Bay called Brenner Bay has perfect shelter but is unattractive and is full of local yachts. There are also several boat yards and small marinas.

Approach

The approach is through a narrow marked channel, the entrance to which bears 315° from the green buoy C1 situated 160m east of Cas Cay. This channel, which goes close to the mangrove islet Grassy Cay, has 2·2m (1988) but a tendency to silt.

Beware of an unmarked rocky shoal (2·1m) 450m east of Cas Cay.

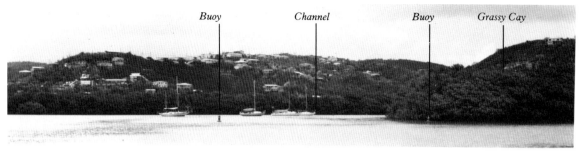

Entrance to Brenner Bay looking NW

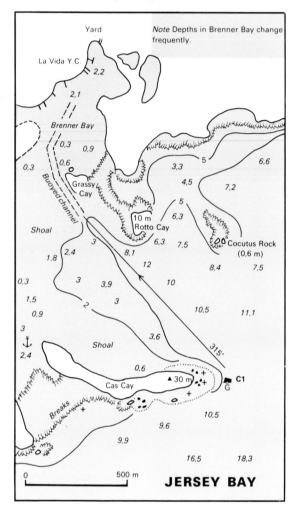

Yard

Note Depths in Brenner Bay change frequently.

La Vida Y.C.

2,2

2,1

Brenner Bay

0,3   0,9

0,3

0,6

Grassy Cay

Shoal

10 m
Rotto Cay

5   6,6

3,3

4,5   7,2

5

6,3

6,3   7,5   Cocutus Rock
(0,6 m)

8,1

12   8,4   7,5

3   3,9   10

0,3

1,5

0,9   2   3   10,5   11,1

3

⚓

2,4

3,6

315°

Shoal   0,6

▲ 30 m   ⊞ C1
G

Cas Cay

Breaks   10,5

9,6

9,9

16,5   18,3

0   500 m
JERSEY BAY

Facilities
Fuel and water at the landing stages of La Vida Yachts Charters. Boat yard with 35-ton travel-lift (Antilles Yacht Services VHF Ch 16).

Islands to the south of St Thomas

Near these islands are fair weather anchorages which are particularly good for underwater exploration.

Buck Island which is very arid and identifiable by its lighthouse is made up of two islands which are almost joined. Anchor in 2·5–5m on sand and rocks in the western bay which is fairly popular and where there is a landing stage.

Saba Island (67m) and Turtle Dove Cay joined by a white sandbank make a single island. To leeward of this island is a pretty and fairly unfrequented anchorage in 3–5m with a sand and coral bottom. The south and south western approaches to this anchorage are unsafe. To enter pass around the northern and north-western coast 200m off the shore.

Lighthouse

Buck Island, St Thomas, looking W

St Croix

The coast, dangers

St Croix stretches for 19 M from east to west. Only the north coast is of interest to yachts.

North coast

The west part of this coast, dominated by a chain of hills from 250–290m high, is comparatively safe as far as Salt River Point which is not easy to distinguish and is surrounded by rocks to a distance of 0·2M. Off the eastern part there are also reefs and shoals some of which extend a mile out to sea.

Buck Island is covered in vegetation, 113m high and is easy to identify. It is surrounded by large reefs (see page 230).

The most conspicuous landmarks on this coast from west to east are:

Hams Bluff the northwest point of the island, massive and steep with a lighthouse 120m high (white tower with a black top Fl(2)30s24M).

A large pylon on Mount Stewart 1·5M southeast of the lighthouse.

The landmarks of Christiansted (see below).

A very large white villa with a domed roof and crenellated towers standing on a height 2M from the east point of the island.

West and south coasts

The west coast of the island forms a very open bay in which the town of Frederiksted (see page 233) is situated. Off the south coast there are a number of reefs and shoals, particularly in the western half where they extend more than 1·5M out to sea. The two wide bays at the western end, the South West Anchorage, are exposed and there is no shelter except for yachts with a very shallow draught.

The best landmarks are the airport buildings and more conspicuously those of the industrial complex and oil depot of Lime Tree Bay.

Christiansted

17°45′N 64°42′W

The capital of the island lies along the shores of a bay which is well sheltered from the north winds by a large coral reef. This is one of the most attractive small towns in the Antilles with alleyways and gardens full of flowers bordered by 18th and 19th century buildings.

Approach

Dangerous shoals (0·6–3m) extend for almost 2M north east of the bay.

The best landmark is a very tall red and white radio mast near the lighthouse of Fort Louise Augusta. A group of green and white oil tanks can also easily be seen to the west of the town. The entrance to the channel which is marked by buoys and tripod beacons can be found on a bearing of 160° to the radio mast. The main channel to the west of Round Reef has clearer markings than the channel to the east of the reef.

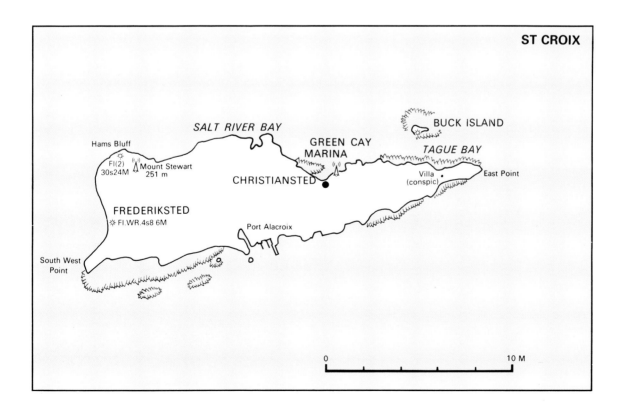

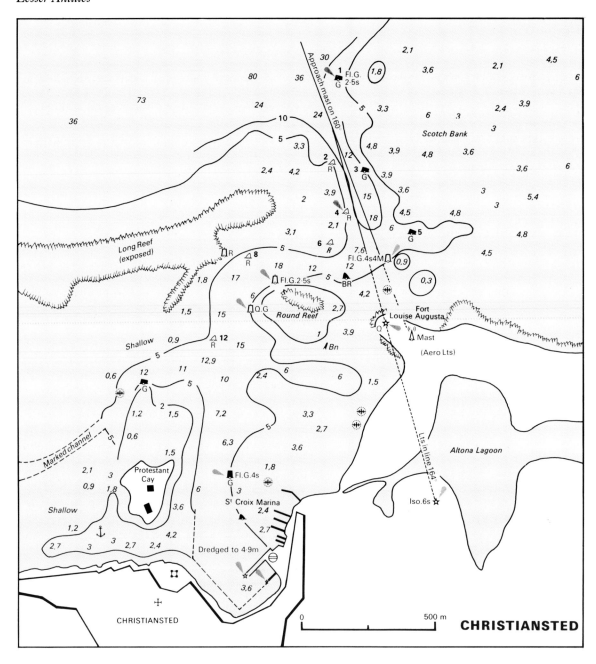

CHRISTIANSTED

CHRISTIANSTED

Anchorage

The best anchorage is in the SSW of Protestant Cay in 2·5–3m depths on sand. Approach this anchorage by passing west and south of this islet. It is possible to go ashore at the landing stages of St Croix Marina (VHF Ch 16) on the east coast of the bay just to the north of the commercial port.

Facilities

Water, electricity and fuel on the quay at St Croix Marina. Boat yard with 60-ton travel-lift (work and repairs of all kinds).
In town: supplies of all kinds (market and supermarkets), numerous restaurants, banks.

Tourism

Some of the oldest buildings in the town may be visited. In particular the fort whose ramparts domi-

nate the town (18th century) and the ancient Lutheran church called Steeple Building (1734–1740) in which there is a history museum.

The north western part of the island is the most interesting part to visit by car via Scenic Road and Mahogany Road, returning via Frederiksted and the Botanical Gardens of St George which are in an old sugar cane plantation.

Communications

Car hire. Airfield (see page 231)

Salt River Bay

17°47'·0N 64°45'·4W

This deserted and indented bay provides the best shelter from hurricanes in the Virgin Islands but it is only accessible to boats drawing less than 1·8m. The approach is through a winding channel which is only scantily buoyed. It is essential to use a local pilot when entering it for the first time. Salt River Marina, situated in the southwestern arm of the bay, provides a pilot service (contact by VHF Ch 16 or ☎ 809/7789650).

Entry

Entry is dangerous in a northern swell. When approaching from the east keep clear of the reef off Salt River Point stretching 0·2M northwards.

Landmarks for identifying Salt River Bay are: a large white church with a red roof standing on a height to the west of the bay and a conspicuous bell tower on the east coast, a white motor launch permanently moored on the premises of an underwater laboratory about 500m NNE of the channel and a rusty wreck on the coastal reef of Salt River Point. A proposal for marking the channel is under consideration (1988).

Facilities

Water and electricity at the quay of the marina, mechanic, chandlery, snack bar.

Frederiksted

17°43'N 64°53'W

Frederiksted is a town of old houses and colonial-type shops situated in the middle of the very open bay which constitutes the west coast of the island.

Anchorage

A landing stage for cargo boats 500m long lies along the front of the town. Anchor north of this landing stage in 5–6m on sand approximately 200m from the shore. This anchorage is subject to swell.

Facilities

Supplies and a few restaurants in the village.

Green Cay Marina

17°45'·6N 64°40'·1W

Green Cay Marina is a recently built yacht harbour in a lagoon less than two miles east of Christiansted. It offers secure shelter and services at the quay in fairly pleasant surroundings.

Approach

Keep clear of the shoals which extend to the NE of Christiansted before heading towards the entrance leaving the islet of Green Cay to the east (17m). To the west of the entrance a hotel with white roofed bungalows is clearly visible. The basin and the entry channel (very narrow and 2·7m deep) are dredged but the channel does tend to silt up. Enter carefully watching the depths.

Berthing

Tie up at the fuel quay or contact the port office by VHF Ch 16.

Facilities

Water, electricity and fuel at the quay, showers, laundry, restaurant and bar, chandlery.

Tague Bay

17°45'·6N 64°36'·4W

Tague Bay is a beautiful lagoon with very clear water and well sheltered by a continuous coral reef. The St Croix Yacht Club is situated on its southern shore and makes passing yachts welcome. There are a number of moorings with less than 2m depths.

Approach

The channel which leads in behind the reef is two miles west of the bay. It can be identified by a square green buoy on the eastern side and a white sand bank partly covered in grass on the western side. An old grey stone windmill on the coast (193° from the buoy) is a good landmark.

The secondary channel 0·5M further east should only be used by those with local knowledge. It is marked by two small buoys. Enter leaving the buoy at least 100m to the east then turn towards the east, sheltered by the reef and watching it carefully taking care to remain closer to the coast than to the reef. Depths are from 4–7m but one must be on the lookout for isolated outcrops of coral which extend from the reef towards the south.

Anchorage

Anchor in the middle of Tague bay in 2·5–3·5m depths sand and weed.

Facilities

Water and electricity at the yacht club pontoons, bar, restaurants, showers.

Buck Island

17°47'·5N 64°37'·2W

Buck Island (103m) and the reefs which surround it form a nature reserve where fishing, hunting and the removal of flowers and plants are forbidden. There is a very pleasant anchorage in clear water close to the west point of the island bordered by a white sandy beach. Approach due east towards the summit of the island where there is a light on a small mast. Anchor in 3·5–4·5m of water approximately 80m from the beach in a large area of sand which is easily visible through the clear water. The lagoon to the south of the island with a marked entrance is only accessible to boats with a very shallow draught.

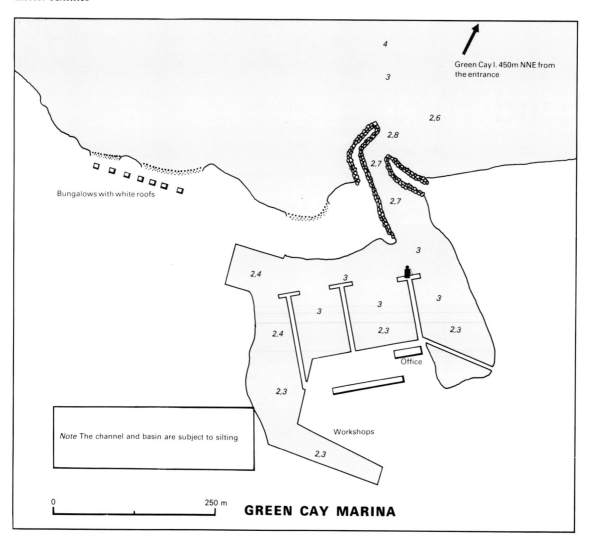

4

3

Green Cay I. 450m NNE from
the entrance

2,6

2,8

2,7

2,7

Bungalows with white roofs

3

2,4

3

3

3

3

2,4

2,3

2,3

Office

2,3

Note The channel and basin are subject to silting

2,3

Workshops

2,3

0   250 m

GREEN CAY MARINA

Appendix

I. HURRICANES

As stated in the main text, the incidence of hurricanes can be summarised as follows:

a. The hurricane season is from June to November; they very rarely occur unseasonably but can do so.
b. The worst months are August to October.
c. There are on average 7 hurricanes per year but as many as 21 have been recorded (1933) and as few as 2.

In June the majority of hurricanes develop west of 80°W, move towards the NNW and thus miss the Lesser Antilles. Between July and September most hurricanes arise in the doldrums of the Atlantic, sometimes as far away as the Cape Verde area. These may enter the Caribbean across the arc of the Antilles. From mid-September onwards hurricanes again develop more frequently in the SW part of the Caribbean and the Gulf of Mexico than in the Atlantic and in November few touch the Lesser Antilles. A hurricane five or six hundred miles out in the Atlantic may still create dangerous swell conditions in the Antilles.

The table on page 8 with lines showing the places of equal frequency of hurricanes indicates that the Leeward Islands lie in the area of maximum frequency.

The signs of an approaching hurricane are:

a. the long, low swell which spreads for a considerable distance from its centre. This may be observed before
b. a drop in barometric pressure. A fall of 3mb below the mean for the time of year signals a probable, 5mb a certainty and one that is close. The measurement must be corrected, in particular for diurnal variation which in this area is consistently of the order of 3mb with maximums around 10hr and 22hr and minimums around 04h and 16hr.
c. a marked change in wind strength or direction coupled with unusual cloud – cirrus, alto-stratus and broken cumulus in the classic pattern of an advancing depression.

If the area is threatened by a hurricane, warnings are usually transmitted by local radio stations several days in advance but bulletins may not be frequent enough to enable the listener to keep track of progress, bearing in mind that a 12 or 24 hour delay can mean missing an advance of several hundred miles and a major change of direction and in any case the position quoted for a centre may be up to 60M out. The Caribbean ham nets on 14313kHz and on 4173kHz may be more helpful. Once the precise area of the threat is known, more frequent, special bulletins are issued stating how the situation is developing. One possible line of action then is to get secured in a hurricane bolt hole. The principal bolt holes are in Grenada, Carriacou, St Lucia, Martinique, Antigua, St Martin and Culebra. No bolt hole is absolutely safe from the elements in a bad hurricane and even in lesser conditions the principal danger is likely to be from other boats breaking away from insecure moorings.

Fuller details about hurricanes and how to avoid them if at sea will be found in the British Admiralty *Sailing Directions* for the Lesser Antilles (the *West Indies Pilot Volume 2*) or in the *Mariner's Handbook* (NP Nos *71* and *100* respectively). If cruising in the hurricane season, navigators are advised to establish for themselves the merits of the various hurricane holes, plan their cruise with them in mind, to have a barograph and to have HF SSB as well as the more common forms of communication.

The following note by Hugo du Plessis may also be helpful.

The well publicised hurricanes which have hit the West Indies in recent years and the pictures of wrecked yachts piled in heaps must have made many cruising yachtsmen wonder about the wisdom of keeping a yacht in the Caribbean, or indeed crossing the Atlantic at all. Eric Hiscock, many years ago, said that no wise person sailed in the Caribbean during the hurricane season, June to November. Since then the position has changed significantly: for the better, due to the good warning system based on satellite and aircraft monitoring; dramatically for the worse, due to the sheer number of yachts now based in the Caribbean.

The chances of being caught in the path of a killer hurricane are small. But make no mistake, if you are, the chances of your boat coming through unscathed are even smaller and she will quite likely be sunk. The danger inshore is not just the hurricane force winds, although only a fool would underrate those, but, far greater, other vessels, anything from yachts of similar size to cruise liners.

What are the chances of a hurricane?

For a start the real killers like *David* (1979), *Gilbert* (1988) and *Hugo* (1989) are uncommon. Only when they hit land do they hit the headlines. Most hurricanes get no mention and more than half wander by harmlessly at sea. *Gabrielle*, which preceded *Hugo* by two weeks, was even bigger and more powerful but missed all islands and the press.

In the Leeward Islands – Martinique, Antigua etc – the chances of a hurricane in any one year are about one in five, though some years can produce two or there may be long gaps. Further south the odds in Barbados are one in twenty-six. In Grenada they are nearer one in fifty, in Trinidad one in a century. The chances of a hurricane are a gamble and the stake is your boat, but it is possible to lengthen the odds.

What is a hurricane?
Tropical revolving storms form in the Intertropical Convergence Zone where the northeast trade winds meet the southeast trades. In the days before scientific meteorology sailors called this area 'The Doldrums'. This zone wiggles and forms waves, known as tropical waves, about four to seven days apart in the summer months. These are normally harmless except for rain and squalls but may develop into a tropical disturbance, at which point watch out. This is where hurricanes start.

If the disturbance develops closed millibars it is called a tropical depression and given a number. Many develop no further, but about half go on to become tropical storms and are given a name. These are not hurricanes, although they may be the next day, but nevertheless a storm is a storm. In an area where gales are rare, a tropical storm means Force 8–11 with the likelihood of onshore winds and seas in anchorages normally sheltered from the steady trade winds. Many sub-hurricane tropical storms do develop into hurricanes, perhaps rapidly, but anyway at the Force 11 margin the distinction becomes academic.

Hurricanes start at Force 12, 64 knots, and are then graded 1 to 5. *Hugo*, with forecast winds of 120 knots gusting 140 was Grade 4 and overwhelmed boats and buildings, beaches, cliffs and landscapes. however most hurricanes are of lesser degree, in the 70–90 knot range, but compare that with a bad Atlantic storm where 90 knots is rare, even in gusts in the most exposed places. A gale Force 8 is 35–40 knots, and wind pressure is a square law.

But the area of the fearsome hurricane-force winds is quite small. The highest winds are near the eye – *Hugo's* eye was 15–25 miles in diameter. The radius from the centre of winds greater than Force 12 was 50 miles, greatest on the northern sector, of Force 10 was 75, and of gale Force 8 125 miles; this is a moving pin-hole compared with the hundreds, even thousand miles of a bad winter gale in the North Atlantic. The speed of a hurricane's advance is a modest at 15–20 knots compared with the 40–60 knots of an Atlantic storm and often drops to nothing, which can leave everyone trembling about where it is going next.

Most hurricanes, which can only form over warm tropical seas, start on a westerly course, perhaps from as far east as the Cape Verde Islands. They then tend to curve in a northwesterly direction, forming a parabola before ending up heading northeast for Europe as a depression and gale. They are cohesive and retain their identity and form for weeks. Their energy comes from the evaporation of sea water – land will cut off this energy source and they then die quickly.

Hurricanes have tendencies but follow no rules but their own, which they make up as they go along. Probably one in ten is a rogue which curves the wrong way, heaves to for a week or even loops the loop and comes back to attack the same island twice. There are however certain trends:

Early hurricanes take a northerly course.

Most hurricanes curve towards the northwest at some point. The problem is to know when they are going to do so.

The northerly or Leeward Islands are more vulnerable than the southern or Windward Islands. The further south the better, but note that tropical storms are still common in the south.

Venezuela is reckoned safe, as is Trinidad. Grenada is also fairly safe and has the best and least crowded hurricane holes.

The worst months are August and September, but the hurricane season is June to November and storms have occurred in every month.

WARNING SYSTEMS

The warning system, based on satellites and aircraft, is good with attention increasingly focussed on a particular storm if it approaches mainland America. The problem is to get hold of the latest information on status and position, bearing in mind that within twelve or twenty-four hours the centre may move several hundred miles and change direction by as much as 90°.

It is well worth having an SSB receiver, which need not be expensive. There are sophisticated transistors like the Sony 2001. MNM, the US Coastguard at Norfolk, Virginia, broadcast six-hourly bulletins at 0000, 0600, 1200, 1800 Caribbean time on 13,113kHz and other frequencies, with hurricane and storm warnings. Their high seas forecast ninety minutes later are often more useful as they cover the western half of the Atlantic, although briefly. Unfortunately a computerized voice synthesiser of unbelievable dullness is used; there are often stupid mistakes, such as forecasting a 500 knot wind, and from time to time it becomes unintelligible.

Twenty-four hour forecasts from island sources, even on islands with major airports and meteorological offices, are apt to be vague and out of date (the time of issue, not of the broadcast, is critical), but are quite helpful if the worst case storm is still more than a day away. Predictions for a forty-eight hour period are less helpful and for longer periods may be influenced as much by politics as science.

The ham net on SSB can provide useful information. The Caribbean net works on 14,313kHz and the unofficial net on 4137kHz but regrettably many ham operators on yachts are ill-disciplined and in times of danger block the frequencies with trivia.

HURRICANE HOLES

There are comparatively few safe hurricane holes, not that anywhere is safe in a bad hurricane. The principle ones are in Grenada, Carriacou, St Lucia, Martinique, Antigua, St Martin and Culebra (see list). It is like musical chairs. Anyone sailing in the Caribbean during the hurricane season must keep an eye on the nearest shelter and its distance away.

However these days the hurricane holes are safer in theory than in practice. Although a sound cruising yacht should be able to look after herself with heavy storm anchors and cables, the greatest danger is not from the hurricane, but from other boats. Against a larger vessel there is little defence. More yachts are sunk by other boats than go adrift. One dragging boat will foul others and pick up the most carefully laid anchors. That boat will collect others and you may be attacked by a pack of entangled boats.

The plain fact is that there are now far too many yachts in the Caribbean for the limited space in the few hurricane holes and very little can be done to improve the situation. Although a careful owner will spend hours laying out his own anchors preparing for the worst, few charter yachts have storm anchors and what they have are light by cruising standards. Big charter fleets are mostly on leaseback or management – there is little personal interest in the boat, only in the job, and to the absent owner it is an insured investment. There are many horror pictures of well sheltered marinas reduced to a shattered pile of yachts. Their staff do not have the time to moor dozens of yachts properly even if they knew where absent owners stow storm anchors and many marina managers, hoping for the best, empty their marinas into the hurricane holes.

CARIBBEAN HURRICANE HOLES

		Grade
Barbados	None	
Grenada	Calavigny Harbour	1
	Egmont	1
	Clarkes Court Bay	3
	Hog island	2
	Secret Harbour	2
	St George's Lagoon	3
Carriacou	The Careenage, Tyrrell Bay	1/2
Grenadines	None	
St Vincent	Blue Lagoon	3
St Lucia	Marigot	1
	Rodney Bay Lagoon	1
Martinique	Côte de Lametin	2
	Trois Ilets	3
	Cul-de-Sac Marin	1
	Anse des Anglais	1
	Petit Grenade	2
	Roseaux Bay	2
	Trésor	3
Dominica	None	
Guadeloupe	Blue Lagoon	1
	Rivière Salée	1
Antigua	English Harbour	1
	Falmouth	2
	Indian Creek	1
	Nonsuch Bay	2
	Parham	2
Montserrat	None	
St Kitts/Nevis	None	
Statia/Saba	None	
Anguilla	None	
St Martin	Simson Baai Lagoon	1
	Oyster Pond	3
St Croix	Salt River Bay	

Note Grade refers to early arrivals. Latecomers may find the best spots, or even the whole harbour, full up and the shelter, if any, is of lower grade.

As shown repeatedly the greatest danger is from other yachts going adrift, and the safest hurricane hole is the one with fewest boats, in particular one with few charter fleet yachts, hurriedly and carelessly anchored. These can make the safest hurricane hole a deathtrap, whereas a second class shelter with no charter yachts may be a lot safer and give a better chance of survival.

LAYING UP ASHORE

In Europe a yacht laid up ashore is considered safe (a strange idea for yachts with masts stepped and flexible fibreglass hulls supported by unbraced wedged shores). Yachts ashore in the Caribbean cannot be considered safe. Normal tides are small – half a metre is a big spring tide – and most boatyards have less than one metre of freeboard, but the exceptional storm surge of a hurricane can reach 3·6m (*Hugo's* was 2·4m). This will submerge most boatyards deep enough to float stored boats and batter them with debris. On top of this will be storm force waves and a big swell. As much damage is done by the high seas of a hurricane as by the wind. Torrential rain too can play havoc with yachts on reclaimed land.

Only a fool would leave his mast standing while ashore in the Caribbean and your neighbour may be one of them. Dry land capsize is not uncommon in winds of much less than hurricane force. In a bad hurricane it is almost inevitable.

A travel-hoist dock or slipway will be an early casualty from storm waves. The yachts may survive, yet be marooned ashore unable to be launched while construction materials and machinery are diverted to more essential needs.

Many anchorages in the Caribbean are open roadsteads on the lee side of an island, safe enough with the steady northeast to southeast trade winds. But one feature of a tropical storm is the reversal of the normal wind direction. Open bays then become dangerous lee shores, and there are often no other safe anchorages near. A hurricane can alter the wind pattern far beyond the area of dangerous winds and send a dangerous swell even further. Hurricane *Hugo* caused Force 5 westerly winds in Grenada 400 miles away, well outside the danger zone, and heavy swells from its predecessor *Gabrielle* nearly a thousand miles away battered the coast, even swinging round to the sheltered side. With a bad hurricane in the offing there is hardly a safe anchorage in the entire Caribbean outside the hurricane holes. The best that can be said is that if the storm is at a safe distance away it is possible to adopt the traditional and seamanlike course of seeking safety at sea – though your insurance company may prefer you to remain at anchor on a lee shore rather than sail at night.

What can be done?

Every skipper will have his own ideas, depending on the circumstances. Make your own decisions, do not automatically follow what other do. Listen to the old hands and ask plenty of questions before the first hurricane comes, then try to decide which of the contradictory advice is appropriate for you.

The following are my own ideas, many of which will not be found in the books.

1. Don't be there. If still in the Caribbean and not being chased by an early storm up Bermuda way, go south to the 'safe' areas of Grenada, Venezuela or Trinidad and stay there for at least the whole of August and September, the danger months.
2. Don't be in the line of fire. Get out of the way if there is time. Sail south if you can do so without sailing dangerously across the path of the hurricane, bearing in mind that most curve to the northwest. You should have at least two days' warning of a bad one heading right your way, long enough to get 200–250 miles away and out of the danger area where at least you could heave to in open water.
3. Wherever you sail keep an eye on the nearest and best hurricane hole, avoiding those, assuming there is a choice, which are used by larger and heavier boats such as island schooners and big charter yachts. Get into the shallowest water you can, although with a storm surge that will not save you from being sunk by larger boats but at least they will start from further away and there is a greater chance they will miss you. Avoid hurricane holes with shallow bars – the depth may change and trap you.
4. Because of their root system, mangroves are almost indestructible and are a soft landing. The best shelter is up a mangrove creek.
5. Do not leave your boat in a marina. Yachts and pontoons will end up in one big pile.
6. Avoid the vicinity of marinas. Managers may empty them, creating more congestion.
7. Avoid the vicinity of a big charter fleet. They may not have storm anchors or the staff to moor them properly.
8. Do not rely on steaming to your anchor. Debris, including ropes from sunk yachts, may make this impossible.
9. If laid up ashore chose a yard with the highest freeboard and a security fence on the seaward side to catch debris. Sheltering land may be submerged by the storm surge or swept away by seas. You may not only be chased around by boats but by houses too, or what is left of them. Lower your masts and chose neighbours who do

so. Make sure the boat is chocked very firmly and the shores braced. The boat will be shaken by the wind, and may be lifted by waves. Shores can be dislodged by surging debris, even on large boats, or settle in waterlogged ground.

10. Take down a furling jib well before the storm while it is fairly calm. If, as is probable, it blows out it will put a tremendous strain on the mast, boat and anchors.
11. If leaving your boat anywhere make sure someone has very clear instructions about what to do if a hurricane threatens. If possible make one person responsible, such as another boat owner. Marina staff may be too busy to moor boats properly or know where your storm anchors are stowed.
12. Find out well in advance the times and frequencies of all weather forecasts in your area, not just the local station, and their reliability. Your local station will probably be put out of action.
13. Plot the storm and its predicted path as soon as it is first reported. A chart of the North Atlantic (e.g. a pilot chart) is essential.
14. Have a range of plans graded from tropical storm to hurricane Grade 1 to killer Grade 5. You may weather a tropical storm or ordinary hurricane. You will probably not weather a killer hurricane.
15. In the hurricane season keep well stocked up with fuel, water and stores, sufficient to last several weeks. Food ashore will be hard to obtain, crops destroyed and stocks damaged. Also being self-contained frees relief supplies for hard pressed destitute local families. Get into a hurricane hole early before the best places are filled.
16. Do not go ashore soon afterwards. You may be shot or attacked by looters.
17. It is a moot point whether it is safer to stay with your boat or seek safety ashore – if it can be found. The natural inclination is to stay with your ship and use your skill and resourcefulness to see you both through. But if, despite all your precautions, it is going to be beyond human ability to prevent your boat being sunk by another boat, it would be difficult and dangerous to get ashore. A dinghy would be impracticable. A liferaft would be blown away. Even swimming would be very hazardous, if possible at all. Common sense suggests somewhere ashore, especially for weaker members of the crew.
18. Keep under cover. Coconuts fly like cannon balls. Tin roofs can slice through a mast like a scythe and that mast then becomes a harpoon. Almost anything can become airborne and even small objects can be lethal. The word 'impossible' loses its usual meaning.
19. In extreme cases consider scuttling your boat in shallow, sheltered water. There will be less damage and it will be easier to salvage than from the bottom of a pile of wreckage on the beach.

II. VHF INTERNATIONAL MARINE CHANNELS

Channel Designators	Operating frequency RX (MHz)	TX (MHz)
01	160.650	156.050
02	160.700	156.100
03	160.750	156.150
04	160.800	156.200
05	160.850	156.250
18	161.500	156.900
19	161.550	156.950
20	161.600	157.000
21	161.650	157.050
22	161.700	157.100
23	161.750	157.150
24	161.800	157.200
25	161.850	157.250
26	161.900	157.300
27	161.950	157.350
28	162.000	157.400
29	–	–
30	–	–
31	–	–
32	–	–
33	–	–
34	–	–
35	–	–
36	–	–
37	–	–
38	–	–
39	–	–
60	160.625	156.025
61	160.675	156.075
62	160.725	156.125
63	160.775	156.175
64	160.825	156.225
65	160.875	156.275
66	160.925	156.325
75	–	–
76	–	–
78	161.525	156.925
79	161.575	156.975
80	161.625	157.025
81	161.675	157.075
82	161.725	157.125
83	161.775	157.175
84	161.825	157.225
85	161.875	157.275
86	161.925	157.325
87	161.975	157.375
88	162.025	157.425
WX1	162.550	
WX2	162.400	
WX3	162.475	
WX4	163.275	
WX5	161.650	
WX6	161.775	

VHF USA MARINE CHANNELS

Channel Designators	Operating frequency RX (MHz)	TX (MHz)
01	156.050	
02	–	–
03	156.150	156.150
04	156.200	156.200
05	156.250	156.250
06	156.300	156.300
07	156.350	156.350
08	156.400	156.400
09	156.450	156.450
10	156.500	156.500
11	156.550	156.550
12	156.600	156.600
13	156.650	156.650
14	156.700	156.700
15	156.750	–
16	156.800	156.800
17	156.850	156.850
18	156.900	156.900
19	156.950	156.950
20	161.600	157.000
21	157.050	157.050
22	157.100	157.100
23	157.150	157.150
24	161.800	157.200
25	161.850	157.250
26	161.900	157.300
27	161.950	157.350
28	162.000	157.400
29	–	–
30	–	–
31	–	–
32	–	–
33	–	–
34	–	–
35	–	–
36	–	–
37	–	–
38	–	–
39	–	–
60	160.625	–
61	160.675	156.075
62	160.725	156.125
63	160.775	156.175
64	160.825	156.225
65	156.275	156.275
66	156.325	156.325
67	156.375	156.375
68	156.425	156.425
69	156.475	156.475
70	154.525	156.525
71	156.575	156.575
72	156.625	156.625
73	156.675	156.675
74	156.725	156.725
75	156.875	156.875
76	–	–
77	–	–
78	156.925	156.925
79	156.975	156.975

80	157.025	157.025
81	157.075	157.075
82	157.125	157.125
83	157.175	157.175
84	157.825	157.825
85	157.875	157.875
86	157.925	157.925
87	157.975	157.975
88	157.425	157.425
WX1	162.550	–
WX2	162.400	–
WX3	162.475	–
WX4	163.275	–
WX5	161.650	–
WX6	161.775	–

III. CHARTS

Imray-Iolaire Yachting Charts for the Caribbean Sea

Chart	Title	Scale
1	Eastern Caribbean General chart	800,000
	Plans: Monjes del Sur	
A	Lesser Antilles – Puerto Rico to Martinique	930,000

Puerto Rico

A1	Puerto Rico	285,000
	Plans: San Juan, Bahia de Ponce, Puerto Arecibo, Bahia de Mayaguez	
A11	West Coast of Puerto Rico	116,700
	Plans: Bahia de Mayaguez, Puerto Real, Bahia de Boqueron, Approaches to La Parguera	
A12	South Coast of Puerto Rico	116,700
	Plans: Arroya, Bahia de Ponce, Bahia de Jobos, Bahia de Guanica, Bahia de Guayanilla, Isla Caja de Muertos, Punta Petrona	
A13	Southeast Coast of Puerto Rico	116,700
	Plans: Pasaje Medio Munda, Ensenada Honda, Palmas del Mar, Puerto Arroyo & Puerto Patillas	
A131	Isla de Culebra	34,250
	Isla de Vieques	44,500
	Plans: Esperanza, Ensenada Honda	
A14	Northeast Coast of Puerto Rico	116,700
	Plans: Cayo Lobos, Marina Puerto Chico, Las Groabas, Isleta Marina, Isla Palominos, Bahia de San Juan	
A2	Puerto Rico to Anguilla	395,000

Virgin Islands

A23	Virgin Islands	282,000
	St Croix	103,000
	Plans: Christiansted, Krauze Lagoon, Frederiksted, Green Cay Marina	
A231	Virgin Islands – St Thomas to Virgin Gorda	88,300
	Plans: Charlotte Amelie, Virgin Gorda Yacht Harbour, Roadtown Harbour, Nanny Cay Marina, Cruz Bay	
A232	Virgin Islands – Tortola to Anegada	88,300
	Plans: Gorda Sound, South Sound, Roadtown Harbour and Approaches, Virgin Gorda Yacht Harbour	

Leeward Islands

A24	Anguilla, St Martin and St Barthélémy	100,000
	Plans: Road Bay, Oyster Pond, Gustavia, Prickly Pear Cays, Crocus Bay, Shoal Bay and Island Harbour, Groot Baai, Simson Baai, Anse de Marigot, Baie de Marigot	
A25	St Eustatius, St Christopher (St Kitts) and Nevis	104,000
	Plans: Saba I	30,500
	Montserrat I	104,000
	Fort Baai (Saba), Basseterre Bay (St Kitts), The Narrows, Plymouth (Montserrat), Oranjebaai (St Eustatius)	
A26	Barbuda – Southwest Coast	28,000
	Plans: Gravenor Bay	
A27	Antigua	57,000
	Plans: Nonsuch Bay, Mamora Bay, Falmouth and English Harbours	
A271	North Coast of Antigua	30,000
A28	Guadeloupe	41,000
	Plans: Pointe-à-Pitre, Anse Deshaies, Gozier, Port Louis, St François and St François Marina, River Sens Marina, Iles de la Petite Terre	
A281	Guadeloupe – Iles des Saintes	19,000
	West Coast of Marie Galante	31,000
	Plans: St Anne, Port du Moule, St Marie, Petit Havre, Anse Accul, Grand Bourg	

Windward Islands

A29	Dominica	73,000
	Plans: Douglas Bay and Prince Rupert Bay, Roseau Roads and Woodbridge Bay	
A3	Anguilla to Guadeloupe	394,000
A30	Martinique	92,000
	Plans: La Trinité, Rade de Fort de France, Havre du Robert, Rade de St Pierre, Cul de Sac Marin, Approaches to Pte du Bout, Mouillage du François	
A301	East Coast of Martinique	55,000
	Rocher du Diamant to Havre de la Trinité	
A4	Guadeloupe to St Lucia	388,000
B	Lesser Antilles – Martinique to Trinidad	750,000
B1	St Lucia	72,000
	Plans: Castries, Gd. Cul de Sac Bay, Marigot, Rodney Bay and Yacht Harbour, Laborie Bay, Vieux Fort Bay and Pt. Sable Bay	
B2	Barbados	56,900
	Plans: Bridgetown, Speightstown	
B3	The Grenadines – St Vincent to Grenada	162,000
B30	St Vincent to Mustique	73,000
	Plans: Kingstown Bay, Calliaqua Bay and Blue Lagoon, Admiralty Bay, W Coast of Mustique, Baliceaux and Battowia, Friendship Bay, Chateaubelair Bay	
B31	Bequia to Carriacou	91,000
	Plans: Hillsborough Bay, Clifton Harbour, Charlestown Bay, Tobago Cays	
B32	Carriacou to Grenada	91,000
	Plans: Tyrrell Bay, NE Point of Grenada, St George's Harbour, Grenville Harbour	
B311	Middle Grenadines – Canouan to Carriacou	25,000
B4	Tobago	63,600
	Plans: Buccoo Reef, Tyrel's Bay, Plymouth, King's Bay, Scarborough, Man of War Bay	
B5	Martinique to Tobago and Barbados	510,700

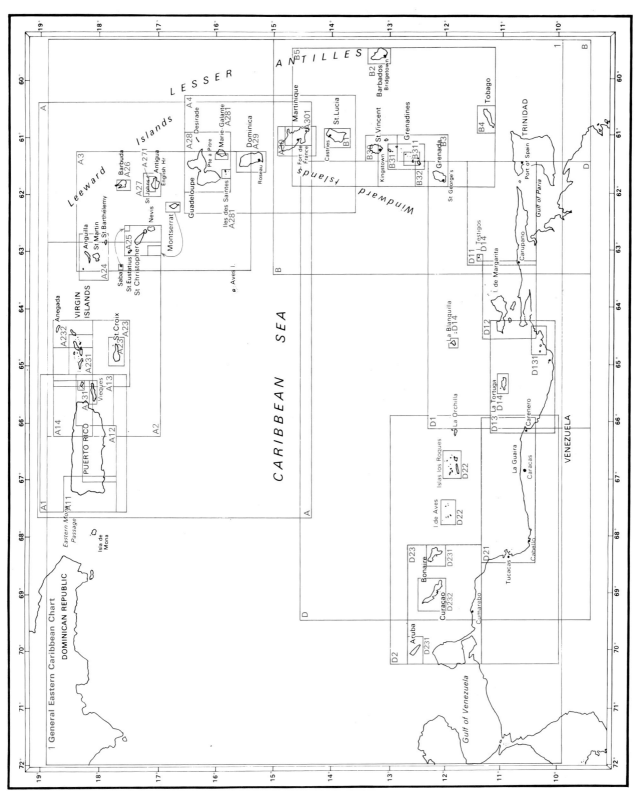

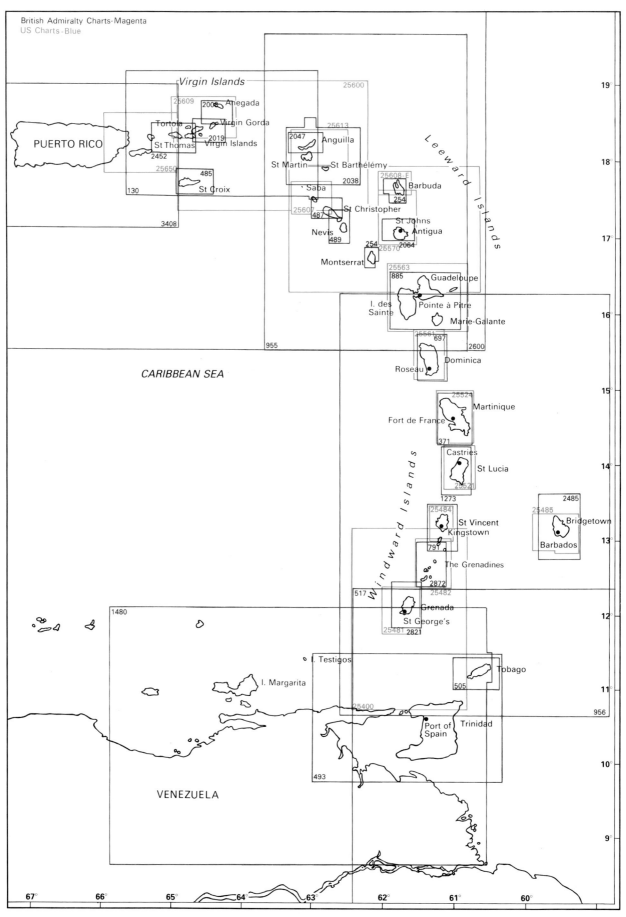

British Admiralty Charts-Magenta
US Charts-Blue

Virgin Islands

25609
2006 Anegada

Tortola
Virgin Gorda
2019

PUERTO RICO

St Thomas
Virgin Islands
2452
25650
485
130
St Croix
3408

25600

25613
2047 Anguilla

St Martin
St Barthélémy

Saba
2038

25608-F
254 Barbuda

25607
487 St Christopher
St Johns
2064 Antigua

Nevis
489

254
25570
Montserrat

25563
885 Guadeloupe

I. des
Sainte
Pointe à Pitre
Marie-Galante

955

CARIBBEAN SEA

25561
697
2600

Roseau
Dominica

Leeward Islands

25524
Martinique

Fort de France
371

Castries
St Lucia
25521
1273

Windward Islands

25484
St Vincent
Kingstown
791
The Grenadines

2872
25482

517
25485
Bridgetown
2485
Barbados

1480
Grenada
St George's
25481 2821

I. Testigos

I. Margarita

505 Tobago

25400
956

Port of
Spain
Trinidad
493

VENEZUELA

British Admiralty Charts

British Admiralty

130	Anguilla to Puerto Rico, showing approaches to the Virgin islands	282,600
	Sombrero island	15,130
197	Marigot harbour to Pointe du Cap	24,100
254	Montserrat and Barbuda	
	Plymouth anchorage	15,000
	Montserrat	50,000
	Barbuda	60,000
371	Martinique	79,700
485	St Croix (Santa Cruz)	58,400
	Christiansted harbour	14,600
	Krause lagoon and Limetree bay	25,000
	Frederiksted pier	7,500
487	St Christopher (St Kitts to St Eustatius	50,000
	Basseterre bay	25,000
489	Approaches to Nevis	50,000
491	Anchorages in Guadeloupe and the adjacent islands	
	Port du Moule and St Anne anchorages:	
	Grand-Bourg	12,100
	Basse-Terre	12,737
	Galet anchorage: Saintes anchorage	15,000
	Port Louis	15,125
	St Francois	20,000
493	Approaches to Trinidad including the Gulf of Paria	300,000
494	Plans in Martinique:	
	Havre de la Trinité, Rade de Saint Pierre	25,000
	Baie de Fort de France	37,500
	Rade de Fort de France	12,000
	Cul-de-Sac Marin	25,000
	Havre du Robert and approaches	37,500
501	Kingstown, Greathead and Calliaqua bays	14,500
	Admiralty bay	12,500
502	Plans in Barbados:	
	Bridgetown harbour and approaches:	
	Oistins bay	12,500
	Speightstown	15,000
508	Ports and anchorages in Tobago	
	Man of War bay: Great Courland and Mount Irvine bays	25,000
	King's bay: Rockly bay	12,500
517	Trinidad to Cayenne	1,500,000
697	Dominica	73,000
728	Prince Rupert bay	22,900
	Roseau roads and Woodbridge bay	11,500
791	St Vincent and the northern part of the Grenadines	72,600
804	Approaches to Pointe a Pitre, Ste Marie anchorage	25,300
885	Guadeloupe with the adjacent islands (Saintes, Marie-Galante and Désirade)	130,000
955	Sombrero to Dominica	475,000
956	Guadeloupe to Trinidad	644,000
1273	St. Lucia	72,000
1480	Tobago to Tortuga	603,000
2008	Virgin islands – Anegada to Virgin Gord	75,000
2019	Tortola to Virgin Gorda	75,000
2038	Anguilla, St Martin and St Barthélémy	174,000
2064	Antigua	50,000
	Falmouth and English harbours	20,000
2065	St John's harbour to Parham harbour	25,000
2079	Plans in Anguilla, S. Martin and S. Barthélémy	
	Baie du Marigot: Groot baai: Port de Gustavia:	
	Crocus bay and Road bay	15,000
2183	Saint Thomas harbour	10,000

2452	Virgin islands – Sheet 3: Tortola island to Culebra, including St Thomas island	70,000
2600	Mona passage to Dominica	875,500
2821	Grenada	71,500
	Northeast part of Grenada and adjacent islands	24,200
	Grenville harbour	12,500
	Part of the south coast	24,200
2872	Part of the Grenadines from Carriacou island to Battowia	72,000
4402	Caribbean Sea	2,750,000

French (SHOM)

1003P	Petites Antilles – De la Martinique à Saint Christopher	418,000
1488	Petites Antilles: l'Anguille, Saint Martin et Saint Barthélémy	250,000
3125	Côte du vent, de la pointe de la Grande Vigie à la pointe des Châteaux île de la Désirade	55,400
	Cartouche: Port du Moule	5,000
3127	Abords de Basse-Terre – De la rivière des Pères à la pointe du Vieux Fort	12,500
3128	Côte sous le vent de Marie-Galante, pointe du Vieux Fort (Mouillage dela Basse-Terre)	25,000
	Cartouche: Port du Grand Bourg	8,000
3200	La Barbade	75,300
3206	Iles Grenadines	73,000
3273	Ile de la Grenade	72,500
	Cartouche: Ile de la Grenade (Suite)	72,500
3287	Grand Cul-de-Sac Marin (Partie Est) de Port-Louis à la pointe Granger	25,000
3367	Grand Cul-de-Sac Marin (Partie Ouest), de la Grande Rivière à l'anse Deshayes	25,000
3418	De la pointe du Vieux Fort à la pointe Allègre	55,400
3419	De Pointe-à-Pitre à La Désirade	55,400
3422	De la pointe Ferry à la pointe de la Grande Vigie	55,400
3423P	Carte générale de la Guadeloupe	130,000
3775	Antilles, la Dominique	110,000
4519	Guadeloupe, ports et mouillages	
	Cartouche: Mouillage du Galet	15,000
	Mouillage du Petit Havre	12,500
	Mouillage de Sainte-Anne	7,000
	Mouillage de Saint-François	8,000
4985	Ile de Sainte-Lucie	75,000
6090	Ile Saint-Martin, baie du Marigot	15,000
	Cartouche: Ile Saint-Barthélémy, port de Gustavia	15,000
	Ile Saint-Martin, grande baie Filipsburg	15,000
6332P	De Porto-Rico au golfe de Paria	1,200,000
6738P	La Martinique – Partie Sud	60,000
6892P	Baie de Fort-de-France	15,000
6948P	Guadeloupe – De Pointe-à-Pitre à Marie-Galante – Canal des Saintes	60,000
	Cartouche: Marie-Galante – Baie de Saint-Louis	20,000
7041P	La Martinique – Partie Nord	60,000
7087P	La Martinique – Havre de la Trinité et baie du Galion	15,000
7088P	La Martinique – Havre du Robert et baie du François	20,000
7089P	La Martinique – Saint-Pierre, Case-Pilote, Cul-de-Sac du Marin, Baie du Vauclin	
	Cartouche: A – Saint-Pierre	15,000
	B – Case-Pilote	15,000
	C – Cul-de-Sac du Marin	15,000
	D – Baie du Vauclin	15,000

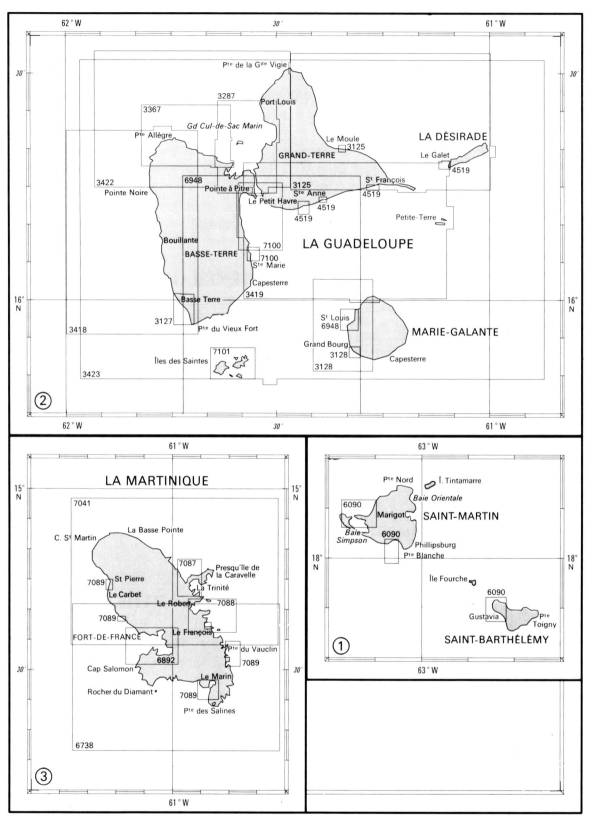

French (SHOM) Charts

7100P	Guadeloupe – Abords de Pointe-à Pitre	15,000
	Cartouche: Mouillages de Sainte-Marie	15,000
7101P	Les Saintes	15,000
7179	Du golfe de Paria à Cabo Cassiporé	1,480,000

P = Printed on *plastic*

US Charts (DMA)

25481	Grenada (West Indies)	72,560
	Saint Georges Harbour	10,420
	South Coast of Grenada	24,320
	NE Point of Grenada &	
	Adjacent Islands	24,320
25482	Carriacou to Bequia (Grenadine Islands)	72,560
	Tobago Cays Anchorages	24,000
25483	Kingstown, Greathead & Collaqua	
	Bays (St Vincent)	14,500
	Admiralty Bay (Bequia Island)	12,500
25484	Saint Vincent	72,608
25485	Approaches to Barbados	100,000
	Bridgetown and Oistin Bay	25,000
	Speightstown	20,000
25521	St. Lucia (UK) West Indies	72,620
	Gros Islet Anchorage	25,000
25524	Martinique	75,000
25525	Plans on the Coast of Martinique	
	Rada de Saint-Pierre	10,000
	Le Havre de La Trinite	14,400
25527	Baie de Fort de France (Martinique)	15,000
25528	Anchorages in St Lucia Island	
	Port Castries	4,840
	Vieux Fort Bay	18,240
	Grand Cul-de-Sac Bay	8,065
	Marigot Harbour	4,840
25550	Saint Barthélémy to Guadeloupe	150,000
25561	Dominica	72,145
25562	Anchorages in the Island of Dominica	
	Prince Rupert Bay	22,000
	Roseau Roads & Woodbridge Bay	12,000
25563	Guadeloupe	131,640
25564	Iles des Saintes (Guadeloupe)	15,000
25565	West Coast of Marie Galante	26,150
	Port of Grand Bourg	5,170
25566	Approaches to Pointe-à-Pitre	
	(Guadeloupe)	15,000
	Mouillages de Sainte-Marie	15,000
25567	Anchorages in Guadeloupe	
	Basse-Terre	12,160
	Moule	4,250
	Port Louis	14,590
25570	Approach to Antigua	75,000
25575	St Johns Harbour to Parham Harbour	25,000
25600	Anegada Passage with Adjacent Islands	250,000
25601	Approaches to Saint Christopher and Nevis,	
	Montserrat and Redonda	75,000
25607	Saba Saint Eustatius and Saint	
	Christopher	75,000
	Saba	25,000
	Saint Eustatius	15,000
25608	Plans of the Leeward Islands	
	Baie du Marigot	15,000
	Port de Gustavia	15,000
	Plymouth	15,000
	Bassatere	15,000
	Approach to Barbuda	75,000
25609	St Thomas to Anegada (Virgin Islands)	80,000
25610	Approaches to Gorda Sound	12,500
	Gorda Sound	7,500
25611	Approaches to Road Harbour	30,000
	Road Harbour	15,000
25613	Approaches to Anguilla St. Martin and	
	St. Barthélémy	75,000
	Philipsburg	15,000

IV. BIBLIOGRAPHY

Admiralty Publications
NP71 West Indies Pilot, Vol II (Lesser Antilles, Puerto Rico to Grenada)
NP82 Admiralty List of Lights Vol J

US Defense Mapping Agency Sailing Directions
SD 147 Caribbean Sea, Vol I Bermuda, Bahamas and the Islands

General Guides
Caribbean – The Lesser Antilles. Insight Guides
The Caribbean James Henderson. Cadogan Guide
Caribbean Islands Handbook. Trade and Travel Publications
Fodor's Caribbean
Penguin Guide to the Caribbean
Adventurer's Guide to the Virgin Islands. Pariser Hunter Publications-Moorland in UK
Berlitz Guide to the French West Indies. Gravette Hipocene Books, USA
A series of books on individual islands and island groups published by Macmillan Educational Ltd

Classics
The Violins of St Jacques. Patrick Leigh-Fermor. Penguin
The Traveller's Tree. Patrick Leigh-Fermor. Penguin

Cruising Guides
Cruising Guide to the Windward Islands. Stevens Tropic Isle Publishers. USA
Yachtsman's Guide to the Windward Islands. J. M. Wilensky. USA
Yachtsman's Guide to the Greater Antilles. Harry Kline Tropic Isle Publishers. USA
Cruising Guide to the Eastern Caribbean. D. M. Street Jr.
   Vol II. Part 1. Puerto Rico, Passage and Virgin Islands;
   Vol II. Part 2. Anguilla to Dominica.
   Vol III. Martinique to Trinidad.
   W. W. Norton USA – Imray, Laurie, Norie & Wilson Ltd UK
Cruising Guide to the Caribbean and Bahamas. Harry Kline Tropic Isle Publishers USA
Sailor's Guide to the Windward Isles. Chris Doyle. Cruising Guide Publications
Cruising Guide to the Leeward Islands. Chris Doyle. Cruising Guide Publications
St Maarten, St Kitts & Nevis Cruising Guide. William Eiman (also covers Anguilla, St Barts, Eustatia and Saba)
A Cruising Guide to the Caribbean. Michael Marshall. Adlard Coles/A. & C. Black

Index